PROFILE OF AN
EFFECTIVE SCHOOL SUPERINTENDENT

DALE BODDY

 FriesenPress

Suite 300 - 990 Fort St
Victoria, BC, V8V 3K2
Canada

www.friesenpress.com

Copyright © 2021 by Dale Boddy
First Edition — 2021

All rights reserved.

No part of this publication may be reproduced in any form, or by any means, electronic or mechanical, including photocopying, recording, or any information browsing, storage, or retrieval system, without permission in writing from FriesenPress.

ISBN
978-1-5255-6463-5 (Hardcover)
978-1-5255-6464-2 (Paperback)
978-1-5255-6465-9 (eBook)

1. EDUCATION, LEADERSHIP

Distributed to the trade by The Ingram Book Company

DEDICATION

My wife, as practical a being as imaginable, did not once question my quest towards a whimsical goal, the completion of this decades old story. A supporter of whatever direction I have chosen, I thank you for this and for countless other gestures of love over our glorious courtship and excellent marriage of 50+ years.

TABLE OF CONTENTS

Preface	ix
Part I: Introduction	1
Chapter 1: The Entry Interview and Study Goals	1
Organization of Narrative	4
Part II: Ed's Key Traits	5
Chapter 2: The Intelligence of Ed Noyce, Our Effective Superintendent	5
Ed Noyce's Intelligence	6
Thinking and Understanding	8
Analysis of Thinking and Understanding	9
Searching for Data	9
Analysis: Did the Education Foundation Need a New Director?	12
"Big Picture" Reality	13
Weighing Choices	14
Trust and respect	15
Balance and moderation	16
Self-Discipline	17
Summary Notes on Ed's Intelligence	18
Chapter 3: The Affable Ed Noyce	19
The Immediacy of Day to Day	19
Three Quick Chats and One Extended Follow-Up	20
Analysis of Three Quick Chats	23
Informal Communications over Bureaucratic Channels	25
Analysis of Informal Communications	27
Courtesy and Humility	28
Analysis of Courtesy and Humility	30
Over the Long Haul	31
Established Integrity	31
Analysis of the Mike Dymtriw Interview and Ed's Affability	33
Chapter 4: Ed's Private Persona	35
Satisfactions	35
The Dissatisfying and Confusing	38
The Disturbing	39
Analysis of Feelings—Especially the Disturbing	40
The Composite Ed Noyce: Intelligent, Affable, Reflective	42
Thinking Ahead to My Dissection Framework	43

Part III: Ed's Leadership Processes   45

Chapter 5: Normal Leadership Processes   45

Process: Trust Through a Shared History   46
- **With Help, Ed Fires a Principal**   46
- **Analysis: With Help, Ed Fires a Principal**   48
- **Eileen's Ultimatum**   49
- **Analysis of Eileen's Ultimatum**   52
- **Trust and Respect Could Not Solve Every Issue**   52

Process: Focus on Students   53
Process: Scanning the Environment   55
Process: Getting to a Consensus   58
Process: Slow, patient, resourceful teaching   63
- **Lesson 1: My Belated Discovery of Cooperative Learning**   64
- **Lesson 2: Observing a Cooperative Learning Lesson**   65
- **Lesson 3: A Sly Test**   66
- **Lesson 4: Recovery After a Failed Test**   68
- **Lesson 5: Strategic Questions Interrupted**   69
- **Lessons 6 and 7: Hexadecimals and Learning-Style Assessment**   69
- **Lessons 8: Patient Planning**   70
- **Analysis of Slow, Patient, Resourceful Teaching**   70

Process: Time on the Job   71
- **Quantitative Work**   71
- **Other Work**   72
- **Time Management**   72

Summary: This Was Just Normal Leadership   74

Part IV: Normal Leadership   77

Chapter 6: The Student Accommodation Committee   77

Student Accommodation Committee Meeting 2: June 7   78
Student Accommodation Committee Meeting 4: September 12   80
- **Table 1: September 12 – Issues Discussed in Student Accommodation Committee Meeting 4**   82
- **Analysis: Student Accommodation Committee Meeting 4: September 12**   85

Student Accommodation Committee Meeting 5: September 22nd   86
Student Accommodation Committee Meeting 6: October 5   87
- **Analysis: Student Accommodation Committee Meeting 6: October 5**   88
- **Table 2: Committee Member "Finds" in the Field Notes of Meeting 6**   88

Application of Ed's Leadership Processes to the Work of the Student Accommodation Committee   88
- **Table 3: Ed's Leadership Processes as Observed in Student Accommodation Committee Meetings**   89

Summary of Normal Leadership in the Student Accommodation Committee   92

Chapter 7: A Newly Discovered Leadership Process: Respect Role Differentiation — 95
    Theory and Practice: Superintendent Role Conflict — 95
    Administrative and Political Leadership — 97

Part V: Leadership in a Crisis — 99

Chapter 8: Paragon Alternative School: Normal Leadership — 99
    The Premise: Alberta Desperately Needed Change — 99
    May 26 to June 10: Paragon Alternative School — 101
        Table 4: May 26 to June 10: Paragon Alternative School Events Summary — 101
    June 22: Dr. Weinard Meets with the Board — 102
    June 23 to September 8: Paragon Alternative School — 104
        Table 5: June 23 to September 8: Summary of Paragon Alternative School — 104
    September 8 (afternoon) to September 26: Paragon Alternative School — 105
        Table 6: September 12 to 27: Paragon Alternative School Summary Notes — 108

Chapter 9: Interviewees Speak to the Paragon Alternative School — 111
    Ed Noyce, Superintendent of Schools: September 12 — 111
    Don Howard, Deputy Superintendent of Schools: September 12 — 115
    Bill Bersche, Assistant Superintendent of Business Services: September 12 — 116
    James Thorborn, Principal, Ormand Mitchel High School: September 22 — 118
    Margaret O'Connell, Trustee and Former Chair: September 22 — 119
    Lydia Jacques, Chair: September 22 — 120
    Herb Bondar, Student Services Coordinator: September 27 — 123
    Marie Noyce, Ed's Spouse: September 28 — 123
    Ann Spencer, Secretary to the Superintendent: September 28 — 124
    Ab Digby, Assistant Superintendent of Human Resources: September 29 — 126
    Interview Summary — 128

Chapter 10: September 27 to October 5: Tensions Increase — 131
    September 27: Paragon Alternative School Meeting with Staff — 131
        Table 7: September 28 to October 2: Paragon Alternative School Discussion Notes — 136
    October 5: The Three Letter Campaign — 138
        October 5: Analysis of the Three Letter Campaign — 139
    October 5: The Regular Workday — 143

Chapter 11: October 5, Crisis—Trust the Parents — 147
    Analysis: October 5, Crisis—Trust the Parents — 154

Chapter 12: PostScript Events with Analysis — 157

Chapter 13: Analysis of Paragon Alternative School Proposal — 161
    Table 8: A Count of Key Leadership Processes Related to the Paragon Alternative School — 162
    Why the Paragon Alternative School Proposal Was a Crisis — 164
    A Newly Recognized Process: Work/Life Balance — 166

Chapter 14: Ed's Hidden Scam — 169
    Table 9: Were There Hidden Scams? — 170
    Is Qualitative Research a Scam? — 174

Part VI: Concluding Remarks in Two Parts — 177

Chapter 15: Concluding Remarks — 177
    Table 10: Critical Aspects on Ed's Paths to Leadership — 178
  Two Beliefs on Organizationally Effective School Leadership — 180
  Ed Nears Retirement — 180
  Overwhelming Admiration — 182

Chapter 16: Concluding Remarks: Ed — 185

Tables — 187

Appendices — 187

Appendix A: Ethics, Validity, and Reliability in Qualitative Studies — 189

Appendix B: A Primer on Educational Structures in Canada, in Alberta, in Wapiti Falls — 193

Appendix C: A District Lexicon — 197

Appendix D: Participants, Places, and Sites, with District Schools Listed Alphabetically — 201

Appendix E: Observation Dates with Time Observed — 207
    Table 11: Observational Tallies and Ed's Workday — 207

Appendix F: June 7 – Tabular Account of Student Accommodation Committee Meeting 2 — 213
    Table 12: June 7 – Items Raised During Student Accommodation Committee Meeting 2 — 213

Appendix G: September 12 – Notes on Seating Plans Relative to Accommodation Committee Meeting 4 — 219
    Table 13: Seating Plan in Student Accommodation Committee Meeting 4, September 12 — 219

Appendix H: October 5 – Sample Discussion from Student Accommodation Committee Meeting 6 — 221

Appendix I: September 28 – Narrative Discussion on the Paragon Alternative School — 225
    Analysis: September 28 Senior Administrator's Meeting — 226
    Continued Observations: September 28, early afternoon — 227

Appendix J: September 29 – Narrative Discussion on the Paragon Alternative School — 233

Appendix K: September 30 and October 2 – Narrative Discussion on the Paragon Alternative School — 241
    Table 14: Grade 9 Mathematics Achievement Test Results - 1992 — 242

Appendix L: Two Case Studies—Summary Timelines — 245
    Table 15: Two Timelines: Student Accommodation Committee Highlights and Alternative School Highlights — 245

Appendix M: Selected Qualitative Studies of Educational Leadership: 1997–2017 — 249

References — 251

PREFACE

While the events in this account are real, all but two names used are fictitious—mine and one other, a deceased friend. I thought I could keep all authors referenced but reporters created a special problem as their accounts might lead directly to events and people, so their authorship has been omitted and their reports disguised. I have also used contrived names for institutions—schools, business, and communities—and described and named locations imaginatively. Throughout this venture, the goal was to tell Ed's story, the real story of the real-life subject, accurately and without disparaging any of the sincere efforts of others. This was relatively easy as everyone was doing what they thought best. Scoundrels would have made for a better story, but they were not present.

Part I: Introduction

CHAPTER 1

The Entry Interview and Study Goals

It was late spring. The lawn sign read Wapiti Falls Consolidated School District #1 offices. The building consisted of two sections, with parts tied together with nearly matching brown metal facia.

The lower, older west section was stucco. With a long wall of classroom-style windows, it was distinctively a repurposed school. The newer east section had prominent dark-coloured metal siding, installed vertically. It would fit into any newer business park. The old was history, the new commercial. Together the message was waste not, want not.

Entering, I noted photos of trustees past, pamphlets describing current programs and services, and an architect's sketch of a nearly completed high school. The photos and pamphlets were real; the drawing rendered an impossible ideal.

Ed's Office in Old School Portion of District Headquarters.

At reception, after stating my business, I received a warm, friendly greeting and an offer of coffee or cold drink. I was early, and a wait of about thirty minutes was suggested. I settled in, comfortable. Passing staff extended further greetings and offered more snacks. One other person waited with me, quiet, but she was gone soon, an appointment, probably. Student art filled three walls. Each identified the artist, their teacher, and their school. Big, bright potted plants added to the clean, pleasant ambience. My subject, Ed Noyce, selected by an expert panel as an outstanding superintendent, appeared at the time we had set, 16:00 hours.

Greetings were quick and cordial. Ed led me down a hallway. A young teacher intercepted him. She was excited, eager to share news of her students' recent success; they had won a music competition. Ed was pleased. She continued, asking hopefully, would she have a job next year? She laughed, embarrassed at her temerity, at the undisguised link between student success and her ongoing employment. Ed offered no assurance. Jobs, he said, depended on the district's new budget. He repeated his message of congratulations, promised that he would tell the board, and it was over. We continued walking and ended in a small meeting room. Alone, Ed wondered if the district could keep her on staff. Like every new teacher, she would only have a probationary contract. An ongoing—permanent—contract gen-

Industrial Design Portion of School District Offices.

erally followed, but would the funds be there? Ed understood why government was effectively cutting educational funding, but how fair was that? I began my questions. Before long, I had completed the entry interview and scheduled initial observations. The study had begun.

After finishing the formal interview, Ed led me on a building tour. We stopped at one office, the one assigned to Joe Pivott. I knew of him. Retired from the superintendency some twenty years earlier, he still had an office? Seeing my surprise, Ed filled me in. When he was healthy, Joe worked part of every weekday. I did not ask the obvious; he worked at what? That answer would come later; someone would fill me in. This was different. What other differences would I observe in Wapiti Falls Consolidated School District #1?

These two side events proved significant. Ed's chance meeting with a teacher outlined a pattern and tone for the numerous interactions described and analyzed in depth here. And when I met this unofficial superintendent emeritus, Joe Pivott, he went to the heart of his understanding of Ed Noyce's success; he declared that it was because of his intelligence and affability.

This study had no guiding hypothesis. As an ethnology, it began as an open slate. A practicing superintendent myself, I already knew something about the job. I did much of the same hum-drum stuff that every school superintendent did—we all worked at

Reception in School District Offices—View #1.

similar tasks; led other educators, did our best to facilitate student learning, and were employed by a lay board of elected trustees. Having worked with other superintendents, I knew, too, that none of us worked in the exact same way. Districts were different; the staff of districts were different; student needs were different; and leaders, those elected and those hired, were different. In this study, Ed, a proven success, would simply do what he normally did.

It was 1994. I wanted to become a better school superintendent. To get there I had read and thought about leadership a lot. John Gardner (1990) noted that the study of leadership drew considerable attention but offered few answers? Why the disconnect? His answer was that leadership was complex. I agreed, understanding was complex, but my task only required watching what an acknowledged leader did. I would observe and make detailed notes, deconstruct them into relevant chunks, and reconstruct them into an explanatory report. It would be leadership as practised in the field. With a naturalistic study, I would thus avoid the contrivance of an experimental study or a survey. It also introduced a different artificiality, namely the reliance of an external observer. I was that external observer, and I show up over and over in this study with various views and interpretations. (See Appendix A: "Ethics, Validity, and Reliability in Qualitative Studies.")

Reception—View #2.

This study started with two goals: The first goal was personal. I wanted to excel at my job. I had worked for and with superintendents with different skills and different approaches to leadership. Not all were stellar. By working with an outstanding individual, I was confident that I would learn more.

The second goal was to share my findings in the form of an acceptable dissertation at Gonzaga University. Fortunately, I had been downsized, so I had time to work full-time on the thesis. I gave myself a year. Unfortunately, I was a mess. Downsizing was not pretty. My self-esteem was shattered and my outlook miserable. With my confidence gone, I struggled, felt alone. My faculty advisor had changed. She was new to me and to the university; we had no relationship and did not develop one. She promised help, but it was mere words. To be fair, since I did not know how to ask for help, it was not offered. I diligently spent the full year thinking and writing, but it was not long enough. With a year gone, I needed a job. I found one and it consumed all my time and energy. My hiatus continued through the entirety of my new career and a year into my retirement. I went from 1995 to 2017 without fulfilling my second goal, the production of an acceptable report on my findings.

These intervening years have changed me. My relatively short time in the field and countless hours thinking and striving to understand my observations have helped. My relationship with Ed has continued. Age has brought a different and better perspective. Retirement also brought a new opportunity. By sharing Ed Noyce's story now, I could finish what I had started and maybe even help someone else.

This is Ed's story. He was the chief executive officer of the Wapiti Falls Consolidated School District #1. He was identified as one of the best. Let me tell you how I found him and why he was so successful. but before doing so, a few details on the organization of this narrative.

Organization of Narrative

This narrative consists of six parts.
>**Part I:** Introduction
>**Part II:** Ed's Key Traits
>**Part III:** Ed's Leadership Processes
>**Part IV:** Normal Leadership
>**Part V:** Leadership in A Crisis
>**Part VI:** Concluding Remarks in Two Parts

As an ethnography, observations form data, and data is followed by analysis. Observation and analysis are separate. Ideally, what Ed and others did—the data—provides the who and what. The interpretation or analysis is my contribution. Sometimes interpretations creep into observations. This occurs naturally when I believed some observation demanded a quick interpretation, namely my explanatory judgment. When it worked perfectly, the actor and the interpreter are clearly labelled, and interpretations are identified as from Dale.

This profile of an effective school superintendent contains multiple appendices. Most provide additional detail and are introduced in the body of the text. Three have content, however, which may be unfamiliar to readers. These three provide missing context and are intended to make a more fulfilling read.

Appendix B: A Primer on Educational Structures in Canada, in Alberta, in Wapiti Falls outlines Canadian and Alberta legislation relating to schools. Care was taken to set out the power of the provincial overseer, previously known as the Department of Education and now called Alberta Education. Legislative support for the two public school districts competing for students in Wapiti Falls, Alberta, is provided. Power was anticipated to be important and is commented on. Ed's school district was described by the numbers of students and staff in 1994.

Appendix C: A District Lexicon contains some of the descriptive words that Ed and other district personnel used. Many are common. Most are self-explanatory. They also reveal a bit of the whimsy that Ed enjoyed.

Appendix D: Participants, Places, and Sites, with District Schools Listed Alphabetically, is an aid to memory. Note that all names are disguised. Other than using one first name twice, names were not duplicated. Following fifty-seven individuals and eighty-seven place names can be confusing. Here, the easy flow of common nomenclature is further complicated by using Indigenous or heritage place names.

There are other appendices that provide detail not found in the body of the report. With too much data to include in the body, the appendices provide missing or different details.

Part II: Ed's Key Traits

CHAPTER 2

The Intelligence of Ed Noyce, Our Effective Superintendent

While data collection started with the entry interview described above, this study had begun much earlier. It began as a university-sanctioned study, and a formal selection process was required. To find a subject, I relied on the panel process Genge (1991) used to identify a sample of Alberta's most effective superintendents. As with Genge, my panel was given no direction as to what exactly "organizationally effective" meant. To avoid personal bias, another colleague, Ron Babiuk from Alberta Education, organized an independent selection panel of senior Alberta educators, people familiar with Alberta's superintendents. Panel members identified their choices for "organizationally effective" superintendents. Ron compiled their choices and passed the results to my faculty advisor, Father Oldham, a Jesuit priest, and assistant head of the Graduate Faculty at Gonzaga University.

Father Oldham contacted me, named two potential candidates, and asked me to select one. I knew both, but I knew one better through our regional meetings and from our work on a provincial curriculum committee. Further, working with this superintendent would make my task a bit more manageable. His community was closer, only a three-hour drive from home, and since I had family in his community, I anticipated free room and board. I phoned him. We started with a telephone meeting in which we interviewed each other. At the end of the call, he agreed to participate. You met him for my in person interview, Ed Noyce.

Over the course of this study, I observed Ed and interviewed his staff and additional contacts for sixteen full days between May 17 to October 5, 1994. We also attended meetings and other events together on another six dates, the last on December 9, 1994. (A full table of the dates and times are detailed in the section, Appendix E: "Observation Dates with Time Observed.")

In the next two chapters I focus on Ed's nature. Joe Pivott, honourary superintendent emeritus, recognized Ed as a strong leader because of his intelligence and affability. He pointed me to where I would start my deconstructive analysis, turning observations into a list of Ed's traits.

Ed Noyce's Intelligence

Intelligence has a long definition. Webster's Ninth New Collegiate Dictionary (1983, p. 629) defines it using a variety of terms: I focused on just four: "thinking and understanding," "searching for data," "forming, then revising mental pictures," and "weighing choices." But then, observations identified one more characteristic that stood out for me, and I added it. It was Ed's self-control. I thought of it as an intellectual strength and added "self-discipline" to the list.

Ed, of course, never talked about intelligence. The closest he came was in referencing the teaching-learning styles described by Bernice McCarthy (1980). McCarthy identified four styles of learners: innovative learners, analytic learners, common sense learners, and dynamic learners. She produced a test that identified each person's individual style. Ed took her test and scored it; he then declared that he was an analytic learner. It made sense to him. Analytic learners constantly gather facts, seek out and rely on expert opinions. They create mental pictures that describe what they understand as their reality. They enjoy the satisfaction of having their theories pan out, but if they find they are wrong, they are content to gather more data in order to revise and form new mental pictures. Typically, their careers are in basic research and planning. Ed saw a fit and an application.

McCarthy designed her work for teachers. By teaching to students' learning styles, they would learn more, and both, students and teachers, would be more successful. This approach suited Ed, as he saw himself as a teacher, before all else. He was a district administrator when he discovered the McCarthy system, and he used it to refine what he was already doing. With it, he did his best to adjust his approach to match the learning styles of everyone else—colleagues, trustees, friends, and acquaintances. He shared the concept extensively within his district. I heard his senior colleagues describe themselves and colleagues using the McCarthy learning styles. It was a productive approach, but I wondered if the fit was as accurate as Ed thought? McCarthy noted that analytic learners typically focused on ideas rather than people, and consequently sought out and landed in careers like basic research or planning. So how did Ed Noyce find himself here, a school superintendent? While no system is perfect and overlaps can be expected, superintending seems far removed from basic research. In education, the focus seems to be more about people than ideas. True, some people find themselves in mismatched careers, but as an educator, Ed did not seem out of place. How did he get here? And why did it work so well?

Growing up, Ed thought he would become a scientist, a typical career for an analytic learner. And Ed was smart enough to do it. Midway through his senior high school year, he realized that he needed another mathematics course. His high school principal, knowing his capacities, helped Ed by making special arrangements. It was double duty. Ed would enroll in math and music at the same time, and would attend each class on alternate days, half-time attendance with full responsibility. It worked. Ed soon vied for the highest marks in math.

How good was he in music and math? During my time with Ed, he talked about his musical career, but as it was off the topic of leadership, I ignored it. Still, I picked up that he was not a fan of rock and roll, because he announced it several times. In a recent exchange, he provided further details.

> "While in high school, the music world was in transition from tuneful dance music to thumping rock. So, our band played a blend of waltzes, foxtrots, polkas, and Bill Haley–style rock. There seemed to be a demand for all in the teenage dance world of the time. My instrument was trombone. And, yes, we had an acoustic guitar, but his amplifier was the size of a small suitcase, and he could play melody or rhythm equally. Later, we had a bass guitar with a huge amp, and we suddenly needed three cars to get to a job. So, the instrumentation was trumpet, saxophone, trombone, piano, drums, and guitar or bass. We relied on the dance hall to provide a piano."

Ed's musical career continued into university. He met his wife Marie while playing for the university's symphony orchestra.

Having learned a bit, I asked for more, asked about a singer for his teenage band, but Ed provided nothing further; he was likely tired of my invasion of his privacy. Fortunately, he had already said more about his professional career as a trombonist.

> "After university, I was active in several bands around Edmonton. The Tailgate Jazz Band was led by Barry Guard, and we played Dixieland style music, mostly. However, a blend was used for most dances.
>
> "With Loren Lindsay it was mostly big band stage work, backing up touring shows or studio recordings, mostly for CBC."

I knew of the Tailgate Jazz Band. It was renowned locally, a personal dance band favourite, but it also used a name borrowed from a more renowned band. And of course, the abbreviation CBC, is the Canadian Broadcasting Company, Canada's national broadcaster.

As to math, Ed pursued it by enrolling in the science track at university, where he obtained a Bachelor of Science degree and began a graduate program. While he did say he was not a fan of some doctoral-level math courses, he was obviously proficient enough at it. It was while doing a doctoral course in quantum mechanics that he discovered teaching.

By then, Ed and Marie had married, and she introduced him to teaching. When her school could not find a certified physics teacher, Ed was hired as a substitute. He liked it so much that he switched studies, abandoning physics and enrolling in education. Ed was obviously multitalented as well as intelligent.

These events have depicted Ed as intelligent, but intelligence comes in many forms. With Ed, one of these forms was as a deliberate and deep thinker, as these three examples demonstrate.

Thinking and Understanding

1. As a superintendent, and needing a better grasp of school finances, Ed taught himself how to program the district computer. He reorganized student data files and created provincial comparisons. With solid data on hand, he developed, and then promoted, a new approach to funding schools. It was designed to improve fiscal equity; he said its purpose was to reduce the disparity between rich and poor districts, and thereby equalize student opportunity, irrespective of local tax assessments. Superintendents and others attended information sessions, where his proposal received serious consideration. Ed modestly thought it was just the typical response of an analytic learner. He had simply marshalled the facts, analyzed them, and developed a compelling argument. It was also confirmation of his careful and deep thought processes.

2. Facing a local contract stalemate, district negotiations with teachers had stalled by late May. With decreased government revenues and increased directives, the district had determined that they could not even afford to keep the teachers they had. While increased enrollment would increase their provincial per capita grants, the increase was insufficient to cover increased expenditures. Teachers were equally firm with their demands. Would the district's long history of labour peace end? As deadlines loomed, Ed focused on the problem. One morning, around 04:30 hours, a solution came to him. He wondered if a one-time payment in the previous contract had not been considered in district calculations. Once again, his familiarity with the district's financial program proved useful. It turned out that while the salary scales had been reprogrammed after the last salary agreement, its lump sum provisions had been left out of the formula—lost, forgotten. Correcting this oversight meant that the district and the teachers could both meet their salary targets, and a new contract was quickly agreed to. Suddenly obvious, discovery required Ed's thoughtful attention to detail. Discovered in the early hours of the day, Ed seemed to "always" be on the job, but of course that would have been impossible. He had another reason for his early start to the day. Over lunch one day, months later, the three of us—Ed, Marie, and I—having finished lunch—watched and listened to the birds. I commented that my wife did not like the bird's sing-song mornings. Every spring they woke her up. Ed understood. He said that they started chirping here at around four in the morning. So that was why he was awake. The chirping birds had roused him from sleep, and once awake, his mind went to work, homing in on his biggest problem, namely district finances, and the teacher contract impasse. Rational. Logical. Typical Ed.

3. My third example of his intellectual capacity was that despite being away from physics for twenty-plus years, Ed had still maintained his expertise. The province liked to involve superintendents in provincial committees, and Ed and I had worked together

on such a committee, years earlier. Ed reminded me and said that he was still doing such curriculum work. He talked about previewing province-wide Grade 12 physics examinations with other educators. For most superintendents, their technical expertise had disappeared—hidden, forgotten, lost. Years out of the classroom had turned most superintendents into generalists. Not Ed. He described taking the student test and easily solving each question. It was as if he had never left his classroom. Ed was a forever "keener," keeping up, updating his technical expertise as well as his administrative knowledge. Then it occurred to me: how dormant was that knowledge? Did it matter that a few years back, Ed had helped his son review the same course materials? Refreshed or not, Ed's expertise was still there. He enjoyed the careful, deep thinking that physics required, that everything required.

Analysis of Thinking and Understanding

Ed was smart; he taught himself computer programming, developed an "equity" solution applicable throughout the province, recalled sophisticated details concerning the district's financial programs, and confirmed the legitimacy of the student's upcoming test by taking it. Of course, he had help along the way, but the fact was that he took on new challenges, thought about them, and applied his knowledge to new tasks.

Searching for Data

Analytic learners are problem solvers; it is what they do. And Ed, the consummate analytic learner, constantly searched for new data—facts, opinions, directions, anything, everything. He needed data to understand the reality of his district. Data, whether existing, newly discovered, or refined, Ed sought it all.

Principals were a primary source of new inputs. So, too, were the senior central office administrative team members. Sharing kept him up to date. Ed was eagerly receptive to data wherever he encountered it, and he actively invited it. When it came, he accepted it graciously. He knew that his mind worked that way, "I need the pieces, and I generate the big picture from the pieces…I have to see the pieces."

To illustrate Ed's penchant for gathering data, I offer three examples, two are short and interconnected, and the third is a longer, more complicated vignette. A detailed analysis follows.

1. Early in my observations, on June 22, the board of trustees rejected Ed's recommendation—his administrative team's recommendation—regarding the lease of the soon-to-be-closed Pawoki Elementary School. While I came late to this specific event, I had followed the full process in similar undertakings and knew that Ed was consistent in all. I therefore knew that this recommendation would have undergone a careful, deliberate, thorough vetting by his full administrative team. After the full process, Ed, supported by the full team, recommended that a native friendship centre be the lessee. At their meeting, the

board considered the administrative recommendation but went with something different. One trustee made the case for a private Christian school. The board adopted this trustee's recommendation over their administrators' recommendation.

This decision was important, and I went back over the events. To make their decision, the board heard both arguments. I watched the body language of both administrators and trustees as this case was made. Something was amiss but nothing was said. And I talked about it with Ed. This is what I came up with: the board weighed their concern for the Pawoki community against their desire to enhance their relationship with the native community. Rent would be the same either way. Rejecting the native friendship centre as a lessee would disappoint them, but the district could help the friendship centre in other ways. This board had previously closed a school and knew that the process and result was painful for everyone. Conversely, keeping a school going would help the Pawoki community—even if it came about by housing a competing school. The board had all the data and they chose the private Christian school over a native friendship centre. An analytic learner like Ed would see the board as community experts. He had made sure that the board was well-informed, and he recognized their legitimacy as his boss. He was, therefore, comfortable with their decision and said so; Ed's team, not so much, as they struggled with it, and viewed it as a personal loss. By Ed's calculus, they would get over it. Either way, Ed's overriding commitment to the district students was unaffected. He had collected all the necessary data and accepted what followed.

2. A second example shows a change in Ed's evaluative calculus, and maybe a change of heart. Several years earlier, when district amalgamation was initially proposed, Ed saw it as efficient and supported it. Amalgamation would increase fiscal efficiency and foster better student programming. He was right. My district was small, and some of our schools were too small and too expensive, and I saw the educational limitations of three and four grades with one teacher. Amalgamation made sense to me and to many others. But as the process unfolded, Ed saw that politics were lording over programs, saw that students were largely forgotten, and saw that people and money were being diverted from their rightful business. Good theory was failing in implementation. Consequently, his opinion flip-flopped. But as in other matters, there may have been more to it. Ed was comfortably ensconced in his larger district and would escape the machinations of amalgamation. They had talked about amalgamation with Roseray County, but neither party thought it was necessary and neither proceeded beyond that one exploratory meeting. Working with me, however, knowing my small district, Ed knew that redistricting would be life-changing for me. Did his views change out of consideration for me? Maybe, but so what? More data and more evaluation meant new realities and new directions. He could and did re-evaluate his conclusions. Additionally, what did it matter, as in the end, his view would make no difference?

3. The final illustration of Ed's quiet process of data gathering occurred on my last day of observation. Ed had arranged a meeting at 14:00 hours, October 5, with Byron, a downtown lawyer, and the volunteer chair of the Wapiti Falls Education Foundation. The foundation, set up to assist the district beyond the government's strict formulas and funding practices, was directed, and effectively set up, by James Thorborn during the preceding year. As principal designate of a school that would not receive their first students for a year, James had time to get the organization up and running. It had been a priority and it filled much of Thorborn's transition year. He liked the work and the contacts. But now, his high school was operational, and he was busy—too busy. Ed had anticipated the coming overload. In the spring, he had talked to James about it and understood that James had not wanted to give it up. But by fall, James recognized that it was too much, so he enlisted Ed's help. Ed agreed and had scheduled this meeting to start the process of finding a replacement director.

Ed arrived on time—he always arrived on time—and was soon ushered into Byron's downtown office. From his chair, Ed could look over the city and its river valley, rich in the golden colours of fall. Spectacular, but Ed did not talk about the view. He came straight to the point; the foundation needed a new director. He proceeded to outline several options involving district assistance. Byron listened and then offered a totally different perspective. He too had spoken to James and was sure that he would stay on if he had an assistant.

What? Two competing solutions were on the table; two conflicting proposals presented at the behest of the same person. James had told Ed that he needed out but had told Byron that all he needed was help. Calmly, without pause, Ed and Byron explored the new direction. Ed expressed optimism about keeping James's enthusiasm and drive. I had seen this before: Ed did what he usually did; he went with the idea newly presented and helped explore it by identifying potential assistants. Of course, district support would continue. And then he casually shared two concerns. Principal designate James Thorborn and his new school, Ormand Mitchell High School, were visible, exposed, and becoming controversial. Second, James needed to delegate more. I watched and thought that Ed was doing more than interacting; he was also deep in thought, and he had just planted seeds that he might reap later. With their exchange over, Ed excused himself to let Byron get on with his busy day.

As we left the office, Ed asked me why I was so quiet. I was quiet because I was in deep thought. I knew that no administrator would want to be put into such a situation. First, it was a surprise, and avoiding surprises is sacrosanct to administrative success. Second, how could he assist James if James did not know what he wanted? Finally, being blindsided was a personal affront. Ed seemed to understand what I was feeling and was soon explaining his lack of reaction. He simply listened to Byron. Nothing further was said about his original plan. I could see that Ed was enjoying my heightened interest. He knew that I would be anxious to hear more, but I had to wait a bit—until we were in the privacy and solitude of his vehicle.

Once we were his car, settled and in private, he explained, answering each of my questions as asked. What happened? Ed said that he now had new facts and would "glue them together" into a new hypothesis. Was he in deep thought? Yes. While carrying on a robust conversation, he had started with the premise that James had "caved," that is he was trying to please everyone. Then he thought that James was agreeing to whatever the last person proposed. With this view, Ed promised himself that he would not play along, that he would not solve James's overload problem. Finally, as he thought more, he began to appreciate the pressure that James was under.

Analysis: Did the Education Foundation Need a New Director?

Ed had answered my direct questions, but I knew that there was still more to this event. Snide personal comments had been directed towards James Thorborn through a letter to the editor (Kroome 1994: A3). I knew that Kroome was not on staff, but he must have had access to someone on staff. I was confident that Ed would have heard the same complaints and would know that district teachers were covetously watching James Thorborn and his new school, with its new appointments, new programs, new everything. While facing hard times in their own schools, Thorborn was receiving everything he wanted, plus fawning attention. They were envious.

Ed told me enough. He might have said more, but as I had noted, he enjoyed having me figure out the rest. He wanted me to reach my own understanding. And I did.

Knowing the system and how information flowed, Ed knew that Thorborn and Byron would talk, and that Ed's concerns would be raised. Thus, James would have an opportunity to reflect and learn. What might he learn? He might learn that it was better to let Ed know before the meeting that he had changed his position, or that he was open to other changes. He might learn to seek further advice before advancing one position and then waffling when finding other directions. And he might have figured out that if it had been someone other than Ed, repercussions could follow. It was best not to put your boss in an awkward position.

There were still more lessons from this short encounter. I had seen Ed plant seeds and had seen him wait for staff to grow. This was part of how he led. First, he did not leap to conclusions. He would chat so that he might learn more. Ed always sought more data. Second, Ed did not disparage his staff, even as they created difficulties. Third, Ed could think on his feet; he stayed cool, stood back, listened, and plotted, all while giving nothing away.

My excitement was also fuelled by knowing that when thrown off-stride, individuals react, revealing themselves. In the world of ethnography, this was ideal triangulation territory. Triangulation is the process of testing emerging patterns and theories. Confrontation would be exciting, and perhaps personally satisfying, but Ed's course of action was simply instructive. Put in that stressful situation, what had Ed done? Nothing. Ed had revealed his true self as confident, non-threatened, and deliberate.

This section has summarized Ed's process of data gathering through three examples. For Ed, obtaining more data was all about better understanding, and with all this knowledge, Ed built, revised, and applied his mental model before acting. This mental model was his "big picture."

"Big Picture" Reality

Ed's "big picture" was his operating reality, but it was not the district vision. Yes, the district had an official vision. Ed knew it, he knew it was important, and he supported it rigorously. But the two were different. Ed's picture was more mundane, more day-to-day. It guided his daily interactions and the bigger projects, and it had become part of district vernacular. So, what was it and how could it be understood?

Student services coordinator Herb Bondar tried to help me understand Ed's thinking process. Eager to explain how similar he was to Ed, Herb understood Ed because they were both "right-brain" thinkers. Right-brain thinking, a feature of the creative-intuitive domain, provided "a very big, whole picture." Wait, right-brain, creative-intuitive? Would Ed agree?

Ed thought of himself as predominately left-brained and rational, but he recognized, appreciated, and used both hemispheres. On one occasion, he described the impact of his favourite opera, "The music wells up in me, just pure emotion. I am tired at the end of two-and-a-half hours." On another day, as we travelled to his home for lunch, he mentioned doing more right-brain activities on the weekend, activities like music. There was a corollary to that singular proposition: during the week, Ed's thinking was more left-brained, and on the weekend, more right-brained.

But getting back to Herb, he saw the big picture as a creative-intuitive dynamic endeavour because that was how Herb interpreted the world. Herb accepted the brain's separate spheres, interpreted events as occurring in separate spheres, and he was right, for how else do we understand the world except in our own terms. But Ed had stated otherwise; his world of events was a continuum, a continuum that he could explore as it suited him. For Ed, the brain's separate spheres could and did work together. Aside from leaving me confused by Herb's interpretation of a right/left brain dichotomy, I recognized that Herb identified with Ed. He was not the only one. Other's saw themselves in Ed, and he saw himself in others. He was empathetic and this left his "big picture" view huge. I might be critical of Herb's "explanation," but no one else did as well in explaining it. Such confusion did not prevent the widespread use of the term.

Of course, there are other ways to view a big picture, and that was literally as a big picture. I recall the impressive dioramas of my youth—calendar pictures in doctor's offices or *National Geographic* stories—with renderings of every species of wildlife in a given setting commingled into one expansive panorama. Ed was indeed visual, but he was also conceptual. I gradually came to understand the big picture as a concept drawing. When Ed spoke of his "big picture," he communicated that he had already accounted for some new bit of data and that all was well in hand. Whatever was happening had not thrown him or his plans off-balance. Somehow it was already or would soon be incorporated into his operating "picture," "puzzle," or "script."

For Ed, the "big picture" was simply his melding of all the available data into a coherent whole. It was his personal guide that he shared holistically with others for their reassurance.

Weighing Choices

Ed's thinking, searching for data, forming, and revising his "big picture" were key to establishing the support needed to act on decisions. It was there, in getting things done, that Ed demonstrated the strengths of his leadership. Ed had significant history in the district. During all that time, he had shown better than just able leadership, first as principal at Walter MacEwan High School, and then as the district's deputy superintendent. Now at the pinnacle of the organization as superintendent, Ed was ultimately responsible for all the administrative decisions made and for the actions arising out of them. With his team's help, most decisions were easy, rational solutions that made sense to most everyone. Sometimes though, a rational decision was unpopular and hard to swallow, but when necessary, Ed made these too. We have seen how he viewed the board decision on a school lessee. While it bothered his colleagues, Ed saw it as rational and implemented it without hesitation. And there were those few decisions that were needed quickly—before supportive data were discovered. Ed quickly acted on these too. There were also those few that could not be justified on any rational footing, but once again, Ed did what needed doing. To face the irrational and to resolve dilemmas, Ed turned to the wisdom of the past. Ethicists and religious philosophers had examined perplexing issues by relying on a set of guidelines, and Ed accepted their expertise. These were moral principles. What were these principles, and where had they come from?

Others talked about Ed's principles. An interviewee declared that Ed possessed a religious presence. Maybe that was because they knew Ed, knew that Ed led an exemplary life. He neither smoked nor drank. He seldom swore. His demeanour and words touched no alarms with the many church-going folks he dealt with. He was comfortable with all these folks—and with the folks who did not affiliate themselves to a Christian faith, those who adhered to other religions, and those outside of any religion. But while some people announced their religious affiliations, Ed kept his to himself. Principal James Thorborn knew the religious affiliations of many of his colleagues but not Ed's. He described Ed as religiously neutral, possessing "strong family values," acceptable to the religious right, but easily accommodating "alternative lifestyles." Herb Bondar, student services coordinator, described Ed as a "small 'c' Christian, a person with a good concept of fairness." If he was religious, Ed kept it to himself. So I asked him. He talked about the "good fundamentalist Christian values" he had been brought up with, and that he and his spouse, Marie, had passed on to their family. Marie identified them: "Being very honest, very moral…a very straight line. I do not want to use the word Christian…all the religions in the world, they all have the same basic moral philosophy, character philosophy…that is very ingrained and very firm. You do not try to tell him that right is wrong when he knows that right is right."

Marie and Ed knew their beliefs, and knew where they came from, but Ed stayed out of any such debate. He offered only the tired adage, "The people that live it don't have to spout it."

Why then did I bring up religion? I did it because in a community that had strong religious elements, it made life easier to quietly fit in. Wapiti Falls was such a community. Ed fit here; he would fit in anywhere. He sought fairness and doing right. For the analytic learner, it was a proven expert system. He had grown up in it, and his experiences had cemented its legitimacy. So, what were these insights? Ed had four inviolable standards: trust, respect, balance, and moderation. Illustrations follow.

Trust and respect

Ed did what he thought right. Prior to moving to Wapiti Falls, Ed had worked in one of Alberta's largest districts. He left that position, and he told me why. Having worked there for some time, Ed had advanced within the district, but he somehow had come to regard their management philosophy as disrespectful. This incident capped off this thinking: When the superintendent's office ordered him downtown, telling him to be there in twenty minutes, Ed thought hard. He knew the district liked his work. He had been told that he could count on future promotions. But his thoughts went deeper; he asked himself if his soul could survive there. Put simply, did he want to work in an atmosphere of disrespect? It was time to test them, and so he arrived late. The meeting happened, and he had made no complaint, but he knew what he needed to do. He would find a better district. But moving required not only Ed's decision. He would need good references. He would need to show a new employer that he would succeed for them. He put all the elements in place, then he sought offers elsewhere. When the Wapiti Falls offer came. he accepted it and began his long career in Wapiti Falls. Respect was critical for Ed Noyce.

Confidence was part of Ed's success as a leader. He earned it. For years he had laboured over critical decisions, made them only when certain. Most had worked out well. It took him to the top position in his district, to the top of his profession. Confidence had allowed him to do what he thought best, what he thought right. His deputy superintendent in Wapiti Falls, Don Howard, described Ed as confident enough to admit mistakes and confident enough to make decisions that others disagreed with. Ed provided this example of a decision that went against the grain. Faced with declining revenues, the Wapiti Falls district had been obliged to cut staff. But contrary to most advice on offer, Ed refused to move quickly. He formulated a plan. It gave staff a full year or more to make their decision. Staff understood the need and responded appropriately. Waiting had reflected the district's respect for them. Staff saw that Ed was doing the right thing for the district and for them, and in return, they respected and trusted their district. Yes, there were incentives, but respect drove decision-making, and respect begat trust. And it worked, for everyone. Respect and trust were mutual.

Ed also trusted parents. He talked about his invitation to a parent council meeting and his subsequent attendance. He was not on the agenda for their first topic, and so he waited, watched, and said nothing. Their first topic was scheduling the teacher's professional development half-day. For students, it amounted to a half-day off school—a holiday. Ed described their conversation. Sides were taken—a long weekend for students or a mid-week break that would leave teachers and students fresher. Which would it be? Ed listened quietly, appreciatively. The discussion showed parents taking the matter seriously, weighing the advantages of each choice. In the end, he knew that they would make their recommendation out of concern for their children. What was their decision? Ed never said, as it did not matter. Ed had seen the discussion, heard parents talk about their children and the children of others; Ed trusted them and their process.

Balance and moderation

Just as respect and trust represent a middle ground, so too did Ed's search for balance. Simply put, he strove to get the "pendulum to the middle" of its arc. He noted and appreciated the balance that new assistant superintendent Ab Digby brought to the senior administration team. We saw that Ed listened carefully for balance as parents discussed their kids' education. Earlier, I identified his proposal to better address fiscal equity and student opportunity for all—fair and balanced. This was how respectful people worked together. Respect and trust, balance and moderation were very personal for Ed. Getting there was not always an easy path, so why did Ed invest his limited time here? Why did he make the effort?

According to the district's psychologist, student services coordinator Herb Bondar, Ed made the effort because he received a payback. The payback was "pride. The concept of wanting to make a difference. The concept of saying I am here; I can help people. It is not the cash." Herb affirmed what I saw, namely that Ed was proud of his work, his contribution to students, staff, and district. I understood that this pride was not hubris, and it was not about personal conceit. It was the pride gained when others achieved their goals. In spouse Marie Noyce's words, "He feels a sense that he's contributing to making things, well, if not better, at least on the road to better." One day, getting up from his desk, Ed opened the door and said, "If I leave the door closed, people go away instead of getting problems solved." Knowing that he was helping made it worth his effort, in the early mornings when he left for work, to working lunches, to staying past quitting time, to taking work home, to taking fewer holidays than allocated. Ed set the example for everyone, modelling trust, respect, balance, and moderation—in everything but work. He did not expect others to work that hard, but he had no problems if they did.

Ed's leadership decisions started with logic, but ended only when decisions felt right. Quick decisions were sometimes required. In our interview, he shared his guidelines for quick decision-making:

> "There are times when I know I can't wait for all the data to make a decision. We have got to move a little more quickly and I will slip myself, if I can, up into type 4 [dynamic learner] and say, here is what I've got, and here is what I think that we should do. Here is what my gut tells me. Let's do it. But I still want to consult with the other fellows around."

When he needed to, Ed took more risks and made things happen, but he did so without being pushy. He was never pushy. I saw him act aggressively twice—once with a parent on a difficult call and once in person with an Alberta Education consultant. The latter occurred when his stress seemingly exceeded his normally high "pain" threshold. (He had wanted to force Alberta Education into admitting that their policies were hurting some Alberta students. He wanted them to disagree with their boss, and I could see that this consultant wanted to do just that. In the end, perhaps after swallowing hard, this official supported his boss.)

Self-Discipline

Ed was disciplined. Is that a form of intelligence? Discipline is not generally noted as a feature of intelligence, but it should be. Three examples follow; they make the case that Ed's discipline was sustainable only through intellectual rigour. He knew what supported his big picture, what detracted from it, and what was immaterial.

First, Ed managed his rather high levels of energy carefully. As he explained, in schools there were more people and more things happening, and all of it happening at once. In schools, the energy needed to deal with all these smaller emergencies was a virtue. In the district office, it would be ruinous. At the district level, events had more impact, and timelines were longer and intensity lower. High energy—especially if it showed up as impatience—was a liability. Ed had to slow things down, and he disciplined himself to meet this need. One of Ed's strategies was to assume the role of an actor on stage. Knowing that others were watching him, he stayed still, and thus he conveyed an image of calm deliberation. It looked like intense concentration, and maybe it was. But at least part of his concentration was on his effort to remain still. In public meetings he sat quietly, stone-faced, almost devoid of nervous energy. He watched others, scanning for their tells, the subtle signs that might reveal their thoughts and feelings. In the privacy of his office, on the telephone, he did not have to do that because he was not being watched. To a listener, he seemed comfortable, quiet, at ease. His voice showed that he was involved, interested, even eager, but he was also relaxed. It seemed that just then he had nothing else that needed doing, that he had all the time needed to listen to an important person—the person on the other end of the call. While he seemed patient, he was not. On the phone, there were the auditory clues when he thought that a conversation should finish. If the caller failed to act on these signals, signs of nervous energy—otherwise concealed—emerged: He searched the piles on his desk for documents; on finding them he took only a brief glance. He played with the phone, fidgeted with a pen in his shoe or on the desk, accessed computer data, kept time with his fingers or pen, discarded his pink call-back notes with an extra flourish, puffed up his cheeks, looked outside in search of any happening, moved his hand through his hair, and on occasion made a note for later use. When on hold, he talked to people in the room. On one occasion, after finishing and forwarding a letter electronically for final formatting and printing, he rose, raced to his secretary's desk, and arrived just as his letter did. With the copy in front of them, he could ensure that his instructions were clear. (To be fair, there was a complication. His secretary was stressed by a death in the family and needed additional support and follow-up. Ed made the extra effort needed, forcing him to check on how well things were completed.) In person, Ed was unfailingly polite, and when he wanted to move on, he stopped asking questions. When the visitor had departed, he was immediately back onto whatever task had been interrupted or was next in his plans. Ed's energy was quietly managed, conveying interest rather than serving as a distraction. In summary, Ed was not as easygoing as his manners and voice implied. Discipline and extra effort made it seem so.

The second example of a formidable discipline derived from Ed's reputation for a strong work ethic. Ed pushed himself. Staff thought that he worked most of the time, slept too little, and yet, he did his job with enthusiasm and energy. Some wondered about the source of his energy. Could it be a reputed high caloric intake? Assistant superintendent Ab Digby referenced this by giving a humorous account about his fondness for sweets, especially for desserts. I wondered about that. The Ed I studied was all about moderation and did not eat a lot. He liked desserts, but his weight, or lack of it, screamed self-discipline. Where staff marvelled at his energy, I marvelled at his discipline.

The third example of discipline came from deputy superintendent Don Howard. He spoke of how personnel issues weighed on Ed. Where others would make judgmental comments about what they had heard, Ed was quiet, concerned about the self-destructive actions or words of others, but mute himself. Don said, they "would just eat away…but he would never say…why the hell did you say that?" Ed stoically waited, patient. Fight or flight would have been easier. Staying neutral, effectively biding his time, required discipline. Did such emotional control affect Ed? In general, Don thought so, "Those are the kind of things that will drag him down." But somehow, it had not. I thought that it was because Ed always had a plan and reacting was never part of it. His intellect overpowered temptation. Ed could stick to his plan because he was extremely disciplined.

Summary Notes on Ed's Intelligence

In summarizing the dominant features of Ed's intelligence, five features were highlighted. Ed was a thinker. He relied on an impressive ability to search out facts and opinions. He could take it all in and synthesize it to form his idiosyncratic "big picture" model of events and needs. While ever the rationalist, leadership events sometimes required decisions before the data supported action, and then again, some problems were not reductive to rational analysis. It was here, where rationality failed, that Ed relied on his gut reactions in weighing his choices, a gut that valued trust and respect for people, and a path of balance and moderation. And finally, Ed was always disciplined, in control of his emotions.

While smart, Ed was not the only smart person. Not all smart, capable teachers want to become a superintendent of schools, but some do. And of those who want to lead and are chosen, once there, some fail. Leading requires more than intelligence. Ed found that he wanted to lead, and once in the role, he earned his success. Why was that? What did Ed have that led to success? We look there next.

CHAPTER 3

The Affable Ed Noyce

Joe Pivott, the former superintendent of the Wapiti Falls district had earned many accolades over a long career. In addition to his success in Wapiti Falls public schools, he was the key figure in starting the local college. He even taught there. A district school was named after him. He retired with a reputation fully intact, and then he continued his work, whatever it was. He even kept an assigned office in the district headquarters. Joe Pivott knew education, and he was esteemed for his knowledge, locally and beyond. He embodied educational leadership. It was fair to say that he was an avatar of education. When he declared that superintendent Ed Noyce was a "good one" because of his intelligence and affability, I took him seriously. It became my starting point. I previously examined Ed's intelligence, and now consider the second quality, affability.

Affability, like intelligence, takes in a broad sweep of skills—being pleasant, at ease talking to others, and friendliness. Affable interactions are comfortable for everyone involved. Actions that invite, reward, and encourage participation are also affable. In his treatise on leadership, Burns (1978) identified such interactional qualities in several lists. One such list contained "prudence, honour, courage, civility, honesty, fairness" (Burns 1978: 75). Another included "honesty, responsibility, fairness, the honouring of commitments" (Ibid: 426), and Burns declared that without them, "transactional leadership could not work" (Ibid: 426). Shortly thereafter, Burns repeated himself and added "honour and integrity—by the extent to which they advanced or thwarted fundamental standards of good conduct in humankind" (Ibid: 426). These basic values—honesty, fairness, prudence, civility, courage, honour, and integrity—served as my guide in the examination of Ed's affability. I started by examining interactions of immediate impact—that is, events that came up in the one-offs of day-to-day events. Then, I looked at ongoing interactions—those with history. From there, the most significant end-value, integrity, became my final arbiter of affability.

The Immediacy of Day to Day

Ed's day-to-day interactions with staff revealed patterns. Ed's most visible activities were informal conversations rather than sticking to bureaucratic channels. Instrumental to this informality were Ed's ingrained courtesy and patience.

Three Quick Chats and One Extended Follow-Up

Thursday, May 26, was my first full day of observation. For Ed Noyce, it was one more day of trying to keep ahead. District junior high schools were transitioning into middle schools, so some staff would be moving between schools and principals, and new teaching philosophies were being integrated with existing teaching practices. Come fall, students who had graduated from Grades 5 and 6 would be in middle schools, and students from Grades 8 and 9 would be in one of the two high schools. It would be double the usual movement. Further, the sparkling new Ormand Mitchell High School would receive an entirely new staff and student body. While they had anticipated some issues, others would surface out of the blue. The reorganized system would have elementary schools from Grade 1 to 5, middle schools from Grades 6 to 8, and high schools from Grades 9 to 12. These changes were significant, and preparations kept everyone busy. (Note: Kindergarten programs might operate out of schools or be otherwise linked, but they were operated by independent societies.)

Staffing decisions were underway, but they were held up because the district's contract with teachers was about to expire, and negotiations were not looking good. The district needed and wanted more staff, but could not afford them. The number of teachers employed would vary according to whatever the new contract established.

The board had also requested that the minister of education authorize a school closure. Having followed all the ministerial requirements, the Wapiti Falls School Board was confident that permission would follow, but until they had it, several staff positions were in limbo. The board had also just downsized central office staff, eliminating several curriculum consultants. No one knew how well the new configuration would fit.

Ed's already demanding environment got more complicated when assistant superintendent Jake Harris unexpectedly decided that he wanted a reassignment. At the regular board meeting the previous night, the board heard about Jake's request. Trustees were surprised, but as superintendent Ed Noyce and his team supported Jake's request, it was approved. Jake would take the only available principalship, and the district would need to find a replacement for this central office role. This left staffing unsettled, meaning that Ed faced a new puzzle. He decided to start with principals, as he now had more principals than principalships.

Change was afoot, and he was busy.

This morning, immediately after last evening's board meeting, Ed wanted to notify three school administrators about the staffing decisions and indecision. He wanted it done before the grapevine did its work. We left his office soon after I arrived there.

By 08:00 hours, he was in Pawoki School. Many staff members had proceeded him there. They were busy, but there was no rush—they still had time before the 09:00 hours start of classes. Ed went to the office and asked to speak to principal Paul Briggs. Paul was there, working, and emerged from his office. Ed greeted him and asked if I could join them in a meeting. I could and did.

Ed came to the point; the board had appointed the current assistant superintendent, Jake Harris, to replace a retiring principal. Jake's request was unexpected, and he had taken the only vacant principal position. With Paul's school due to close, Paul was suddenly redundant, the odd man out. With one fewer school, the district now had one principal too many. If the game was musical chairs, Paul would soon have no chair. Would this become a contractual problem, as the district had effectively fired a principal without cause? An obvious predicament, Ed advised that he would "take care" of Paul. Come fall, if there was no suitable administrative placement, Paul would be placed elsewhere at full principal salary until there was a suitable opening. Paul took the message quietly just as Ed had predicted. The conversation soon turned to other staff and students, and they speculated about another school in another district. This diversion had given Paul time to think, and Paul's thoughts had gone to the district in-service day, June 8. In-service, or professional development (or just PD) days were days that teachers worked without students. It was a day off for students, and a day of preparation for teachers. This particular day was designated as staff planning, preparatory for next year. With all the changes underway in the district, planning had increased significance. As to Paul, having no assigned position, what could he prepare for? And so he asked, could he go golfing instead? Smiling, he waited. Instead of answering, Ed changed the topic; it had been heard but unacknowledged. Having delivered the news—with still no decision for Paul—Ed was off to the next school.

Next up was a meeting at nearby Alexo Elementary School. On arrival, Ed confirmed an administrative transfer. Just that. A bit of chit-chat, and he left for J. M. Kovach School. That would be the third quick meeting that morning.

By about 08:30 hours, Ed was parked across from the J. M. Kovach School. It was nearly half an hour before the start of classes. As he crossed the street, he heard a call-out, "Hiya, Ed." Ed smiled and returned the greeting. He explained that he had met this youngster a few years back, and the kid remembered it well, and he obviously enjoyed the notoriety of knowing the top dog in the district, the superintendent of schools. Ed continued his trek and talked about the meeting ahead. He would be the bearer of bad news, and there could be sparks. To minimize the hurt, Ed wanted to be alone with vice-principal Sandra Jenkins. His message: she had not been selected as the school's principal next year; Jake Harris would be. Arriving in the office and seeing her there, he greeted Sandra, and they departed to a quiet office. They reappeared as classes were getting underway; their business was done. Retiring principal Magnus Petersen walked Ed to the exit as he reminisced about his own career. Ed listened politely.

In the car, Ed indicated that he had not been early enough. Despite his request that Jake wait with the news, that Jake say nothing about the change, Jake had informed Magnus Petersen. In turn, Magnus had organized an impromptu staff meeting for 08:00 hours. Consequently, Sandra already had received the difficult news before Ed had arrived. So how did Ed use his time with her? He told me he talked about the position and about her. He offered her support, told her that she had been strong candidate, and suggested that her future administrative prospects were good. Quick but not quick enough, Ed's direct efforts to soften the blow of a failure had been too late, and he quietly returned to his office and other morning tasks.

By June 8, Ed had thought about Paul Brigg's request, and he had consulted others. Paul would not have to pretend to be in preparation for next year; he had official permission to be out golfing. And why not? Closing Pawoki School was already traumatic. Everyone was doing their respectful best to mitigate the loss. Pawoki staff, for example, had invited district staff to their final staff celebration. It was their gesture of good faith, but Ed understood—and he made certain that district level staff understood—that if they attended, they would be viewed as gate crashers. Consequently, they acknowledged the invitation but declined attendance. They would not rub salt in fresh wounds.

Before the start of the next school year, a principalship came open, and as Ed had promised, Paul Briggs, the principal with no school, had been reassigned. He was now principal of Etzikom Community School.

Ed visited principal Briggs in his new school one fine fall day. On arrival, he checked into the school office, asked for Paul, and learned that he was teaching. Not one to wait, to waste time, Ed wandered the hallways and observed all that could be seen. He soon encountered the itinerant music teacher. With her students elsewhere, she had time to chat, and she told Ed how happy she was with her job, her schools, and her system. Meanwhile. Paul's class had ended, and he had learned that Ed was in the building—and looked for and found him.

Back in his office, Paul reported that his year was going well. He and his vice-principal had discussed enrollment with a prospective Grade 4 pupil and her family. He was optimistic about her enrollment, and the appeal of a small school. Theirs was an open enrollment system, meaning that parents could choose his school if they wished. Ed was pleased; he knew of this family and had their "story" somewhere in the back of his mind. He would "get it glued together," if Paul wanted details. They chatted about other things—students, parents, staff, and their upcoming in-service. Ed acknowledged Paul's efforts, a "great start here, Paul," and he laughed with him. With the chit-chat done, Ed moved on to business, his purpose for being there. Another potential challenge had come up.

Ed told him that he was working on his Student Accommodation Report. The committee was looking at school attendance areas again, and school closure was back on the table. At their last meeting, the talk was that Etzikom Community School would remain operational, but would have fewer bus students, forty-seven fewer. This school community—its attendance area—was already unable to fill the school. Students were bussed in to keep it viable, which made busing the school's lifeblood. Since his previous school—Pawoki—had closed in June, Paul's ear was keenly attuned to discussions of school closure. He listened carefully, repeated some of Ed's words, including the clunker, "back to Pawoki." Ed heard his concern—that Paul feared that he would once again face the trauma of another school closure debate—and proceeded carefully, crafting his massaging deftly. He knew that he had to prepare Paul in case it happened again.

Would Paul hear it as intended—preparation? Or would he hear it as a threat—a repeat of last spring's heartaches? And so, Ed elaborated; he would recommend that the Etzikom receive additional students bused in from the newer sub-divisions. This would further expand their attendance area eastward. Still, Ed expected questions, and if asked, Paul should be prepared. Paul understood. He replied ironically; he was "very familiar" with the district's school closure policy. Ed's critical messages had been shared and understood, but the conversation continued.

Paul noted that his parent council was energetic (and potentially political, should the need arise). Was he messaging Ed? Telling him that the school had powerful backers who would fight any school closure attempt?

Having delivered the hard news, Ed shared the bigger plan. He identified the district's most pressing concern, namely the "pieces still missing" in the provincial restructuring plan. He drew out a confidential memo on district finances. This led to a further a review of the general directions of the Student Accommodation Committee and its focus on the district's unused student capacity. All of it was about money. Paul appreciated being in the know and was satisfied with prospects for his school, for now. With their business really wrapped up, Ed asked Paul to tell me his story of "the Rileys." Paul did so, identifying issues with this family, and the resolution eventually reached. Paul's descriptions were colourful; his solution was novel and pragmatic. Pleased with my reaction, Paul took the opportunity to further demonstrate his resourcefulness, and luck. He shared additional intrigues, and then he extended his support to the board and to the superintendent. Ed acknowledged the pressures on the board and that further committee decisions were expected, perhaps by December. Paul repeated his thanks to the district. They had sponsored his attendance at a summer leadership workshop, and the program was "super." He said that Wapiti Falls looked especially good in the face of indiscriminate cuts elsewhere. Their discussion had reached a natural end, and Ed excused himself.

Analysis of Three Quick Chats

This section started with three June meetings held in quick succession. The first advised Paul that he was a principal without a school. The second meeting, the one at Alexo School, was short—face-to-face congratulations on an upcoming transfer and promotion. The final meeting that spring day involved Sandra Jenkins.

There were two meetings with principal Paul Briggs, once in June and a follow up in September. These two encounters will be considered last.

With Sandra, Ed had attempted to beat the grapevine, to deliver difficult news respectfully. In communicating a non-promotion, Ed had reached out to Sandra Jenkins. He was too late. Jake had jumped the gun. While the immediate purpose was sidelined, Ed still met with Sandra; he offered support and encouragement. At no time did he complain about Jake. The impulsive Jake would face no repercussions; Ed did not work that way. Ed would always be the better person. The district relied on Ed's capacity to forgive, to focus on the important matters rather than personalities. This meeting had a single purpose, and further follow-up was not called for.

In the second meeting, Ed was in and out of a school, able to offer news and congratulations on a promotion.

We saw more in the two tête à têtes with Paul Briggs; the content was richer. But in all these conversations, Ed demonstrated his affability. With Paul, both conversations were about a school closure, one that was happening that June and one that might happen. Closing a school is challenging. Beyond the hard work of presenting a rational financial justification for an event no one sought, it was a human event that sometimes ended careers. It soured relationships. It changed people and communities. It was political. Paul had already faced it once, and perhaps he would see it once more. Ed thought that such situations required attention, an appreciation of the human context, and he made that effort.

Note the conversations between Ed and Paul. Their friendly chit-chat flowed easily, pleasantly, and as with the other conversations, they wandered around the topic. It was evident that their relationship revolved around friendship, trust, and respect.

In June, school closure had helped solve last year's financial problem, but in this new term, the board faced the same financial dilemma. Tough decisions would be required once again, and the board, through a committee, once again seemed to be asking themselves what schools and programs could they afford? It put Paul where he had just been—still recovering from what might have been the end to his administrative—and perhaps his teaching/administrative-career. Would he now be asking himself if he was on the cusp of the plague's second wave? Ed felt for Paul; he put himself in Paul's place. And so, in the second meeting, he made every effort to accommodate Paul's fears, to reassure and support him, and to let him vent. Ed also honoured Paul, giving him an opportunity to brag a little, to demonstrate his resourcefulness. As ever, exchanges were honest and reciprocal. Both were comfortable discussing their business—planning for future student populations. Ed was honest, fair, factual, patient, and sincere. Ed respected Paul—applauded his energy and enthusiasm, and heard his acknowledgement of, and compliment to, the district. Paul was strong once more and doing his best for the district. Because Ed was candid, Paul now understood more about the money pressures on the board. And there was a bonus: Ed had Paul's testimonial to share with others. He found this personally satisfying; together they were making a difference. Being affable reflected who Ed was, and it served his leadership goals.

It would be easy to discount the value of dealing with the people issues. Ed could come right down to business, but he was comfortable going beyond the facts, comfortable dealing with people issues too. He did it in simple chit-chat in which relationships were renewed, connections were made, and sensitive issues were shared. When meeting with Paul, both men gained new knowledge, and learned some unexpected things. In these flowing, dynamic conversations, people felt safe and respected, and when relaxed and unguarded, background matters emerged. Trifling details came to mind, points that might be bothering them surfaced. They revealed themselves. Small talk was vital to leadership in this district.

Informal Communications over Bureaucratic Channels

Burns (1978) argued that values underlie leadership. Consider it so; this made the values evident in Ed's interactions critical. Examined here are four open, affable interactions occurring within the organization. This section starts and ends with matters related to department head Herb Bondar, Student Services Coordinator. The middle interactions involved outgoing assistant superintendent, Jake Harris, and considered one of his final staff placement decisions. However good he was as an administrator, Jake was flighty, and this attribute drew my attention throughout this study. We had already seen how he pre-empted Ed's meeting with Sandra Jenkins on May 26. Jake's actions and interactions will keep reappearing, not because they are unusual—they are—but because they reveal less obvious features of Ed's leadership. The first vignette began at Ed's open door, a sacrosanct policy of his.

Staff knew the symbolism of Ed's open office door; it announced that he was open to issues and suggestions. They knew it was more than symbolism; it was also true. Susan Bakker, secretary for the student services coordinator, Herb Bondar, took Ed up on it. They met late Friday afternoon, June 10. Its immediacy and brevity were typical, less than ten minutes. Their goal was to share perspective on what Susan saw as an administrative issue and to start thinking about a solution. Notice the mutual respect in the following:

Having finished a conversation with the assistant superintendent of business services, Bill Bersche, Ed returned to his office, no doubt thinking about money. That is what he had talked to Bill about. Money issues were always at the fore in Wapiti Falls, so Ed and others did their best to stay on top of money matters. Back in his office, he received a call from secretary Susan Bakker.

Shortly thereafter, Susan stood in Ed's doorway. Invited in, Susan described problems with the district's in-service on student cumulative files. Since the files were in schools, it was the job of school secretaries to keep them current. As Susan saw it, the in-service designed to establish and reinforce uniform district standards was not working. School secretaries had changed, and their responsibilities had increased over the years. Getting files done right was becoming ever harder. Susan thought that a dedicated part-time staff member was needed. Someone hired centrally and specializing in cumulative files would do a better job. Ed asked, Would the school secretaries like this? They would, Susan explained, schools were frenetic at year-end. That was it. She asked Ed to think it over. Ed had not just listened to the suggestion; it drew his response.

Ed recognized it as a good idea but difficult to implement. And it would be the opposite of the current direction—centralization rather than decentralization—but as schools were constantly being asked to do more, some of these extras were done poorly. Ed identified the central irony. If monies were available, it would only be because of the savings realized by cutting centralized teaching consultants. Susan was asking the district to add central services, while the district was reducing central services. Still, he thought, the district might combine other part-time tasks to accomplish this and more. The matter of cutting expensive professionals to add less expensive non-professionals was left unsaid.

Their business done, the conversation shifted to personal matters. Susan talked about her daughter; she used to help with the district files. Older now and going out with friends, she no longer had time to help Susan in the office. Ed asked about Zach, her son. With family updates complete, Susan and Ed both turned to me and asked how long my district kept cumulative files. This topic was soon exhausted—I had no idea. That done, Ed asked Susan about her job. He teased her, asked if her boss, Herb Bondar, student services coordinator, was still miserable. Susan laughed and deflected the question. She talked instead about being busy. June was always busy. Their conversation was beginning to repeat itself. They recognized the repetition and let it end. Susan departed, and Ed began a call-back to a school on another topic.

The second of these quick chats offered a different lesson. Openness did not mean that Ed was unfailingly candid. There could be complications. Jake Harris, assistant superintendent of human services, had a challenging job, and Ed knew that solutions were often complicated. Here, two meetings flowed out of just one decision.

One June day, Jake Harris appeared in Ed's office. While he was leaving his current job for a district principalship, in June he was still there, still keeping Ed apprised of staffing decisions for the upcoming school year. He had told Ed that Janice Wong's position would be split again—she would be full time—but in two schools and that she was satisfied. Ed listened agreeably. As soon as Jake left, Ed carried on with another task. He had not said that he was meeting with Janice that afternoon—at her request. Something was up, but Ed did not know what.

That afternoon, Ed listened carefully to Janice. She wanted her own classroom, not a shared classroom, preferring Grade 2 or 3, but other elementary grades would be fine. She would be patient, waiting for the right assignment was no problem. Ed assured Janice that her "stock" was high. They would try to accommodate her. With the gist of the conversation done, Janice departed, and Ed returned to other work.

Two interactions out of one decision is a typical illustration of the interconnectedness of work for Ed and for every superintendent. The issue here, openness, will be soon be explored.

The fourth vignette involved Herb Bondar, student services coordinator, again. Imagine Herb, what he must have felt when Ed brought parent news to his attention. A parent had called; Ed got the call and was passing it on to the right person. Herb looked surprised and listened intently, silently. Herb was relatively new to the organization, and he seemed mystified. Perhaps he did not expect to have this kind of informality. He must have thought, what was up? What he heard was not insignificant, but it was not critical. It did not involve some screw-up or something that had been ignored or mishandled, but still, it had made its way to the superintendent. Why did this issue get to Ed? Why was he giving it his personal attention? More than likely, Herb was still thinking about such nuances when Ed finished by stating his expectations. Ed wanted the matter followed up on; he thought Herb might call the parent. Shortly, Ed followed his verbal report by handing Herb his little note. It was his job now, and it came without further ado. The two men parted.

Analysis of Informal Communications

These short vignettes, pulled out of hours of observation, were selected to relay information about the Wapiti Falls district, a hierarchical organization that Ed led in a distinctive non-hierarchical style. Notice first the conversations, their easy openness; they were amiable and purposeful.

In the first vignette, Susan and Ed interacted on a district issue and then moved into relationship building when Ed asked about Susan's family. Susan left feeling respected and appreciated. Notice too that Ed explored Susan's relationship with her boss.

In the two parts of a second event—staff placement—Ed withheld important information from both parties. Ed prided his open relationships, but here that was not in evidence. Ed had not warned Jake of his meeting with Janice. Had he been candid about meeting Janice, the impulsive Jake might well have rushed in, possibly reducing Ed's options. With Janice, Ed listened and promoted her professional status. But what was left unsaid was as important as what was said. Yes, Ed thought Janice was great with children, but outside the classroom, he was aware that she had had difficult communications with adults, specifically with some principals.

I do not know if Ed did anything with either of these matters. Jake would soon be in a new position. Janice's issues were not of immediate impact.

Finally, consider Ed's short meeting with Herb: probably some parent had called and asked to speak to the superintendent. Parents do that; some of them start at the top. While the front office probably knew who normally dealt with such matters, Ed had given explicit instructions. They were instructed to forward such calls for Ed directly to Ed. They complied, and Ed took the call, listened, and made his tiny notes on a tiny slip of paper. When he saw Herb, he passed it on. Herb, after all, was the person who normally handled this particular student issue. Why did Ed do this? He might have done it because there could be more to it. He had asked Susan about working with Herb. Through these two interactions with Susan and Herb, he might learn of matters that were working or not working, of solutions or of issues getting bogged down—and such matters had caused some grief in this department before. Ed was unobtrusively gathering data.

Despite the easy flow and candid details shared in Wapiti Falls, not everything was or should be shared. Decisions were still required, and some details were extraneous to successful implementation. Return briefly to the interactions involving Jake and Janice. Ed had been less than fulsome with both. No doubt Ed had faced similar situations before. And no doubt he had used this very strategy before, but somehow, he was not tagged as selectively accommodating, or as slippery and duplicitous, or as a rationalizer who only gave easy, kind messages. Instead, I saw that his discretion was valued. He was the bulkhead supporting those left out, or hurt, or short-changed. He left the "Jakes" alone, waited for them to grow. Failing remediation through gentle nudges, he would be patient and supportive—unless such words or actions damaged the district or its students or staff. Ed was disciplined enough to be politely silent or consistently steady and positive—building staff morale, encouraging people, and stressing the positives. It worked for Ed, and it worked for the district and its people. And why not? Ed had determined that confrontations were unproductive. Ed was fair, considerate, and careful. Adroit balance was essential.

In these scenarios, the approach taken was informal, outside of the bureaucratic hierarchy. Still, I heard no one complain or even mention proper channels or line-charts. They existed and were utilized, but informal channels were often considered superior. Ed wanted information to flow, and the channel was immaterial.

Finally, it was abundantly clear that Ed relished details, grassroots details. There was enough information for everyone, and Ed's leadership processes ensured that he had his share. The more information coming to him, the better he functioned.

Courtesy and Humility

Ed told me that he been looking forward to the Kananaskis Middle School year-end Science-Mathematics Olympiad for several weeks. This event helped me visualize the importance of hierarchical rank in the district by providing further details on how Ed viewed his status as chief executive officer of an important school district.

With his early arrival at Kananaskis Middle School, Ed had time to chat with principal Sam Belterlaben. Sam was concerned: would there be a job next year for the young teacher who organized this event? Ed did not know. The board/teacher contract impasse needed resolution, and until then, new contracts would be held in abeyance.

We made our way to a large room—a gym with a high ceiling; tall, large windows; and a brick feature wall—altogether an attractive space. Students had finished filing in and were sitting in theatre-style rows directly on the floor. Chairs were reserved for the teachers and the few dignitaries present. When all were ready, the program began. The teacher in charge of the program called on the district's science consultant to speak. Next, he invited a representative from Union Gas and Electric, the school's business partner, to the front. He, too, had words to share with the assembly. With recognitions and speech-making complete, it was the students' turn for recognition. Those meeting the Olympiad standards were called to the front of the assembly, where they received medals, to the loud applause of their classmates. While not everyone was focused on the program, everyone in the audience enjoyed their brief respite from the classroom. It was June. The school year had been long, and that routine was now old. Students grew restless; some were talkative and noisy. The program finished, a long twenty minutes or so, and the audience departed. A reporter was present, and she interviewed the presenting dignitaries. Alone, Ed slipped away. He had had no role in the program. He received neither honour nor mention. And yet he held a key to the future of at least one of them—the probationary teacher's ongoing employment. I asked Ed about being ignored, about not being acknowledged. All fine, he told me. His thoughts went to the young teacher who had excited students in his science classes. Ed, like the school principal, wondered if the district would have the funds to keep him employed with them next year. He hoped so.

Back in his office, Ed went straight to work. This included a review of his evening schedule. He was to attend a district art exhibit. An hour later, he reviewed it once more. He was confirming the time for me. The start time would be 19:00 hours, not 19:30. Shortly, he ended his workday, leaving for home at 16:30, earlier than usual. With free time unexpectedly available, I read the community's daily newspaper, the *Wapiti Falls Cascade*. They had promoted the evening's exhibit with a student's artful rendition of a TV celebratory. It was well done and captured my attention.

I arrived at the venue early and read the building plaque. The building had formerly been a post office, and the plaque pointed out the building's classical features. Its façade was made from local bricks and stone, and built in 1895. I researched further details. Most of the façade was the typical red-brick found everywhere, but with an added touch. The red was highlighted by the brown-white hues of Tyndall Stone windowsills and lintels. The stairs and the two-storey portico featured columns with more of the same stone, the not-quite-white dolomite. And then again, a flat roofline circumscribed by a thin belt, the final display of Tyndall Stone in a wide red-brick facia. The windows showed peeling paint, with cracked and missing putty. The exterior doors needed work. Overall, a tidy exterior "with good bones" (a term favoured in real estate to describe a good property which had been left to run down, fade, age). Had the polish all been started on the inside?

Venturing inside, I saw that it had. The high ceilings were old-time tin tiles. Polished brass hardware adorned the stained hardwood doors. Wide floorboards sparkled—a clean wood grain with a high gloss finish. The totality of the inside was eye-catching; the outside needed its turn. It was once a glorious addition to the city. Back in its days as a post office, its presence had announced that Wapiti Falls was a town with a future. But Wapiti Falls had outgrown it, and it was abandoned. But someone saw opportunity, and the city purchased it at a nominal cost. It was once more returning to its glory years. Tonight's student art exhibit was one of many cultural events that this fine old building hosted.

The young artists, with their families, teachers, and members of the local art community, supported this exhibit of student art, and there was a crowd. They gathered in its large open room and spilled into the foyer. The exhibit started with speeches, short thankfully. Soon Ed and others were making their way through the exhibit. Almost immediately, a young teacher captured Ed's attention. He had organized the event and had purposefully invited Ed. Ed, polite and apologetic, admitted that he had missed an earlier part of the program. (Was there an earlier part?) The two visited briefly. Soon Ed quietly slipped away, resuming his role as my host and guide.

As we walked along, Ed was drawn into conversations with various other attendees, some as he encountered them in our tour, and some who, on seeing him, approached. I was invariably introduced. Everyone, everything cordial. Ed drew my attention to some, works created by student artists with connections to district staff. He talked about their families. At one, Ed mentioned that the artist was the child of a former refugee. The parent, now a district custodian, had once coached Olympic wrestlers. Ed shared other histories as we walked. The tour completed, I met Marie, Ed's wife; we were already acquaintances. She was just as I remembered, friendly and a good conversationalist. Ed and Marie signed the guest book and left. It had been a good day, but long. Ed was already at work when I arrived at 07:50 hours, and the two left for home at approximately 20:30 hours. Evening functions created additional demands.

Analysis of Courtesy and Humility

What was my takeaway from these two celebrations of student achievement? First, Ed's leadership put students at the centre of the district achievements. Both events recognized successful students and teachers. The Science-Mathematics Olympiad also let a young teacher shine. The exhibition of student art showcased yet another young teacher. Perhaps both events would be instrumental to their continued employment. Of the two, the Olympiad was richer: Olympiad winners were rewarded and recognized by their friends. The district science specialist, having survived the recent staff cuts, saw his value reaffirmed. Similarly, by promoting the school's business partner, the community profile of that business would be enhanced. Value added for all the participants. All in all, a successful event. Ed might have been recognized but he was not. He saw no need to have his ego stroked. With no direct work-related payoff, why had he even shown up? A whistle-stop check-in would have worked. But Ed was there, and for the full program. He wanted to see and recognize the students. He felt no compulsion to insert himself, saw no need to settle down the boisterous students or to complain about them. He enjoyed successes vicariously, through others. It was a pattern I observed over and over again.

The art society had a full display, which was well received by the public and by parents. It was another success. The artists were recognized and valued. That was enough. That evening, Ed introduced me as his guest, a visiting colleague; it hardly drew any attention. If observed on subsequent occasions, I could be identified as a visitor, who was simply learning how Wapiti Falls Consolidated operated. Ed liked this; it did not need further attention, the attention that might come from Ed being recognized as a "noteworthy" subject, someone of research interest. In short, it preserved his low-key style. Marie Noyce was accommodating and unassuming, just as she had been when we had met on other occasions. Neither had airs; both served their community with courtesy and humility. Appearances and reality were never in conflict.

Before moving on to other matters, think about the extra time it took Ed to be there. He never drew attention to his needs, or how long his day had been, or how tired it made him. He was there simply to smile, to chat, to engage. District students and staff were important to Ed, and he was there for them. Staff sought him out, sharing their concerns, joys, hopes, and recently, fears about their jobs or about the jobs of colleagues. Ed turned no one away, and no one left feeling unappreciated, even though he could not ease their concerns or address their issues. He knew his staff, their backgrounds, and the names of many of their children, and he worked at keeping current. Additionally, he had reams of information pouring in, helping him to identify where he might help, or who needed help, all while filling in the missing pieces to the puzzles of leadership.

Emeritus superintendent Pivott viewed Ed as affable. Others might see Ed as respectful. Both terms work. Donna Hicks, a Harvard professor and an expert in conflict resolution, recently described her approach: start small, in individual interactions. Focus on dignity. Learn from students. "We are equal. This is the heart and soul of my mentorship relationships" (O'Donnell 2017:1-7). Hicks was pointing out her process of resolution, after the fact steps; Ed's work was proactive and preventative. What she did, Ed did. He preserved dignity. He learned from everyone. He understood that everyone was his equal. He was generous with his time and interest. He was affable.

We have seen and adjudicated on Ed's interactions in the day-to-day of events. At their heart, these were the interactions that kept people involved, that effortlessly took in every available detail, that valued individuals over formal channels, and finally, that let colleagues and students shine. This open system was polite and invariably affable, and all of it suited Ed's ongoing need for information. It reflected his nature; it was who he was.

Over the Long Haul

When I observed Ed, he had already been in the Wapiti Falls Consolidated School District for eighteen years, first as a principal, then as a deputy superintendent, and finally as the chief superintendent. The next events show how his long-established reputation helped him every day. It was through these years, when his unshakeable integrity and mutual trust had been established, that gave Ed the latitude he needed to keep things moving in healthy directions.

Established Integrity

Surviving and prospering in the district demanded more than just being pleasant and attentive. Ed had been there when leading was easy and during the hard slogs. Time-tested and found true, Ed's integrity was unsullied. He had integrity, the "trustworthiness and incorruptibility to a degree that one is incapable of being false to a trust, responsibility, or pledge" (Webster's Ninth New Collegiate Dictionary 1983: 579). He had earned this reputation in spades. People identified with Ed. People saw that he was like them, only better. They wanted to be mutual friends.

In an interview, Mike Dymtriw, a maintenance staffer and president of the district's Canadian Union of Public Employees (CUPE) local, spoke easily of Ed's integrity. In some districts, the superintendent and a maintenance staff member would, at best, have limited contact. Dymtriw did not report to the superintendent. Their formal contact came only through confrontation, "union versus management" issues. Such relationships would seldom be viewed as collegial, but what I found was unexpectedly just that. Consider first how I found Mike.

As Ed and I chatted about my upcoming interviews, Ed saw Mike outside his window and immediately suggested that I interview him. Excellent, someone other than the current list of professional or central office sources. In study terms, Mike was not one of "the usual suspects." Ed invited Mike inside. Greetings were exchanged, and I was introduced as a colleague and a researcher. Ed had a request of Mike; he wanted Mike to grant me an interview. Mike hesitated; he was too busy. He had a job to finish right now, before classes. When Ed suggested using district time, Mike relented and agreed to Ed's request. We scheduled a meeting for 12:30 hours that day. I wondered if he could really be as busy as he had said, but so what? He left, and Ed went back to work. Observations continued until my meeting with Mike that afternoon in his shop.

The maintenance shop was one of a collection of World War II armouries, formerly part of the A-8 Air Force Camp. To the west and nearby were residential homes, slightly newer but of similar vintage. Celebration Hall, another remodelled, repurposed, and renamed armoury was the next building to the east. Still further east lay Walter MacEwan High School and its playing fields, also formerly part of the Air Force grounds. Stepping into the shop, the aroma of new wood filled my lungs. It was a sweet, comforting smell on a sharp, windy September day. As it was still lunch time, and seeing no one around, I ventured further inside. I saw refinished desks piled high. The smell of varnish permeated another room. Wood-working equipment filled another room, and still other rooms were obviously storage. Voices came from upstairs, a mezzanine, and in a few minutes, men descended the stairs. Mike greeted me and led me into a paint storage room, a locker really. There we sat, a desk between us. He explained that today he was a painter. I imagined a brief and unproductive interview. But I was wrong. Mike had lots of insights. He gave a new viewing angle on Ed Noyce.

They had known each other for twelve years, but Mike had had little to do with him until five years ago, when Ed became superintendent. Then contact had come through a union grievance, issues unresolved in a preceding lockstep process involving strict procedural rules. Grievances, I learned, were rare—two in seven years—and nowadays informal meetings sufficed. Mike explained, "About every time I'm in the [district] office, Ed always calls me in his office, and we sit down, and just really, don't talk about anything, just how things are going." Mike talked about solving union and district differences through the give-and-take of both parties; they met "in the middle." Ed was "easygoing," "fair," and "open-minded." He was someone you wanted to talk to all day, "just, you know, bullshit with." Mike said that he could lay the "cards down" with Ed because they understood and trusted each other. Each helped the other. He talked about that happening just the other day. At any point in the interview, Mike could have closed off the conversation, could have turned circumspect—cited union business—but he did not. He continued, "He's really a good guy," and tellingly, Mike and his colleagues were not "just a bunch of maintenance guys." This was mutual respect.

Mike looked back to a month earlier, when Ed had addressed all the staff, shared district directions, and talked about government plans. Ed made it clear that he did not know where the government was heading, or how they would respond to the district's constant shortage of money. Mike appreciated the information, valued the inclusion. Then he talked about the tradition of the district and his union, said that they had never gone on strike. Mike talked about other staff—teachers, principals—they were fair too. With the interview nearly over, Mike summarized what was important to him, "I like Ed. Ed is no pushover. I mean, he is a smart man." In fifty minutes, Mike had clearly, honestly identified with Ed as his partner and his equal. Mike walked me out of the shop, and we chatted about his own farm background, about his goal of moving to his acreage, and about his future there, in the berry business. I had entered as a stranger but was departing as his guest. Wapiti Falls School District was more family than a multimillion-dollar business, and Mike was a proud family member.

Analysis of the Mike Dymtriw Interview and Ed's Affability

For this analysis, consider these three issues: First, would Mike be an accurate observer—consistent, dependable? These concerns went to his reliability. Second, would his comments be valid—that is, well-founded, accurate, meaningful? Third, would Mike have relevant, worthy insights?

The first consideration was whether Mike Dymtriw was simply putting in time with me, perfunctorily doing what the district's "big" boss had requested, an unwilling participant, a coerced "volunteer?" While arrangements might have looked coercive, this ignored the context. Ed had anticipated a reluctance of staff to talk to a stranger about their district, to share private insights about their ultimate boss. While known to the professional staff and those in the district office, I was also someone poking into their family; I was putting my nose into their business. Mike only agreed to participate because Ed Noyce asked, nearly insisted, that Mike help me out. Initially, Mike was guarded, but this reluctance soon disappeared as evidenced in clear and forthright statements. I heard his tone and watched his body language, and I knew that he was a truth-teller. He wanted to share his assessment of Ed Noyce. He wanted to be helpful without being patronizing. His comments were consistent. Mike Dymtriw was eminently reliable, but were his insights valid?

Validity is the second in this triad of considerations. Did Mike Dymtriw know what he was talking about? In my view, he did. As a maintenance worker, Mike and his co-workers logged more time in schools than anyone else. They were silent observers and almost invisible—ignored. Family members, but barely. Mike and his co-workers had lunch together where they shared facts and gossip. Mike claimed that Ed was no "pushover," but neither was he. He could force issues through a formal process. But he did not do that. Instead, Mike wanted to be fair to the management of the district, as long as it was reciprocal, both personally and as union president. Mike was indeed a truthful and objective observer possessing informed, valid knowledge. He brought a perspective that was unseen by most.

My third task was to identify what I had learned and to look hard at what Mike had said. Mike's comments rang true to what I had seen, and what others had told me, plus they were the careful, consistent observations of a well-informed lay person. Mike, the union president, and Ed, his employer's man, represented different interests, but they understood and respected their differences. Each trusted the other and knew that each would do their best to work out any differences. Their problem-solving focus was even the same, getting to the "middle" ground. They found excuses to help each other, to keep each other in the know. Mike, bordering on effusive, was positive about Ed and the district. For Mike, Ed was the district. What Mike spoke of was integrity and honesty, established and maintained throughout their work together.

Qualitative research is a natural process—observing and thinking about what was seen—and it requires valid and reliable observations of people and documents. Reliable data is consistent, dependable, and in so far as possible, without error. Valid data consists of grounded measurements that reflect the true and accurate representation in that environment. (Appendix A: "Ethics, Validity, and Reliability in Qualitative Studies" provides more detail about qualitative research.) This interview had the unmistakable consistency that signifies reliability and validity. Ed was truly what he appeared to be. Could all this be accurate? Was Ed too good to be true? Were faults hidden, or simply not observed? Was I missing something?

Not so. Former chair and current trustee Margaret O'Connell marvelled, "I mean, I have never heard a bad word said about him." Neither had I, and I looked for it. Ed had also asked me to look for and to enumerate his faults. Perhaps he thought I could make him a better leader or a better person. I failed to find the "dirt," but was this failure simply not finding what was not there? In the end, I heard no whispers, saw none of the downward glances of avoidance, and identified no hints, no whiff of sentiments left unexpressed. In his eighteen years in the district, despite storms that might swirl around him, Ed Noyce had an air of unperturbed probity.

Joe Pivott described Ed as affable, and Ed was that. But it is easy to be friendly and easygoing when leadership is easy. It becomes harder when the difficulty increases. Ed had faced the full continuum, from tough sledding to easy glides, and was affable through them all. He promptly attended to all, including the hard interactions: telling good people that they would not be promoted, advising a successful principal that his job had disappeared, sharing with all his concern that the waters ahead could get rough. Ed was there in the background, too, helping others in low-key informal processes that might ignore hierarchies. He had time for people, listened respectfully, and empathized with them all. Ed knew that everyone was worthy of being heard, knew that everyone was striving to do their best, knew that everyone would and was contributing. Affability was his inherent to his nature.

CHAPTER 4

Ed's Private Persona

Why was Ed so darn nice? Could it be that he was smart and had concluded that being affable was good business? After all, it was only logical that interactions should demonstrate respect and trust, and should reflect moderation and balance, because this brought more data into play. More data, more discussion, more thinking—it all led to better decisions. That was all true, but how did he stick to his tight game plan? Why do it? The answer to both questions was that it was rational. Hard, but all of Ed's efforts delivered something that he needed, that he could feel good about.

Feelings were important to Ed. We learned that he relied on his gut feelings to make some decisions. He told me that on hearing an opera performed in a language he neither spoke nor understood that his emotion "wells up." If inanimate music produced such strong emotion, imagine the feelings that emerged through events he was directly involved with, the interactions that challenged him, and those that occupied his inner thoughts. Ed seldom talked about himself and what he was feeling. Such reticence made me dig for data. I found tiny glimpses and extrapolated. This section examines such feelings and classifies them. I concluded that some feelings satisfied him, others dissatisfied and confused him, and a few disturbed him.

Satisfactions

Ed found satisfaction in his interactions with family and colleagues, in district accomplishments, and in intellectual challenges.

Family values and enjoying life were important to Ed and Marie Noyce. Marie described these, "Having a little bit of fun each day, or each week, or each month, to go along…visiting with your friends, visiting with your family. I think all of those are important." Asked if time was enough, she thought it adequate, but barely, and laughed as she asked, why had he agreed to so many meetings? Overall, both were content. While never effusive, Marie and Ed were clearly proud of their children. Ed was especially pleased that their children shared a love of music. Bright and talented young adults, the world challenged them, and Ed knew that he and Marie could not fully protect them. Not that they did not make the effort. Ed also enjoyed humour, even humour involving his most private subject, his family. In a group of superintendents, Ed chuckled as he asked for advice on how to get adult children to move out. It was a theme he repeated later, "We obviously didn't teach them how to raise a family…so grandparenting is a long way away." Enjoying his quip, he added, "We've got some more work to do there." Having shared it publicly, I was confident that it was a sentiment previously discussed at home, in private.

Work and staff were another source of satisfaction. Telephone conversations were light and breezy, often punctuated with wit and laughter. He enjoyed jokes, but seldom told them. Elementary coordinator Katja Virtanen, goaded by fellow administrators, related how she had gone into his office one day to retell a joke. Ed had somehow misunderstood references in a story told in a principals' meeting. Her job was to clue Ed in. She retold it, augmenting it whenever necessary. Ultimately, she was rewarded with Ed's hearty laughter. Ed enjoyed kidding others. He liked to put me on the spot, forcing me outside the silent observer role. He told staff that I was after a job, perhaps their job. I had no choice but to explain further. On the first occasion, I fumbled, went from embarrassment to a full explanation. Ed laughed. (In this tight job market, the lingering suspicion that I was trolling for a job would not have been welcome. But by directly confronting this suspicion, there could be no mistake, no fudging, no chance that something untoward was happening. Ed was their unassailable witness.) From gentle teasing, word plays, or mildly self-deprecating comments, Ed enjoyed laughter. One day, in the face of mounting problems, he announced, maybe we can "turn this mole hill into a mountain." Discussing his imminent retirement, I suggested that he write children's novels. He laughed, talked about poetry, and laughed again as he quipped, "How many lines rhyme with blue?" Ed's laughter never—well seldom— came at the expense of others. Appendix C: "A District Lexicon" is a compendium of his expressions, and the whimsy and wit that he enjoyed.

Difficulties that Ed and staff had faced and overcome were cause for celebration. Looking out his window late one September afternoon, Ed spotted a "speechie." This was Ed-speak for speech therapist. It became his opportunity to share the dynamics of a previous decision. Back then, expenses were heavily scrutinized, and cut wherever possible. He discovered that their immediate supervisor had approved the attendance of the therapists at a conference in New Orleans. While the funds involved were immaterial, attendance would create a symbolic and political target—a New Orleans conference looked less like a need and more like an extravagant waste. Since good fiscal stewardship meant making cuts where possible, Ed cancelled the authorization. He communicated his decision in his typical "gentle" manner, whereupon the speechies "gently" invited Ed and Marie to a house party. Naturally, the theme was New Orleans, and while Ed was the brunt of numerous jokes, he was magnanimous. He said that he thoroughly enjoyed the "set-up." Times were once again fiscally tough, but the political climate was better, and so once again, the speech therapists requested support to attend this same conference and same location. Once more Ed discovered it, and he ordered the "speechies" and their supervisor to his office. It was a party, a time for cookies and reminiscences. Approval followed. Looking outside now, Ed realized that they were just back from this very conference. He enjoyed these moments, and he enjoyed sharing them with me. Ed took joy in life and people.

The opportunity to work with people is what brought Ed into teaching because he felt that it was the right thing to do. People, especially students, filled a need that a budding research career had not. Ed's job as a graduate student over one summer was to produce a piece of copper "less than ten angstroms thick at the tip." (Ten angstroms are one millionth of a millimetre.) He called it the "most incredibly tedious summer of my life." When he was asked to substitute teach in a senior physics class, he discovered his calling. Nuclear physics out; teaching in. Ed talked about teaching:

> "I really enjoyed working with kids at the school and I got a lot of satisfaction from it. And discovered, I guess, through a few experiences, that I kind of enjoyed working with people beyond the limits of my classroom. I got involved with the Students Union and…worked with teachers on a couple of projects in the school…"

Now at a different point in his career, Ed looked ahead to retirement. He even had a plan of sorts; he talked about teaching physics in a high school, college, or overseas.

Ed took pride in the district's "growing community support," in the breadth of the district's programs, and in the district's students and staff. No surprise, students were front and centre. "The fine arts kids, we've got a marvelous jazz choir over at Walter MacEwan [High School]. They are fantastic. That teacher is being sought by districts all over the place and we have got to keep her there if we can." A colleague identified Ed's reward, the satisfaction he gained from work, it was "the growth of other people."

Intellectual challenges were also inherently satisfying. Travelling from Taiwan to Japan, he played chess on the plane with a ten-year-old Chinese boy. Clearly beaten in his first game, Ed managed to get one back. "It was a close call. This kid was a flyer in chess. I love it! It is a strategy game. It is a detective story game. I love a puzzle." He saw work as an invigorating puzzle. "I love it when there are fifteen things happening at once." He might laugh or engage in wordplay when staff approached him with problems or complaints. Such laughter was eager anticipation, the pure pleasure of taking on new challenges. A faint smile would emerge when he recognized an approaching quagmire or when he pictured the fallacy of a simple solution applied to a complex problem. He loved finishing a task—the announced "swoosh" as call-back sheets flew into the garbage—or when a bigger project was complete. A well-designed plan invigorated him. He found it satisfying when participants enjoyed their work or when they understood or appreciated the rationale for a decision or direction. The recent endorsement of the district's strategic plan by the community, staff, and board was a source of satisfaction; he proudly identified it as his current "big picture package." Pride in his district was the most ego involvement that Ed revealed. That and his refusal to wear a hat despite frigid weather.

We have seen here that Ed's satisfaction came from basically two sources: people and problems. Family life and an overriding belief in people gave enjoyment and meaning. Addressing problems confirmed his big picture. Troubles came when irrationality intruded. He confidently solved rational problems, but was confused and frustrated when duplicity, irrationality, inconsistency, and unreasonableness violated his "big picture." Sadly, life did not always deliver satisfaction.

The Dissatisfying and Confusing

Not unexpectedly, Ed often dealt with his frustrations through humour. He used puns, and he enjoyed the wordplay of idiosyncratic terms—intriguing, novel, alliterative—words that both revealed and hid underlying issues. "Bizarre," he said, when a school's partner sought written clarification, when the real issue was control over how "their" money was used. He knew that the "no strings attached" gift giver would never make their concern explicit—that would be unseemly. It was also "bizarre" that the updated, provincially mandated accounting scheme had dropped the junior high accounting category, leaving just two categories, Grades 1 to 9 and Grades 10 to 12. It was a simple scheme from a bygone era. But most districts had schools with elementary, junior, and senior divisions. What would happen here was obvious—more fudging and more work. I heard the term bizarre with a tinge of annoyance, but the district had also gone against the flow when it created middle schools. Their new scheme fit neither the old nor the new accounting classifications. Yes, the new accounting scheme was irrational from the perspective of Wapiti Falls grade divisions, but their grade divisions looked odd from the perspective of the typical district. Here, "bizarre" was a location-dependent judgment, dependent on your side of the fence. The bigger question was why the province had bothered. "Bizarre" was judgmental and personal, but some frustrations went deeper, to more substantial matters.

Occasionally, Ed was seriously frustrated by "the odd parent that comes out of left field and doesn't know where it's at, and is not prepared to listen." A telephone conversation with one such parent revealed problems at both ends of the phone. The child of this parent was currently suspended from school, a school decision that culminated a long disciplinary history. To resolve the suspension, Ed tried to get the parties together by setting a date for further discussion, something suitable for parents and teachers. That was not to be, as the father simply blamed staff, and as to a meeting, he neither negotiated nor budged. Ed's conciliatory tone became more abrupt: "No sir, I am not…That was an unfortunate comment…No, I'm afraid you don't." This parent was frustrated, and Ed was moving there. In the end, though, Ed's final appeal was to work together. This call showed Ed as firm and professional, but when pushed, he could be blunt, even aggressive. For me, it was a rare revelation!

His "unpredictable" board was also frustrating. With previous boards, Ed could anticipate their vote, "I used to be able count hands really well before they went up." Now, that was impossible. This board was inconsistent, talked out of both sides of their mouths. They acted as individuals rather than as a cohesive body with a guiding plan. It left him frustrated, knowing that he would be unable to adequately assist his board. Their perceived needs exceeded his capacity. They needed unity, a plan, their plan. Ed had a plan, but he was determined that their plan would not be his plan.

An unpredictable board and unreasonable people might frustrate Ed, but he denied having other work-related frustrations. He might ask, what job did not have issues? Always resourceful, he would just do a workaround, but others in the district disagreed on his success with that strategy.

I learned that deputy superintendent Don Howard thought that such "tough" personnel issues weighed heavily on Ed, and he listed student suspensions and teacher terminations as among the heaviest issues. Here, Ed would make the decision when it was required, but not easily. Ed told me that he analyzed everything and then summarized its salient features, "carefully, done by letter." We will soon learn about his follow-up when one student expulsion looked suspect—that is, unduly harsh and applied inconsistently. Ed disliked and vigorously avoided championing political positions with bosses, his elected board. He shared an example: Faced with a 3-3 vote, Ed "inserted" himself into the debate. Doing so revealed his beliefs—he had picked sides. If they had failed to pass this motion, the board would affectively abandon an established principle. Ed entered the debate and used up time until a seventh trustee arrived and broke the tie. In the end, the board's principle held. While he had helped the board maintain their consistency, helped them stick to their principles, he described his feelings as far from elation or satisfaction. Instead, he was dismayed for he had violated what he had promised himself. He had entered a political debate and that was not his place. Inserting his views made him a participant rather than a resource, and this was unacceptable, and a personal failure. While personnel issues might challenge Ed, playing politics meant abdicating his code of conduct. Ed understood the separation of elected and appointed roles as a rational construct and sacrosanct. If only people were rational!

Some unacknowledged signs of frustration worried his colleagues. Ab Digby, assistant superintendent, commented, "We see Ed being more pensive than he was when he was deputy superintendent, and I think that is simply because he's taken on the total load of the superintendent, and that responsibility weighs on him." Marie, Ed's wife, talked about his worries, specifically a political climate that was fragmenting educational delivery. She added that Ed tried to separate home from work, but he never quite succeeded. I understood that these were pieces of the puzzle that could not be chucked aside. On encountering them, on trying and failing to discover a satisfactory resolution, his mind would experience no rest.

As the previous school year had wound down, and getting the "pieces to fit," or "glued together," the demands had grown and challenged his abilities. It was in such a situation that his focus would momentarily lapse. One day, faced with a long list of "to dos," he forgot what was next. A vague sense had him searching for loose ends. He paused, left his office, and returned. Then it came to him; he had agreed to an interview with the local television station. He made his interview on time—just. At other times, deep in thought, he might acknowledge conversations, but decline participation. On this, Ab Digby said that he had "disappeared." Then—being nice—Ab added, Ed still had fun, just less frequently. What were these challenges, the pieces of the puzzle that weighed most heavily, that had him "disappearing?"

The Disturbing

Ed, though occasionally dissatisfied, mostly moved on. Unfortunately, some matters stuck. Lacking resolution, never absent, their niggling accumulations gnawed at Ed. Naturally private and careful, Ed was reticent to reveal vulnerabilities, and so he hid them. Some of these issues were serious threats to the district's culture and values. How could such entrenched feelings not detract from Ed's well-being? And recent events increased his disturbance. Ed felt his purpose slipping away, and his private, internal debates intensified. He even admitted to some of them privately to me.

Believing that the deputy minister of education would be pleased, Ed had organized a closed-door meeting for June. It would involve the deputy and twelve educators—six board chairmen with their superintendents. (See Appendix B: "A Primer on Educational Structures in Canada, in Alberta, in Wapiti Falls" for further details on the structure and power of Alberta's Ministry of Education and its officers.) To his surprise, the deputy's assistant slammed the meeting—strenuously—and aborted it. Ed was "perplexed" and said that walking away was "bizarre." Why reject direct information from a strong field of elected representatives and their senior officers? Would Ed's bewilderment pass?

Summer brought new hope. After meeting Marvin Hendriks, a provincial education official, Ed became more optimistic; provincial funding was changing. A new equity formula was in the works. Ed shared the news with trustees and staff. Told them that fiscal disparity would be addressed. They could expect more money, soon.

It was disconcerting, then, that official fall announcements talked of less money, substantially less. Something had happened, and Ed investigated. At a zone superintendent meeting, Ed carefully probed their guest, Marvin Hendriks, the source of his earlier hopes. Out of character—aggressive—Ed interrupted to seek clarification. He was unrelenting, and Marvin said too much; he revealed fissures within the department, and he essentially agreed with Ed. Hendriks was sympathetic, but what could one do when your boss had decided otherwise? "Do nothing" was Hendrik's answer, but Ed did not accept that. With different guests the next day, Ed again sought clarification. Challenging them, doubting their intentions. Was the fault with Ed, rather than with their policies?

Analysis of Feelings—Especially the Disturbing

Ed's satisfactions and dissatisfactions were those of every leader; in fact, they were those of every sentient being. Ed's heightened feeling, his disenchantment, and lack of agency related to this specific time. Those details have been covered and consequently, this analysis focuses on Ed's disturbing dilemmas.

I understood some of Ed's angst; other superintendents also understood. Start by focusing on the deputy's assistant nixing a meeting of chairs and superintendents. The gossip among superintendents had this assistant to the deputy (minister) "dissing" superintendents as the problem and not part of the solution. Did the assistant speak for his boss? Probably. Was this deputy and staff blindsiding their political boss, the minister of education? Maybe. Was this a conspiratorial cabal? Probably not. The often heard official statements about cooperation and partnership were just talk, empty phrases. In general, superintendents saw that the department's words and actions were contradictory. Ed did not want to believe that, did not want to believe that Alberta Education was not interested in a partnership. That had been just gossip, but now, now Ed had incontrovertible evidence that the gossip was correct.

Walking away from meetings and blaming others was wrong-headed and irrational. How would this solve problems? How did that serve students? Fundamentally, it was disrespectful, and that alienated Ed. As the deputy minister of education struggled to implement his plan of change, he increasingly blamed superintendents for its failures. Ed recognized the change in tone and mission. He felt cut off, abandoned, and his feelings metastasized. No longer would he be the hopeful organizer of problem-solving meetings. While analytic learners like Ed were predisposed to trust experts, his trustful predisposition was abandoning him. He asked himself "if he could live with it…this government doesn't give a damn. And I don't believe that my agenda is in tune with their agenda at all." And so, he retreated inward with occasional outbursts.

Ed questioned if he even wanted to fit into the "new education." He had believed in the Ministry of Education role and purpose, and believed that the well-being of students was at the department's corporate heart, but events were forcing him elsewhere. Was the department still a force for good, or had that disappeared? Imagine the thoughts burrowing into his mind. Is that why his thoughts turned to retirement? If the deputy minister of Alberta Education was the most disruptive element to his peace of mind, retirement was next.

Ed had asked his board chair to lead the board on a discussion on his imminent retirement. He did not hear back; the matter was ignored. Maybe she was busy elsewhere, busy perhaps in searching for and then persuading a good candidate to replace her, for it turned out that she also wanted to retire, and her need came first. That fall, at the organizational meeting, a new chair was elected by the seven trustees. Excellent, it would mean that current directions would be maintained. To Ed's knowledge, no one had raised the issue of Ed's retirement in public or privately with the board. Still, Ed assumed that the two chairs, the outgoing and the incoming chairs, had discussed it. He was so very sure, maybe he had heard some oblique reference to it, but there had been no progress, nothing official or unofficial. That was hard on Ed. His retirement plans would not disappear, and he did not forget it. Once again, he knew that he would have to take the initiative, start the discussion, propose a timeline, and outline a process. But Ed's need to examine retirement went deeper.

Years earlier, as a fresh, new superintendent, an expert had declared that five years was about the limit to a senior executive's effectiveness. Thereafter, complacency crept in. Ed believed it. He described his first four years as exciting—new responsibilities, new directions, new achievements—but that phase had passed. In this, his fifth year, he declared:

> "I am starting to go off the boil. I can feel that a lot of what I wanted to accomplish has been done, so what am I going to do? What am I going to do next? I have to find a big project or move. Well, what is going to keep me excited…and keep me energized about my job? I have to find a big picture change, Dale, or this place is going to go down, and I am going to go down… so I have to keep getting better."

He was concerned, but there was a solution. He said it himself; he might have to move or find an exciting big project. He had choices.

Ed's dilemma somehow became my dilemma. How hard is it to find a worthy project in a school system with all those unanswered needs? How about superintendent emeritus Joe Pivott? While retired, Joe had projects, so why couldn't Ed? Why even think about a move? Ed already had a good job in a good community. Why contemplate retirement when he was so young? He loved the job and was extremely good at it. Why all this soul searching?

But Ed was searching, recalibrating, letting me follow his thoughts in our formal interview. He wandered in and out of discordant propositions. At one point, he said, "I probably should have been an engineer when it comes right down to it." But that was contrary to what he had said minutes before when he talked about finding teaching, "So I made the switch to education, and I have never for a moment regretted it." And then again, closer to the end of our long session, "Maybe the ego should be a little bigger in a leader, so that you protect things a bit more. I don't know." Ed was confused and he confused me, worried me. I saw drift, vacillation. How should I understand this? I saw great work, exceptional leadership. Could this be the mind of a rational analyst at work? But how was this rational?

Perhaps Ed was other than he thought he was. Was he really the rational analyst that he wanted to be? He had, after all, abandoned the rationality of science to enter the people business of teaching. Hardly the rational analyst's preference for "things before people." People would always frustrate, but people issues also invigorated. He found that he could help others. He liked helping; it was satisfying. But as issues accumulated, Ed's world and his understanding of educational leadership and its purpose clashed with reality, and it drove his feelings inward, invisible. And it would not get better as events became a crisis, but more about that later.

The Composite Ed Noyce: Intelligent, Affable, Reflective

Ed Noyce was smart in his job. His intelligence led him to gather copious quantities of information and allowed him to think about how individuals might think, act, and react. With all this knowledge, he developed a big picture of events and potentialities in his district. He even had a fall-back strategy: if a decision was required and his knowledge was insufficient, then he relied on his moral code. Intelligence was the foundation of Ed's leadership, but not every intelligent person was successful. Ed had more.

Ed was thoroughly nice—decent—as he went about his business interacting with others. Comfortable in most interactions, he had time for everyone, and he had empathy for those facing difficulties. He was such a good listener that others sought his presence and his counsel. The conversational techniques of "deference, demeanor, and face" that Goffman (1967) identified as essential were ever-present. Affable when decision-making was easy, and affable in the difficult interchanges where generosity and genuine interest won over friends, colleagues, and even those who were disenchanted with what they knew was coming. He supported those on the way up and those spiralling down. He was trusted, and in eighteen successful years in the district, his integrity was uncontested. Ed was indeed affable, exhibiting the critical values that kept him in the know, that made transactions possible—honesty, responsibility, fairness, honouring commitments, prudence, civility, and ultimately integrity. Ed was smart enough to lead with good manners.

And he was rewarded. His work challenged and satisfied him. There were frustrations—every job had them—but lately, he was discouraged, and it turned him inward.

Thinking Ahead to My Dissection Framework

At this point in my journey through Ed's story, I have inventoried the intellectual and affability traits of Ed's nature—inward intelligence, outward affability, and the feelings that tagged along. Now I was ready to do the same for his leadership. As I went through the field notes, I deconstructed leadership events into its constituents. Two issues came to my mind.

First, leadership is complicated and, hence. difficult to describe.

Large Committee Room.

Mathematical tools provided me with a supportive metaphor. Consider Venn diagrams, the overlapping, ill-defined, and fuzzy entities. They would serve as my metaphorical framework. The leadership lists were Venn diagrams possessing tolerable imprecision. These lists did not have to be perfect.

Small Committee Room.

The second point requires a personal story. I once enrolled in a class where I was to observe nature. It was enjoyable and ultimately useful. I discovered that the more I looked, the more there was to see. With Ed, this experience repeated itself. The more I saw, the more I discovered, and the more I discovered, the more I understood, or thought I understood. I tried out the deconstructive process and found that I could identify and name leadership actions, but I was never sure if my process lists were exactly right, somewhat close, or vaguely resembled the names I gave them. Again, I pictured the Venn diagrams—indistinct shapes and forms, but ultimately helpful. I strove for utility, even if the processes lacked precision. The next chapter starts this process of looking at Ed's everyday leadership and taking it apart bit by bit.

Part III: Ed's Leadership Processes

CHAPTER 5

Normal Leadership Processes

In detailing Ed's smarts and affability, we see a self-sustaining circle: his search for information gave him things to think about. He knew that by being pleasant, interested, and empathetic, he would have still more information brought to him. Thinking about all the accumulating information required that he create a picture or conceptual model in which all of the cogent data would fit. The more he knew, the better the decision. Life worked, and overall, Ed was very satisfied. Yes, he was always self-reflective, and currently some issues gnawed at him, accumulated, and turned his thoughts negative. These hinted at future problems. The Ed described here was well-known, well-understood, and appreciated. Now we need to see Ed at work. How did he lead?

Through deconstruction of the observations, I found key leadership processes, or repeating action series. They reflected Ed's personal intellect and manners. Whereas some leaders seem to present two faces, two versions of themselves—the public and the private—Ed led as he was—consistent, genuine, thorough. There were no airs. Deconstruction yielded leadership processes which I group qualitatively, as the "whos," the "whats," and the "hows." The "who" processes relate to Ed's philosophical bent towards trust and his focus on students. The "whats" are the processes of continuous scanning, and then synthesizing through sharing. The final two processes focus on the "hows," how decisions were made and how he used his time. These six processes are the answers I found, identifiable pieces of the leadership puzzle, but before the answers emerge, I start with halftones, the bits of evidence pulled from events. As in old newspaper pictures, the half-tones combine to form an identifiable picture.

Bennis and Nanus declared, "Trust is the lubrication that makes it possible for organizations to work" (Bennis 1986: 43), and so, I start there.

Process: Trust Through a Shared History

Deputy superintendent Don Howard linked Ed's tenure with high levels of trust:

> "It comes from trust relationships that develop over time. You know, he says that he is going to do something, and he does it. People phone him, and he eventually gets back to them. You know all of those things add up. So it is, within the district, people trust the superintendent…they know that…the recommendations that he is going to be making are ones that he has thought out, and [they are] maybe not the best for everybody, but [they are] probably going to be the best for the building."

How had Ed earned this trust and loyalty? Two vignettes help, and both describe history. While they started with observations and my questions, Ed filled in the details. In the first, Ed was recognized for adhering to exemplary standards of professional behaviour. In the second, a principal achieves long-term success through Ed's help.

With Help, Ed Fires a Principal

June 8 started out busy, and it stayed that way. Ed had met with his senior administrators, then privately with his deputy superintendent. He had talked on the telephone with a parent, checked his electronic correspondence, and worked on an old personnel file. He was ready for coffee, but even there the diversion was minimal, for the topic of conversation was work. Different location, same focus. It was 10:40 hours, the end of his coffee break, when Ed checked in with his secretary. Done there, he returned to his office, prepared comments for a retirement ceremony, and began attacking his growing pile of call-back requests. The organizer of a provincial fact-finding committee dropped in to give his regards. One half-hour later, Ed was on his way to Snipe Lake Middle School. His car was loaded with plaques for a noon-hour presentation. I learned that one of the retirees, a secretary–library assistant, was getting out before she was fired. The principal had done his homework and was helping her leave gracefully. This firing was a harbinger of another firing, something from Ed's past. This morning, filled with events and requests, was like every morning.

At the school's entrance, Lydia Jacques, vice-chair of the board, met and greeted Ed. She bubbled over with ideas gleaned from a recent conference. One of the school staff arrived and led us to the library. The hallways were oddly dark, vacant, and quiet—no students. Aha, it was the districtwide in-service day. It was nearly noon, and staff at Snipe Lake had set aside planning for next year's teaching assignment to honour their retirees. The plan was that Ed would address each retiree, and Lydia would present each plaque. The principal began by introducing the guests, including me. Soon, Ed was talking about the secretary–library assistant. Staff listened politely and watched. Lydia had the congratulatory plaque ready. Staff all knew the score. They would; it was their school. Finished, the secretary–library assistant sat, another retiree followed, and she was in turn followed by Dennis Llewellyn. Dennis would provide a significant insight into how Ed lead.

Ed stood, summarized Dennis's history with the district. This was easy and uncomplicated, as Dennis had been an excellent teacher. Staff were enthusiastic as Lydia presented the plaque, but unlike the previous retirees, Dennis wanted to address the group. He began, "Chairs come and go" and looking at Lydia, "so do vice-chairs." He turned to the staff and said, "But superintendents stay." His audience was attentive because Dennis had something to say, and nothing would stop him. He continued; thanked Ed, elaborated on what Ed had done for him, and for education in their district. It was quite a compliment—clear and to the point. Dennis tacked on a thank you for former superintendent Joe Pivott. Done, he sat down. The ceremony was soon over, and Ed drove me to his office.

I asked Ed what had just happened? Plainly, Ed had been acknowledged, and elected leaders had been snubbed—Lydia was right there. A long-gone superintendent received a compliment, and there was the pointed, no doubt planned, omission of the two superintendents who served between Ed Noyce and Joe Pivott. Dennis was clearly not one to mince words, and his comments were heart-felt. Ed understood the references Dennis had made. Dennis had acknowledged Ed's professionalism from an event that took place years earlier. Back then, Ed's ethical approach had led to the removal of a principal, a cancerous principal. Dennis was involved but had said nothing of his own role. Ed supplied such details and more. This event provided an important insight into this tight and polite family, the Wapiti Falls family.

On the drive to his office, Ed talked. Years ago, he had led a school evaluation in Snipe Lake Middle School. Fortuitously, as the evaluation began, he became aware of lewd, sexist comments attributed to the school's new principal, Jerry Boyce. And so, he prepared for problems just as he typically did. Interviews with staff commenced, and soon one teacher started what seemed to Ed as a criticism of principal Boyce. Ed stopped her, asked her about the teachers' ethical code, the "Code of Professional Conduct" (Alberta Teachers' Association 1994). Ed's question alerted her to a problem, and she stopped talking. And so did Ed. He did not need to stop the interview, and typically he was eager to get every morsel of data, but here he stopped; in fact, he left the school with a promise that he would be back the next morning. So, what was this "code" that stopped the school evaluation and why was it there?

The code required teachers to adhere to three principles: that a teacher would criticize the competence or professional reputation of a colleague only in confidence, only to the proper authorities, and only after informing the colleague. Consider these three: First, the meeting was private and confidential. Second, Ed was the proper authority, but third, there had been no sharing of concerns with the principal. This conversation, therefore, would be a code violation. If she had broken the code, the union could discipline the teacher. Additionally, as the principal was a union member and had been wronged, he would be regarded a victim. The union would be obliged to step in to defend him. These were not idle threats; history said that they would pillage the teacher for unprofessional conduct. In its defence, the union wanted "bad" teachers gone, but claimed that there was a better way to remove them; namely that the parties initiate the complaint in a face-to-face process—that is, through direct dialogue with their colleague because that is what professionals did.

On Ed's return the next day, he learned that some of the school's teachers had spoken to their principal, criticized him face-to-face. Those teachers could now share their criticism with the proper authority, and they did. Ed finished staff interviews by 10:30 hours and met with principal Boyce. He recalled Jerry Boyce's exact words, "I'm in a lot of shit." Had principal Boyce hoped that Ed would deny it, and smooth things over? But that is not what happened, and Boyce knew what would follow. Ed and principal Boyce arranged a noon meeting at the district office. Jerry Boyce arrived early, his resignation in hand. Ed accepted it.

Analysis: With Help, Ed Fires a Principal

Consider these events from the perspective of these actors: Dennis Llewellyn and his colleagues, the union, the district, and Ed Noyce.

In his retirement comments, Dennis acknowledged Ed's contribution but was silent about his own role. As related by Ed, Dennis's role was not insignificant. All those years ago, Ed had given Dennis and his school colleagues a chance to prove their professional mettle. Ed had not told them what to do, but they already knew. Dennis knew and acted. He had gone to the teachers and persuaded them to meet with principal Boyce and state their concerns. They only needed to be honest with their principal. Doing that would respect the "code." Professionals, after all, discipline themselves. Dennis's appeal worked. Half the teachers delivered their criticisms directly and having done so, they could tell Ed. Ed listened, and executive action followed; as described, the principal had no choice but to resign. Years later, in celebrating an entire career, Dennis shared one critical career moment, and that moment was about the professionalism of teachers and their duties and obligations. He and other teachers were professional, and Ed had provided a way for teachers to give expression to these obligations. On this day of tributes, Dennis recognized two well-regarded leaders, Ed Noyce and Joe Pivott. But there were four superintendents over this time span, and I knew something about their history in the district. Dennis had ignored two in-between superintendents—one mediocre and one confrontational. I saw it as a sandwich with two nutritional slices of whole wheat bread between two layers of stuff that Dennis thought best forgotten. Impolite, but meaningful!

The teacher's union was often criticized for upholding a code that protected bad teachers and bad actions. In Alberta, principals were part of the union, and they still are today. But here, one of their own ended up out of a job. The "code" had worked just fine. It was more than a "code of silence"; it required respectful adherence to procedural rules about fairness. Superintendents looking to fire teachers, but who failed to, or did not bother to follow the proper procedures, ultimately failed. Ed followed the procedures and succeeded.

The district was also a winner. Keeping unprofessional teachers and administrators on staff satisfied no one. Had the rumours been ignored, the district would soon be facing complaints from parents and teachers, and rightfully so. Instead, by respecting the professionalism of teachers, the district had removed a problem that could only get worse in the future.

Ed had enabled this to happen. He did it by taking his professional obligations seriously. He did it by working with his professional colleagues, trusting that as professionals, they would self-discipline their fellow members, their colleagues. Ed's plan had worked, and he had earned a lifetime of respect. That was why Dennis had made a point of thanking Ed. Dennis was grateful.

In his short, simple thank you, Dennis celebrated a shared history of trust and respect. It reinforced the lore of the district—working together, overcoming obstacles, doing their best for children and each other. With each retelling, and there would be retellings, Ed and the teachers would be heroes, protecting students and staff, fostering learning, and making a difference. The next vignette related to an important event, and it too came with a history.

Eileen's Ultimatum

By June 22, Ed knew that he should talk to Eileen Gatenby, principal of Waputiuk School. It concerned the district's practice of providing schools with discretionary funds. At Waputiuk, discretionary funds were distributed through a decision of staff. The staff had voted, and Eileen had forwarded their decision in accordance with that vote. Ed had it and sat on it. He was thinking, waiting.

Provincially, school-based budgets were viewed as better, closer to students, and more efficient than spending decisions made at the district level. But while clamouring for greater school-based funding, the province offered platitudes rather than direction. It was all talk; they had no route map with their normal definitions, regulations, procedures. The district wanted to comply, but how, specifically? They already had an account that allotted small monies to schools, but these allocations were restrictive, smaller than what the province was talking about. The district would change, but Ed anticipated unforeseen wrinkles—problems.

In Wapiti Falls, there were many fiscal issues, and discretionary funds would add to a long and unsatisfactory list of who got what, when, how. By Ed's calculations, Eileen's request would be the first of several tests. Ever cautious, Ed wanted to avoid the dead ends created by taking paths with no exit, paths created by premature decisions. It would be best to think, discuss, mull over how financial responsibility would be shared. In his previous district, Ed had seen battles over rebalancing school and district fiscal authority, and it had not been pretty. He looked first to what he knew.

He knew that on June 9, Mark Cobb, representative of the teacher's union, had expressed concerns about discretionary funds from a union perspective. Then the next day, senior administrators brought up the same topic from a district perspective. There, assistant superintendent Jake Harris added further details. He had learned that during their school's budget debates, Eileen had held to the current expectations, and staff had disagreed. They saw money and wanted it put where they thought best for them, the district be damned. As Jake described it, her own staff had beat her up, and she reluctantly acquiesced. Ed quietly sighed and agreed that he needed to do something, but what? And so, he waited. Then in the following week, Walter MacEwan High School requested district approval for their discretionary allocations. Now Ed had to deal with it because a line was forming; a second school had requested authorization for their allocation of discretionary funds. There would be more. The two requests were different, but the issue was the same. Ed needed a plan.

And so, that morning, the morning of the June 22 board meeting, Ed and his senior admin team discussed discretionary funds once more. Hearing their opinions, Ed summarized: schools were hard-pressed to manage with less money. They needed direction in spending the little extras that discretionary funds allowed. Would discretionary funds be for staffing, professional development, or other everyday uses? The Walter MacEwan request vaguely fit previous practices, while Eileen's school, the Waputiuk School's request pushed out further. It crossed boundaries. It mattered not how the spending decisions were made, namely by a staff vote. It mattered only what the funds were to be used for. What to do? It was decided, agreed; Ed's senior administrative team would recommend that the high school's request be approved with a caveat. They also decided that the Waputiuk request was not acceptable and would be turned down.

That afternoon, the high school's request was duly placed on the board agenda. The board would receive an explanation and discuss their administrator's preferred direction.

In a separate letter, Ed summarized the Waputiuk request, denied it, logically defended the denial, and unequivocally restated the decision. He would be prepared to defend the rejection should the school or the teacher's union challenge him. Further, Ed would deliver the decision in person. He had to wait though because the board had yet to set their ultimate directions. He anticipated what they would say but could not act until they had said it. He might find that the board had other concerns, or that they wanted to deviate from past practices, or that they wanted to totally change existing expectations. In short, he did not know what the board would do. But why not just wait a bit longer, why take the time to prepare before the board had made their decision? The why now was because once discussed in the public board meeting, the media would get the message out, and Ed's experience was that they would muddle it. The media would get it wrong. The media were not the only concern. The district was very open, and that was not just about students moving to the school of their choice. Information flowed in Wapiti Falls Public; gossip was quick and efficient. Therefore, it had to be first thing in the morning—immediately after the board's decision. Ed prepared his letter and made his appointment to see Waputiuk principal Eileen Gatenby early Wednesday morning.

At the evening board meeting, the Walter MacEwan High School's request was discussed, and trustees had their questions. Each of the three senior administrators (Ed Noyce, Don Howard, and Jake Harris) answered them and supported their proposed solution. Come fall, the administrative team promised the board that they would be asked to comment, review, revise, and ultimately approve a new school-based fiscal policy. Thus assured, the board approved Ed's recommendation. It left Ed's letter as the right instrument for the next morning's task.

Early Wednesday, on our approach to Waputiuk Elementary School, Ed pointed to one of the attached portables. It was a daycare, city-owned and -operated. The school considered the daycare as their partner, as well as part of the school for events like Christmas pageants, Halloween, Easter, and more. The Waputiuk School was inclusive.

Ed parked, walked past the daycare to the school's entrance, past the travelling art display, and into the general office. Principal Gatenby greeted Ed and quickly ushered him into her office. She was anxious, worried about what might be happening? Ed began with a background statement on discretionary funds and then shared his thoughts on the matter, including the unresolved, underlying issues. With the preliminaries done, Ed gave his written decision to Eileen, and spoke directly to it; her request had not been approved. He waited, and her reply came, but it was not what he had expected. She nodded; she agreed. She said that she understood Ed's reasoning and admitted that she had not expected approval. Her feelings bubbled out, relief. How was that? She explained that when the call came, and Ed's appointment made, her staff began to worry—they were afraid that the superintendent was visiting because he was about to transfer Eileen to another school. That would explain why she barely glanced at the letter Ed had presented. Reading a letter would have gotten in the way of listening. She liked her school; her staff liked her. No one there wanted her gone. And Jake, who had said that Eileen had been beaten up by staff over the allocation of discretionary funds, had perhaps overreacted to events actually witnessed by others. Or maybe he had it right; maybe the staff had cause to worry, worry that they had gone too far, first by ignoring their principal's appeals, and then through a vote that aggressively thumbed their collective noses at their principal, maybe at their district. Suddenly, whatever the reality was, it was now immaterial. There would be no showdown.

Their business done; conversation turned to summer holidays. Eileen was going to her hometown, Victoria, British Columbia. Ed knew Victoria, and they chatted about places and experiences there. She invited him on a school tour. He accepted. This tour proved significant to my understanding of the district milieu.

Although the day was hot, the portable classrooms attached to and part of Waputiuk School were cool. I said so, and this prompted Eileen to talk about her earlier experiences with portables and summer heat. As the new principal in a previous school, she reminisced about inviting former superintendent, Milt Palmer, to visit her school's "sauna." It was a double entendre, humorous as well as a complaint about the school's hot, humid portables. I heard Eileen's laughter, but I also recognized sub-textual context. I guessed that superintendent Palmer had failed to appreciate the humour intended. As she described events, I formed a picture of big, strong, in-your-face Milt Palmer. I waited. Our tour continued into the main building. Eileen and Ed observed events there and chatted with teachers. When he departed, Ed knew that discretionary funds would not be an immediate issue, and I knew something had been left unsaid.

In the privacy of Ed's car, I asked about former superintendent Milt Palmer's reaction to Eileen's invitation. He explained that Milt had not been pleased with the not-too-subtle complaint about the portables. In his view, Eileen was already on thin ice. Her comment added one more item to his growing list of her shortcomings. In fact, Milt had subsequently had Ed serve as a witness, in a meeting where Eileen's weak performance had been discussed. Milt had given her an ultimatum: fix these problems—or else. Right after this "or else" meeting, Ed hurried back to Eileen's school, expecting to find her devastated. Instead, she was unconcerned; she had not understood Milt's message. She failed to understand that her job was on the line. Ed explained the situation so that she did understand. Where superintendent Milt Palmer had delivered ultimatums, his deputy, Ed Noyce, had provided support and guidance. It worked. Eileen was here, still in the district, still a principal. In fact, she was a well-regarded principal. That first year, though, it was tough.

In this meeting of late June 1994, Ed accomplished what he wanted: he gained time to address school-based funding issues. True to his word, that fall, Ed and staff were actively investigating school-based budgeting.

Analysis of Eileen's Ultimatum

Think about the effort Ed made to reach the administrative decision about discretionary funds, the unified direction Ed's team presented to the board, and finally Ed's face-to-face discussion with the principal. All that care and preparation. He was ready for a confrontation, but it never came. Staff might still disagree with the rejection of their request, but Eileen would make it work. With Eileen, Ed's decision had simply been trusted to be the best for the district. Eileen trusted Ed. She knew it would be fair because he was fair. That was their history.

Consider too the contrast in leadership attributed to Milt Palmer and that observed with Ed Noyce. Milt was confrontational; Ed was conciliatory. Milt demanded; Ed assisted. Milt burned bridges, including his own, eventually; Ed built relationships and trust that paid off when he needed a little extra support or latitude.

Trust and Respect Could Not Solve Every Issue

Trust and loyalty made people cooperative but, as one further illustration shows, neither one nor both can solve every problem. Ed had spent considerable time preparing for a meeting with Natalia, a teacher who had previously retired from the district. Natalia had returned to teaching; she was helping the district by accepting a term position to the end of June. It was June, and her contract would soon end, but now she wanted to stay on. To do that, she needed Ed's help. In their meeting, Ed listened and understood; he recognized her pain, her frustration. But when the year ended, Natalia was once again retired. Perhaps she was better prepared because of Ed's obvious empathy. But it did not bring her job back.

Process: Focus on Students

Ab Digby, assistant superintendent, identified the critical aspects of Ed's job:

> "His main job is to make sure that we are providing quality education to our students, and I think that he realizes that is his first job, and he makes that his priority…every time you talk to Ed, it seems to always come back to what is important. Where are we coming from? What's our mandate? Our mandate is to make sure that our kids are having quality education in their classrooms."

Yes, education exists for students, but students seemed far down on the superintendent's list of active tasks. Despite the distance, Ed made the effort to stay in touch with their needs when decisions were made. He had enjoyed the student calling out, "Hiya, Ed." He saw students at work in their classes and chatted with them. He attended their programs of celebration and recognition. He was also there when they were removed from school. It was an ugly part of his role, but it was required.

One September morning, without saying hello, Ed walked past me, past two school administrators, and past several parents. A student hearing was about to start in district offices. It was 07:49 hours, and Ed was almost late. And he was preoccupied. Removing students from school weighed heavily on him. After thirty-six minutes in a private hearing, the two school administrators and Ed were excused from the meeting. So, too, were the three participants, a parent, a male student, and his representative—a young, short male, dressed in a suit. Each party had made their case, and trustees were deliberating in private. Ed seemed okay with that. He was chatty, talked about his weekend in the mountains with Marie and about their treks. He was likely deep in thought, but you would never have known it. I had thought that the meeting was a simple suspension, but it was more—this student was a repeat "client," and the hearing was formal, quasi-judicial. The parties waited outside until 08:34 hours, when they were asked to return. Decisions were about to be communicated. Left alone, I chatted with the school's administrators, who for some reason had not been invited back into the hearing room. Then, it was over. Expulsion! Out of school for the balance of the school year. The student's former principal and vice-principal wished the student well. The representative in the tailored suit turned out to be from the John Howard Society, the society named after an English prison reformer. Evidently, the issues were dire; they went beyond, school issues. These participants left and were soon replaced by another group. This one consisted of three individuals, all Indigenous Canadians. They waited in the foyer. Ed joined them and introduced himself. It was 09:00 hours, but soon Ed, the school team, and family members were called into the hearing. Alone again, I amused myself by chatting with people I knew—former colleagues—and I found homemade cookies. Took one, maybe two. Fifteen minutes for the initial part of the hearing, and then the student and representatives were all excused. Once again, the trustees would discuss and make their decision alone. Ed sat with the family. He spoke with them, talked about appreciating their support, and tried to get a conversation going. It was stiff and awkward, but Ed kept at it, trying to involve the student. He asked the young lady, Val, what courses were going well, what did she like best. Predictably, her answer was "none." Ed changed tack and asked which course was better. Ed was not going away, and Val became a bit more animated, more willingly involved. Math and drama were her favourites.

I listened, watched, and began to realize that Val would soon be having more conversations like this. She too was facing legal charges as well as a school expulsion. People would be trying to figure her out, and she would be doing the same, trying to figure them out and looking to get a handle on her situation. Everyone would be searching for ways to help; it would all be invasive and intrusive—"in your face." And the tall gentleman, family I guessed, was also facing criminal assault charges.

Shortly, all of them—the school administrators, Ed, Val, the parent, and the tall gentleman—were invited back into the boardroom to hear the outcome. Then it was all done. Short, not so sweet; it was another expulsion. They left in silence. Still, smiles were exchanged.

Had chatting helped? Maybe it had showed consideration. Maybe somebody had cared. It had not been the best start for anyone's day—not for the students, not for the parents, not for the family or extended family, not for the two school administrators trying to make their school work better, and not for those doing the judging—the trustees. It was also hard for Ed, and he was less than satisfied. His thoughts whirled. Had all this been fair?

Later, while writing one of the two expulsion letters, Ed remarked that the girl had already received a harsher punishment than another student involved in a similar incident. He would be following this up with a counsellor.

Events then seemed to conspire to bring further student suspensions into focus. Only two days later, a principal called Ed about another suspension. It was different this time, and Ed wondered out loud—what were schools expected to do? He told me how the media had recently chased down another superintendent, a colleague, and asked why a student was not suspended? Suspended for a fight outside of the school, a fight well beyond the school grounds? Clearly, a suspension for events beyond the confines of the school or its grounds would exceed a school's powers, but expulsion seemed to be the media's preferred response—until some school did it. Then the cry would reverse. Ed was trying to figure it out. Why was the "big picture" changing?

I empathized with Ed, said something ham-handed, stated that at least it was about students. He let it pass. Ed was committed to supporting schools, and that meant supporting student suspensions. Although removed from direct contact, Ed's commitment to students was always central to his thoughts and decision-making.

Another event, a sexual concern, added to the evidence of Ed's overriding attention to students, but before learning these details, some background. Sexual matters are always sensitive, but now, school folk were extra-cautious, their senses on high alert following local press coverage of a nearby sexual abuse trial. The headline, "Judge blames the teacher," screamed out at everyone involved with schools. No one would just sit back to wait and watch. Principals, staff, parents—everyone—would want to avoid a similar incident playing out locally. And then Ed got a call.

During two related telephone conversations, Ed listened carefully as principal Jeff Mackellar relayed a parental concern. The Bowdages had informed him that their Grade 5 daughter was being sexually harassed by two boys. The boys, he said, were in Grade 3. Surprised, Ed repeated it, "Grade 3?" The parents were insisting on police involvement. Ed learned more over the next twenty minutes, and then he voiced his preference. As of right now, he did not want to involve the police, but the Bowdages were free to do so. Instead, he suggested that they tell the Bowdages that the school regretted the incident and would deal with it directly. Still, to clarify his thoughts, Ed asked for more time to think. Within minutes, he was back to principal Mackellar. Would it help to have the parents and the district police liaison officer talk, to meet each other? They reviewed what they knew—back and forth, back and forth—and then agreement; there was "potential" to that approach. Ed would discuss the incident with the police liaison officer, but he needed time. He requested one hour.

Knowing these details, Ed acted. When he was unable to reach the police liaison officer, he left for his next appointment. Later, back at the office, he went for coffee. Out of a side window, he noticed a police officer. He rose—hopeful—chased, and having caught up, saw that she was the police liaison officer. Perfect. They met in a nearby room. Ed summarized the concern, and the parent's position that he described as upset, but supportive. Could she help? Calm them? Address the issue? The officer highlighted previous situations. She thought it might work; it was worth trying. With this agreement, she promised to investigate it, likely tomorrow. Done, their conversation turned to another student and another issue. Back in the office, Ed immediately updated principal Mackellar and asked that he report it directly to the parents.

This student concern drew Ed's immediate attention. It was one example of a consistent leadership focus. Staff, parents, and trustees saw and understood that the interests of students would always be paramount with Ed. Outgoing chair Margaret O'Connell talked about the board's dilemma, balancing student needs with limited fiscal resources. "Ever since I have been on the board, we have been hacking and chopping, and Ed isn't [doing that]. I mean, his main focus is the kids, and he always brings you back to that."

Process: Scanning the Environment

Ed Noyce's intelligence made him curious about everything. A similar process existed professionally. Ed talked about his strategies:

> "I do a lot of reading, Dale, but a lot more skimming than reading, looking for the nubs in *Ed[ucational] Leadership* or *PDK* [*Phi Delta Kappan*, a professional policy journal for K–12 educators] or those kinds of things. I really value *Ed Leadership*. I think that it is a marvelous journal, and that one I tend to digest."

In his office, he had one tall, slim shelf of mostly binders. Other print materials were piled on anything that would hold them: his desk, the coffee table, and the floor. In June, his coffee table included a haphazard collection: a CD of "Prairie" music, numerous administrative papers, and a book, *Learning to Succeed: A Radical Look at Education Today and a Strategy for Tomorrow*. Ed identified the book, open at chapter five and left upside down, as one recommended by friends from England, and he talked about its message. It was not just accumulated stuff; Ed knew what was there.

The district office held other print resources. When Barney Hepworth, the district computer specialist, asked about a total quality management (TQM) workshop, Ed left, and then reappeared with a related boxed set of books. He outlined their content and encouraged Barney to take them, to read them.

Everything interested Ed. He listed them for me: "Computers, physics, math, the world in general. I am interested in whatever is around, and learning." One day he demonstrated the broadness of his reach in a conversation with technicians. It was a discussion of amplifier circuits in their largest computer. They followed his thoughts; I could not.

Ed at Work.

He handled mail and telephone inquiries that I was certain would not have reached the desk of other superintendents. His secretary wanted to cull some, but she knew that Ed wanted "a feel for it." She described him as easy to please, just keep him up to date. Staff knew that they were to help him stay well-informed. A former executive assistant recalled that one of his roles was to be "another pair of ears" for Ed. When staff alerted Ed to a potential problem, he typically concluded the session with a polite request: if things change, please advise.

Listening carefully was his best strategy for collecting information. New chair Lydia Jacques marvelled at his listening skills, "Ed is a good listener," and rephrased the thought for emphasis, "Somebody who actually listens." I was at the December zone meeting of superintendents when Ed casually mentioned that closing the provincial land title offices between Christmas and New Year's would save money, but it would also hurt some businesses. Superintendents perked up. Were business professionals tiring of the government's "attack, slash, and burn policies"? Ed said that this little gem came from a Rotary meeting. While not an enthusiastic club supporter and only an occasional attendee, when there, he paid attention. Business leaders were paying

Ed's Office: Principal Thorton described Ed as a "piler rather than a filer."

attention as well. Soon this analysis became prescient news for a provincial daily that subsequently published similar views.

Sometimes Ed's sources were wrong. He repeatedly heard rumours that government would be reversing its "attack and cut" mentality. Here, he had heard the wrong rumours, as these hopes were repeatedly dashed by government's continued enthusiasm for the cuts he viewed as devastating to districts like his.

Ed also sought out visual data. That fall, faced with the prospect of retrofitting a school for a possible new program focus, Ed toured the Kananaskis School. The Student Accommodation Committee was considering a retrofit. How easily would space designed for special education convert to French immersion. How much would it cost? He needed a "reminder" of how this space was configured. From the school's basement entrance, he walked into a large vacant classroom with a smaller side room. Next, he examined the wood-working shop. Students were elsewhere, but the teacher was present. Seeing an opportunity, the teacher pitched a capital purchase, a specialized welder. Ed listened, acknowledged the request, but made no commitment. Then upstairs, he knocked on a classroom door. The teacher greeted him enthusiastically. She, too, had a "wants and needs" list. Her class enrollment was on the high side, and it was loaded with children requiring special education or English as a second language (ESL) instruction. Once more, Ed politely listened to her concerns. She saw that there would be no commitment, not even much of a comment, so she demonstrated her resourcefulness. Her student choir needed an audience, and Ed would be perfect. The kids sang; Ed listened and enjoyed it. Finished, he visited students. Before leaving, he peered into another classroom and found that the students were gone, but the teacher was there. They chatted. She was enjoying her break. Ed's tour had only been fifteen minutes, but it was enough. He was ready and he had the images he needed firmly in his mind. He would be a ready resource if the Student Accommodation Committee asked for ideas or details. Looking back, I recalled a previous tour.

Late one June day, Ed toured the district's portable classrooms. It started at the J. M. Pivott Community School—yes, that Joe Pivott, the retired superintendent emeritus. This was a community facility with the public school at the north, a Catholic school to the south, and community facilities between the two—a pool, a library, and a skating/hockey arena. Starting from the community pool and library, we entered the nearby portables. These were the standard 1970s model—wood frame boxes set on piles, and like boxes, they had a nearly flat roof. Inside, carpeted floors, panel walls, limited windows, and ceilings of long tiles. Classrooms were connected by narrow hallways. The smell was distinctive. Stale! A teacher, Kimberly, was still at work. Obviously, Ed was examining the portables, and she had opinions about them. She told Ed that they affected student and teacher health. While the air conditioner made the spring and fall heat bearable, it added humidity, maybe enough to grow mould. Her students missed more school days than those in the core building. Teachers also had more absences. The concrete block construction of the core building was obviously superior to the portables. Ed and Kimberly agreed—these buildings were unhealthy. We left and walked through the core building and entered still more portables, the west wing. There, a teacher meeting was in progress, and quick greetings were exchanged. Ed excused himself continued his tour and soon I followed Ed to his car.

He filled me in; the school's west portables were newer and better, but he did not like them, either. The latter were better than their older neighbours, but they were still trailer-type construction. He continued to Nakiska School, where we walked through more portables, and then he drove past more at Coalspur Middle. We chatted—the portables had served a need, the district had critically needed more student space then—but the construction had been quick, hurried. With the economy booming, and workers hard to find, professional standards were lower. Ed wondered how they would fit the coming middle school concept. How would they meet future needs?

Ed was deep in thought. So was I. This visual tour was in response to another direction being pursued by the Student Accommodation Committee. This committee was eating up his time, clock time, but also his cognitive need for more details, more visualizing and more tidying it all up. As a visual tour—the big picture—it all fit. It made total sense. Still, I would not have initiated it, and was surprised that Ed had done so. What was I missing?

Ed's extensive network produced wide-ranging details that not everyone picked up on, but he did. Ed focused on being well-informed, especially on matters relating to his schools. To accomplish it, he took in all that he could. He read, watched, and listened. And then he did what thinkers do: he made it all fit.

Process: Getting to a Consensus

During our September interview, I asked Ed Noyce about a phrase that I kept hearing, "It makes all kinds of sense." Had he heard it? He had, "Yeah," then he went quiet. He waited. He was not about to be sidetracked by a cute phrase. Finally, I filled the void; did he have notes on what he wanted to talk about next? He did, and he talked about needing input, and what was personally satisfying. He was helping me stick to the meat of the interview, providing good data, addressing real questions. Ed was disciplined. He had volumes to say about involving others, his leadership focus, the team, and what he tried to avoid and what he tried to do. Consider his words:

> "First is teaming, and for me it is very important that we not run the district…with a single person so clearly [at the] helm that everything hinges on that one person. Everything we do now goes back to our Wednesday morning admin meetings. I don't take a single step with the board without discussing it with them. Making sure that they are onside with it, listening to them, adjusting it from them [sic]. Making sure that they are onside with it, discussing it with them. Many of my memos to the board that are the big memos—new directions or suggesting a project or proposal—go to the admin team, and get chewed apart pretty thoroughly, and approved. And I

think, as a team, we are stronger. Cooperative learning, cooperative teaching, cooperative administration, I guess, is sort of where I am coming from.

"I try to get people to go from their individual perspectives to a team perspective. To hear others, to get the pendulum to the middle, to look at the goals of the district, and to identify with the mission. That, to me, is the ultimate responsibility.

"Trying to read the styles—learning styles, teaching styles—of people and use their strengths, help them to understand themselves, and why they might be in disagreement with somebody else, and where that other person is coming from. And recognize that a good team is a blended team; not everybody of all the same perspective.

"What works? I think, listen to the team, focus on the team, and admit errors, but avoid errors by listening to the team. Go back to rule number one: listen to the team."

The terms Ed used to describe his leadership process—team, middle, cooperative, blended, listen—I observed repeatedly. And the team got it. Bill Bersche, assistant superintendent of business services, stressed the "team concept" when interviewed. He, like the others, was following Ed's quiet lead.

In the interview, Ed stated that his priority was the team, and my observations confirmed it. But who was the team? Obviously, he wanted and needed teachers and consultants to buy in, and Ed saw to it that they contributed to the development of the district's vision and the action plan that followed. They owned it; they implemented it. He involved principals in the same way. He also had various other players who got to know and trust each other. For example, at the September 28 semi-monthly board meeting, trustees heard from a team of four teachers and two central office consultants. This team described a remedial language arts program and then a French program. Other teachers chimed in with further comments, with support and explanations. A principal followed, offering up his team's report on a school evaluation. Such strategies developed and enhanced mutual trust. A whole range of others were involved in creating their district vision—principals, middle managers, parents, students—and all would again be involved in the next steps of strategic planning, the implementation phase. Ed revelled in the wide involvement of others. When asked what work was most personally satisfying, he identified three items, all from the strategic planning process: working with his various teams, involving others from throughout the district to create the district's strategic plan, and finally, the support the district received from parents and the community. Recall Etzikom School principal Paul Briggs's compliment to the board for facilitating his attendance at a summer workshop, and their consistent, deliberative support for teachers and others. Ed took comfort in knowing that Paul had recovered from a difficult school closure process, and that he recognized and supported his board and employer.

Part of Ed's leadership involved building a consensus. I felt it was epitomized by the phrase, "It makes all kinds of sense," but Ed dismissed it. In our 140-minute interview on September 12, Ed used the phrase, "it makes all kind of sense," zero times, and when asked, declined further comment. But the phrase was used in other contexts.

On Tuesday, June 7, 1994, the Wapiti Falls School District held what they called their central office planning meeting. It dealt with the upcoming school year and as it was held in the yet-to-open Ormand Mitchell High School, it was a private, quiet, and largely empty venue. It was away from central office distractions—phones, e-mails, secretaries, colleagues, and visitors—and all at no cost. In attendance were five senior administrators and four curriculum consultants. These four consultants were the only survivors remaining after recent cuts.

The day started at 08:30 hours. First up on the agenda was an opportunity to re-examine and revise the prepared agenda. Then came "Priorities for 1994-95" and "District Calendar Review." A break was scheduled from 11:30 to 14:00 hours. Two-and-a-half hours seemed excessive for the mid-meeting break, but I'd learned that unscheduled time would not be wasted. The afternoon's items included "Issues and Directions Arising (Sr. Admin only)" and "Other." It was a skinny agenda, and I was surprised that, "Other" was only allocated thirty minutes allotted, 15:30 to 16:00 hours. Would that work?

The morning went as planned. Participants were prepared. They stated their individual priorities and coordinated their plans with others and with district events. Discussion was comfortably informal and productive. At 11:52 hours, Ed stood, said that he had a meeting with the Student Accommodation Committee, and quietly left. Others also had other commitments. They too left. The afternoon session would be smaller, as four participants were not part of the discussions.

Shortly after 14:00 hours, the senior administrative team had all filtered back. Everyone seemed ready to continue. Now there were just four: Bill Bersche (assistant superintendent of business services), Don Howard (deputy superintendent), Ruth Thompson (assistant secretary-treasurer), and Ed Noyce (superintendent). Outgoing assistant superintendent of human resources, Jake Harris, would have been there but instead opted to attend his last meeting with the Tallgrass Human Resources Officers. Jake's focus would soon be entirely on his new role as principal of a district elementary school. I wondered how would this meeting be different from a regular senior administrator meeting. It wasn't different; it was like other meetings only longer, and it produced another consensus.

Ed began by asking what items from the morning needed discussion, but then he continued, "Let me start." This was different; Ed was starting the discussion. Maybe he wanted to set the tone, maybe his goal was just to get the ball rolling. What he did was simple; he wanted follow-up on the job changes that Jake had proposed in the morning. He reviewed them.

I could see that this would be the morning discussion with a new focus. Earlier it was about coordination, while the afternoon was about personnel. It made sense that fewer people were in on these private details.

Discussion was robust. Ruth Thompson, new to her expanded role and new to the group, was asked to contribute her thoughts, and did so, with some hesitation. She seemed reluctant to say too much, too soon. Ed listened while everyone had their say. True to form, the discussion began its normal drift; it wandered, meandered, stalled. New directions were introduced, but invariably the talk returned to personalities, strategies, roles, all private stuff. Ed summarized, suggested that they wait to firm up the details of several roles until they had filled Jake's recently vacated position. This would prevent "fragmenting of staff…piecemeal" changes. Waiting would let them work the role description around the new appointee's skills. Nothing came of Ed's remarks, and their discussion moved on to other topics. Ed followed along—listened carefully, nodded agreement, and waited—then belatedly, he repeated his earlier suggestion, namely that they keep a position open until they had a new assistant superintendent of human resources. Finally, it seemed, they had a decision.

Next, Bill Bersche, assistant superintendent of business services, raised a money issue and led the discussion on it. Money matters drew extensive discussion—the district was, and needed to be, extremely frugal. These various financial concerns were hashed over until there was general agreement. Ruth agreed to do the appropriate follow-up. Ed agreed, "It makes all kinds of sense," and then he summarized. Done, and on to the next topic.

Ed said that he had a personnel matter; a principal had requested an invitation to attend their "Senior Admin" meeting. Nothing happened. Ed offered clarification; that principal was James Thorborn. He was the incoming principal here, at the new Ormand Mitchell School. Ed asked for Don's views on it. Don led from his perspective, and then Bill added related information; he talked about the fiscal resources James wanted to make his start-up work, come fall. Like Ed, he wanted to talk directly with the principal, but nothing came of it. Instead, the group attacked other topics. They were busy, and their time passed quickly. At approximately 14:45 hours, plans for a Teacher Centre were on the table. This morphed into discussion of a computer program for human resources. Ruth was assigned another report. Ed repeated his request for additional items. He received them: Should funds move with students transferred from their soon-to-be-closed school; topics were identified for tomorrow's regular senior administration meeting; and further requests from the soon-to-open Ormand Mitchell High School were mentioned. This last item led. Ormand Mitchell School wanted an outdoor storage—a garage—and had plans for its construction. They also proposed a charge for student parking. Ed, Bill, and Don were all involved. Don gave his support, "It makes all kinds of sense."

Bill shifted the discussion to another of the school's requests, this one was for surveillance cameras. These topics, and more, were discussed and wrapped up when Ed asked if he should invite Ormand Mitchell principal James Thorborn, to their next senior administration meeting tomorrow. He had suggested this earlier, but only after forty-five minutes of discussion around this and other new topics, was the group ready to deal with Ed's query. When it finally came, everyone agreed; principal Thorborn should be invited. No new topics were raised.

This was the second delayed decision on a topic Ed had introduced. Ed had not pushed to have either of his topics addressed sooner. The group discovered the correct topics, established their own working order, and finally, made informed decisions. They were fully engaged—comfortable, busy, and productive.

Ignore, if you can, the wandering, the seemingly unfocused discussion. The purpose of the meeting was to reach a consensus, and one phrase summarized the process. Twice in the afternoon's conversation, someone had said, "It makes all kinds of sense." Twice was maybe less than a pattern, but I felt it was worthy of further exploration.

The phrase, "It makes all kinds of sense," was important enough for me to pursue its meaning in most of the interviews that I conducted. Chair Lydia Jacques recognized it as a pet phrase of Ed's. She thought he used it to mean "common sense." Don Howard understood it similarly, "Common sense prevails. That things are well thought out." Student services coordinator Herb Bondar knew the phrase and provided nuance. He explained it by relying on the psychologist's knack to have it all ways:

"It is the gestalt of the whole situation. It makes all kinds of sense, and not necessarily… sense in a logical-rational domain. It also makes sense in a big picture, knowing what the big picture is. It is right-brain thinking. Reading between the lines, being able to take a look at something."

"Gestalt" of the whole? "Right-brain thinking"—intuitive, thoughtful, subjective? Good psychological terms, but what did they mean? Herb was as comfortable with its holistic gestalt and with its opposite, the "logical-rational" explanation, left-brain thinking. He had eliminated nothing, informed nothing, had it both ways, and agreed with everyone. Perfect for him, but what did it mean for me?

Ed's spouse Marie Noyce recognized it as a general phrase meaning, "I can kind of agree with you, but I'll have to think it over for a while." That was a hedge. Consider Ab Digby, assistant superintendent. When asked, he laughed, "Yeah, Ed says that a lot." He then added,

"It's his way of saying to you that, hey, you have the knowledge. You have the background… It sounds like it'll work, and…I'm throwing it back to you…Now you prove to me that it makes sense by going out and implementing it, or carrying it through."

"It makes all kind of sense" was district lexicon. (Other terms idiosyncratic to Ed and the district are identified in Appendix C: "A District Lexicon.") Its meaning was contextual and fluid; it seemed to mean whatever the hearer thought it meant or wanted it to mean. As district lexicon, it would likely wither to be replaced by the vigour of some new expression. Was it any wonder that Bill Bersche—an aptly cautious money man—declined further explanation? He needed context before volunteering any meaning to it.

For Ed, the phrase was a distraction of little import, but he was wrong. It was heard and used everywhere. But again, for the man who basically owned the phrase, he offered no comment.

I concluded that Ed used the phrase, "It makes all kinds of sense," to signal that the topic has been thoroughly vetted and ready to be put into action or ready to be introduced to bigger audiences—the board, teachers, community, or provincial superintendents and officials. There, it might initiate a new round of consensus building. The phrase mirrored Ed's personal process of searching out everything, but it was more than a search. It involved more information, more sharing, and more reflection, all among an ever-increasing circle of contributors. Leadership in Wapiti Falls involved many people and covered a wide swath of the district's business. Everyone had opportunity to share their thoughts, and to hear and understand those of other contributors. "It makes all kinds of sense" signalled that a consensus had been reached.

But Ed's leadership process required another step. Consensus was the goal, but getting there required skillful teaching.

Process: Slow, patient, resourceful teaching

Serendipity had taken Ed out of his physics lab and put him in a classroom as a substitute teacher. He found it was surprisingly satisfying, enough that it changed his career path. And so he trained as a teacher, worked as a teacher, and thought that even as the superintendent of schools, he could still be a teacher. The youth of his classroom days had been replaced by colleagues, but these adults could still be students. His bosses were also students of a sort, learning about education as they guided it. Yes, some trustees were former teachers, but the others came from multiple endeavours, professional and non-professional. Ed taught them all. In effect, he had become the district's lead teacher. He led as the resource person: providing information, broadening perspectives, and helping everyone evaluate possibilities. Occasionally, he challenged them. Guided by the grand vision of the district and his own day-to-day "big picture," Ed could patiently wait for teaching opportunities. When opportunity presented, he created and delivered appropriate lessons. He did so without patronizing, lecturing, or rendering harsh judgment. His secret was to listen and respect all who made the effort to contribute. His process was self-maintaining.

Ed delivered a variety of lessons, and I collected several, put them on a metaphorical shelf, and called it a library. Ed's pedagogical library contained many lessons. The first and most important lesson was my discovery that Ed was a practitioner of cooperative learning, and then I witnessed Ed use cooperative learning with his new assistant superintendent. Teachers are also test givers, and Ed, the typical teacher, was no different. Two such tests are described here. One was the sly test executed on his deputy superintendent. The second was uncomfortably close. I took his test, failed, and then did a make-up test. Each lesson and each test helped him plan for his next lesson; each would guide to some future interaction. Some lessons, while not exactly the classic didactic lessons of Socrates, consisted of a series of instructive questions. In one such setting, Ed, with the help of his colleagues, adjusted, reformulated, and changed a series of strategic questions after a recalcitrant colleague used the answer sheet to dress up, misconstrue, and exaggerate through grandly formulated replies. And he sent two fun lessons my way. These two were to be neat and tidy bookends, but I could not resist adding one last tactical lesson. It further demonstrated patience as a key component of cooperative learning.

Lesson 1: My Belated Discovery of Cooperative Learning

I observed Ed carefully and soon recognized that he was a teacher. It was hard to miss. After watching him deliver numerous lessons, a niggling issue stood out, left unresolved. What was his teaching model? He was providing a lesson, but I did not understand what I was seeing it until twenty-plus years later—September 13, 2017. It was an important day. I had just reviewed my notes, looked to confirm a bit of analysis, when a new insight hit. In re-reading deputy superintendent Don Howard's interview, I noticed a thin thread. Don referenced Ed's "non-directive" style. I linked this to Ed's reluctance to "insert" himself into discussions—insertion was another puzzling observation. Under the auspices of non-directive instruction and inductive reasoning, I thought that Ed's reluctance came about because "inserting" his personal view would prematurely limit discussion or narrow the focus. Insertions would give the answer away before the student really understood the concept. Avoiding insertions was good teaching, but there was more; I discovered that it was a whole instructional system. My thoughts wandered, took me back to my time in teacher education classes.

Inquiry education was a big deal in my training as a future science teacher. Then, in my first teaching assignment, an inquiry text drove me crazy. It posed questions but offered no answers. My students disliked the questions and resisted them, resisted me. I struggled. I needed to learn more and was soon doing a master's degree in curriculum. Our group dumped our professor. We would teach ourselves and set our own course of studies. We fumbled. I hated it. That was my second inquiry project, and both had run amok.

But with Ed I saw the familiar signs—non-directive inquiry, a teacher-facilitator purposefully leading discussion—and with Ed, it worked. Where my teacher-facilitator lessons failed, Ed's succeeded. Why? I googled another thought, a similar teaching strategy: "discovery education."

"Discovery Method: Noun, Education. A largely unstructured method or philosophy of teaching whereby students are permitted to find solutions to problems on their own or at their own pace, often jointly in group activities, either independent of supervision or under the guidance of a teacher" (www.dictionary.com). Was there more? I re-examined the data, re-read interviews, and found, hidden in plain sight, Ed's reference to cooperative learning. I had even quoted it but had found significance elsewhere in the quote. I looked further afield. Wikipedia described "cooperative learning" as more than "merely arranging students into groups…and structuring positive interdependence" (https://en.wikipedia.org/wiki/Cooperative_learning). A check on inquiry-based learning yielded similar results: active learning starting with questions and assisted by a facilitator. Inquiry education and discovery method

"Hidden in plain sight."

were both part of the same learning movement of the 1960s (https://en.wikipedia.org/wiki/Inquiry_education). Under all four banners—"non-directive education," "discovery education," "inquiry education," and "cooperative education"—the teacher role changed from spouting information to facilitating student problem-solving. All described Ed's teaching style. I had a fit. While my science education referenced "inquiry" and "discovery education," Ed labelled the process "cooperative learning." That was acceptable, and so, I started thinking of Ed's teaching style in his terms. I found that cooperative education solved another issue, the "insertion" problem. Avoiding insertion, I concluded, was in part tactical. Ed was teaching his way. I learned Ed's lesson in cooperative learning, but it took until I was ready to learn it—just shy of twenty-three years.

And so a key component of Ed's leadership process was identified. The second lesson shows how Ed used it.

Lesson 2: Observing a Cooperative Learning Lesson

First thing on September 12, Ed's secretary, Ann, let him know that Ab Digby wanted to see him. Ed got up from his chair and went to Ab's office. Ab, the new assistant superintendent of human resources, wanted to talk about intern teachers. Interns–fully trained, full-time hires–had employment contracts, but they were not recognized as teachers by the teachers' union. What were they then? Ab was concerned about board approvals for their hiring. Ed watched as Ab reworked some financial calculations. No doubt they were recalculations. Ed saw the numbers, saw that Ab wanted further explanation, and so he discussed how these new interns came to be employed. Intern hiring recommendations had gone to the board and were approved. While interns were not specifically mentioned in the omnibus staffing resolution, the board knew that interns would be part of the package.

Maybe Ed thought that his explanation would take the issue off the table, but Ab had further follow-up. He wanted to drop the intern contract and replace it with a regular teaching contract. Ed thought this move would please the teachers' union. More back and forth discussion, but Ab was still not satisfied, so Ed asked, "But you're nervous about it?" Ab was, "Yes." Ed took another stab; he said that on first blush, the board liked the cost savings, but that was the wrong way to look at it.

By now Ed's interest had apparently moved on. He changed the subject. He asked for details on student enrollment, different details than Ab had already provided. Ed said that Ab's charts were confusing; the numbers were accurate but jumbled for his purposes. More full-time equivalent students had enrolled, but the numbers were so small that there had been "no growth." Enrollment was essentially steady. Ab nodded his agreement. Satisfied, Ed was done with his enrollment quest. So true to pattern, he asked about Ab's weekend. Ab replied, "It was all right," but clearly, matters were still unsettled.

While Ed had talked about enrollment, Ab had only nominally followed along. He was still thinking about interns. He must have finished his internal processing, for he declared, "I agree." Agree with what? Ed had given neither answers nor directions. He had answered Ab's questions, but had not asked any. By then, Ab had the information that he needed. He would revert to regular teaching contracts. No more special "intern" contracts. Ed understood, and with Ab's firm decision, he finally he offered an assessment. He said that the existing intern contract was "abusing people." He offered reassurance; the board would have "no trouble with this, Ab." They would want interns properly assigned.

I thought about Ed's strategy, his teaching lesson. From 07:50 hours to 8:10 hours tops, Ab raised questions about the intern assignment. Ed answered his questions but gave no direction. I saw Ed's strategy as holding out, keeping his own views to himself until Ab had made his decision. Ed's questions about enrollment data were a distraction. By month-end, I had interviewed Ab. There, he spoke comfortably about Ed's leadership style, "He gives you permission to go for it [and] the consequences that go with it." Ed had given permission and had used good teaching practices. But what was the lesson?

Ab was new to this position. He had replaced the previous assistant superintendent on the first day of this new school year. Nearly three weeks into it, Ab discovered some troubling aspects to "intern" contracts. The previous approach saved money but was dodgy; it circumvented the normal rules—union rules. Ed understood the concerns and saw that Ab had a workable solution. Ed followed along but avoided taking the lead. By the time Ab had made his decision, Ed had changed topics, twice. In the place of a directive, Ed had danced around his view of intern contracts. He did it by making up a skit about enrollment. Neither men referenced nor mentioned Ab's predecessor. Calling him for comments or advice would have been easy; he was still there, in the district. It was Jake. Several weeks later, possibly with further discussion out of my hearing, Ab was more comfortable in his new role. And Ed would no doubt be encouraged with the new approach; it was an ethical upgrade.

Ed had been thinking about interns for some time. During coffee chit-chat on June 23, he mentioned that the intern salary was low; the context and his tone implied too low. I asked, what were interns? Later that June, I heard more: "intern" had casually been alluded to in discussions with the teacher union representative. Mentioned and gone. But was it gone? Why had it been mentioned? Ed had all this background. He had allowed the previous incumbent to incorporate something that he might not have been keen about, or maybe it had slipped in before he knew it. So, he waited, perhaps thinking that Ab might discover issues. Ab might figure out a better approach, and he did.

Ed's teaching method was slow, patient, and cooperative. Next, Ed did something teachers do on a regular basis. He tested his deputy superintendent, Don Howard.

Lesson 3: A Sly Test

On my last full day of observation, October 5, during the regular Wednesday morning meeting of senior administrators, Ed listened carefully as a team member raised a new concern. Ed seemed to have been waiting for such an opportunity, and when it appeared, events unfolded quickly.

As usual, the first task in senior administrators' meetings was to set an agenda. Deputy superintendent Don Howard identified one agenda topic: school priorities. Others added their items. After constructing the agenda, discussion followed. With earlier topics addressed, school priorities were next. Don was concerned about school maintenance; specifically, he noted the limited progress on projects at Snipe Lake Middle School. Principals, he explained, wondered how important schools were? A district office renovation—a teacher centre—apparently had priority. No one spoke of the new high school, Ormand Mitchell, and their start-up problems. Everyone knew that Ormand Mitchell High School was perceived as having a stranglehold on both maintenance staff and financial resources, but discussing it seemed mean, off limits. Predictably, discussion started with the ever-present issue of money and moved to its consequence—a paucity of maintenance staff. The five administrators were engaged and respectful. Ed listened, leaned into the group, tapped his pen softly on the table. Shortly, he summarized what others had said and concluded with what they all seemed to be thinking—namely, that maintenance staff needed to be pulled out of Ormand Mitchell, maybe out of the central office. This would free up staff to work in schools. But doing that, he continued, would not make maintenance problems go away, as the source of this problem was insufficient staff. Don nodded an agreement and then steered the discussion back to his concern, school priorities. He was, in effect, saying, help me help Snipe Lake. He thought that the team should have one unified direction; that was how they worked. The discussion continued; everyone participated and offered their ideas until Ed asked that they put these priorities into a larger context.

He let his team know that several schools faced maintenance issues. His biggest concern was that the portable classrooms at the Pivott Community School could be making staff and students ill. Perhaps the problem was in the carpet or maybe it was the walls; conceivably it could be both. They were substandard. They jeopardized student and staff health. Others identified more maintenance issues. Soon they realized that principals were not seeing the total picture. Principals complained because they did not know why some projects had a higher priority than others. Don shared rumours about the government's new capital (facility) plan. He asked, could the old portables be replaced under the new plan? Student safety was his, and the district's, number one priority. There had been no resolution, but this discussion was complete for now. Ed moved their discussion forward to the next agenda item.

So, what happened? While this exchange looked innocent, it was much more for Ed. When we were alone, he explained. Principals were going to Don to solve various problems, and Don solved them by assigning funds at his disposal. By linking facility maintenance to health impacts, he could gauge Don's reaction. He got it. Don's raised eyebrows—surprise—informed Ed. Don did not know or had not thought about maintenance issues districtwide. For Ed, the heart of this discussion was not maintenance, it was Don bypassing the team process. Ed had communicated preferred directions on two levels. On the first level, the team knew that overall maintenance issues needed attention. By working together, they could make their limited resources work. On a second level, Ed had offered a rational illustration of why colleagues needed to share concerns. He never said that, but he hoped that Don had received this part of the message. He knew Don would think about this conversation Would he learn from it?

When next asked to "grease" the squeaky wheel, Ed hoped he would go to the senior admin team or to Ed. If this subtle message had not been received, nothing more would be said. Ed would wait for a different context, for another teachable moment. (To nit-pick, perhaps the solution was to discuss the priority of the various maintenance projects directly with principals. This solution did not come up, at least not then.)

In interviewing Don, I came to understand that Don did indeed pick up on subtle messages. He described Ed as "very non-directive." People could carve out their own niche; he let them. Not exactly the message that Ed delivered on this day, but he was getting there.

Ed had held onto his concerns over portables until that item was useful. What else could he do with the knowledge? The solution required money, and they did not have it. We had toured the portables in late June. It was still a problem on October 5, four months later. Ed had not known how this concern could be shared. He held it until a fit appeared. Patience was one of the many aspects of Ed's leadership key.

Lesson 4: Recovery After a Failed Test

While Ed helped me interpret Don's test, I realized that he had tested me. Earlier that fall, at lunch in Ed and Marie's home, I flubbed a response, thoughtlessly repeated statements heard at home while growing up. I had stereotyped Indigenous people, members of the First Nations, the people we had grown up calling Indians; some of them had been my classmates. Having said it, I heard it differently now and knew that it was wrong—I was wrong. What might have been accepted years before, or quietly tolerated in later years, was no longer conscionable. Nothing more was said, and while I had fumbled through an explanation, I also knew that I had crossed a line. On the way back to the office, Ed drove around older parts of the city and pointed out the stately homes close to the river. Strange—why use up his day in this way? Then it came to me: he was not simply wasting time; he was thinking. I felt guilty, and then it registered—his thoughts were about me, about my foolish comments. I had created an unnecessary distraction from work. Could it be something else? A clue came later that afternoon: Ed was offering me a lifeline, a way to absolve my guilt. I took it.

When Ed mentioned the hardships facing a native man and his family, I responded, instantly, spontaneously. I blurted out, what had we, society, done to the native culture? It was heartfelt and our conversation continued, but the mood, my mood, had changed. Given a second chance, I was able to show that I was a better person. I felt better, and if this was indeed a test, maybe I had passed. I hoped I was back in Ed's good grace.

Lesson 5: Strategic Questions Interrupted

Strategic questioning was another of Ed's instructional skills. Ed related the details of a meeting he had helped initiate. While the deputy minister of education had rejected Ed's attempt to get a previous meeting, this same deputy now agreed to meet with a group of superintendents. Nothing was said about who initiated it, only that the deputy had requested the questions in advance. It would help him prepare, help him provide more thoughtful answers. With input from other superintendents, Ed amassed a series of questions for the deputy minister and forwarded them. The meeting date arrived, the deputy was there, and question period started well—too well. His answers were contrived, inauthentic—too perfect. He was skirting the intent of the questions. His responses ignored the reality of his policies and practices. Feeling sidestepped and cheated, Ed passed a note to his colleagues. It asked that they change up their questions. They did. Facing new questions, the deputy went off stride. No longer did he have the neutral answers that could be delivered smoothly, professionally. He was suddenly awkward. Superintendents watched, listened, and understood; it confirmed their thoughts on his shortcomings. But why had the deputy gone to that much bother? I was not in attendance, but I had seen similar examples of this man's hubris. My thoughts were that the deputy saw the superintendents as rivals and assumed that each of them was out to show him up, to ambush him. His predecessors provided leadership; this man sought power. His approach was inferior.

Lessons 6 and 7: Hexadecimals and Learning-Style Assessment

Finally, the fun lessons. I had finished Ed's interview by 13:10 hours on September 12 and waited to interview the deputy superintendent at 13:30 hours. Ed, doing an unusual project involving the district computer, had his scientific calculator in hand. As he worked, he talked about hexadecimals. I knew about them and had used them in university computer classes and assumed he was doing a similar task, programming something involving the district computer. I showed some interest, and Ed could not resist. We played at converting decimal numbers into hexadecimals, back and forth. I was rusty. We did several examples together before he returned to his conversion project. At 13:20 hours he announced, "This is confusing." Apparently, his conversion skills were a bit rusty, so maybe we had both lost our edge. I smiled.

September 22 was another day of interviews. Before leaving for my first interview on what was going to be a full day, Ed gave me a learning-style assessment form and the Grace McCarthy instructional materials I had requested. When I had finished taking the test, he wanted to talk about it, to mark it, to study my results. He was not kidding. Okay, I thought; there would be free time between interviews, and I said that I would do my best to finish them.

I was at a school for my nine o'clock interview at 08:40 hours. I looked over the McCarthy materials, started the questions. I made all my interviews on time, and I used the slack time between them to complete the test instrument. Back from a full day of interviews, I caught up with Ed. He and a principal were in discussion. The customary pattern was followed: finish business and then share family stories. The principal left, and Ed turned to me and asked, did I do the test? We studied the results. Ed and I were in the same quadrant, and the results were similar, but his score on the "abstract" axis was higher. Why was that? Together, we examined the questions, figured out where and why our scores differed. Apparently, Ed wanted to understand me better, or perhaps he wanted us to understand each other better. Another teaching opportunity utilized.

Lessons 8: Patient Planning

The previous lessons provided a representative look at Ed's role as a teacher, but one additional lesson merits further emphasis. Consider the time Ed allowed for cooperative learning to take hold. I knew he had waited four months to share the health concerns learned about in his June tour of the portables. And I took me twenty-plus years to figure out cooperative learning—but I was not a work project. This next look had another extended time framework—in terms of workaday standards. For several years, the district had planned for grade changes in a transition from junior highs to middle schools. That would take place in September, and it seemed unlikely that further grade changes would occur. And so, Pivott School principal Gavin Emerson had likely not thought about still another grade configuration for his school. But Ed had casually mentioned it in June, putting it out as a possibility, a maybe, and moved on. Gavin had heard it but offered no comment. I wondered at the time what was that all about. Like other unknowns, I thought all would be explained in due course.

That September, Ed repeated it; he asked Gavin for his thoughts about future grades in his school. Gavin's school was still unusual for the district. While it had lost their Grade 9 class, it was still the only Grade 1 to 8 school in the district. Was Ed talking about a change to an elementary-only school—Grade 1 to 5? Gavin had not reacted; he may have shrugged, but he said nothing more. Again, my previous thoughts returned, what was that about? Back in his car, I pursued it and Ed walked me through it. "Here is an opportunity to tell me if I am going the wrong direction. That's what I was listening for with Gavin on Friday." Hearing no comments about such a move, Ed understood that another change, if it came about, would be supported. Nothing else was said; nothing else needed saying. Gavin had listened carefully and was prepared should more changes come about.

Analysis of Slow, Patient, Resourceful Teaching

Gavin, Don, Ab, and others all listened carefully to Ed's comments, to what was said and not said, and they were comfortable knowing that Ed would not intercede unnecessarily. He would give them whatever scope they needed, but if change was necessary, whatever Ed decided, it would be fair. So again, having heard his comments, they thought hard about what might come next. They learned.

But why have I viewed Ed's behaviours, interpreted them as teaching lessons, and concluded that such practices were important to his leadership? They were presented as teaching lessons because that was how Ed saw himself, as a teacher. It took me some effort to identify his teaching style, but once I arrived at his model, I was rewarded. I saw that Ed used his team to do what he could not accomplish on his own. Every leader does that. Some utilize careful job descriptions and assign clearly defined tasks. There were no such marching orders with Ed. He had a team that built a consensus about what they would do and how they would do it. He respected their abilities. He let them do what they thought best. He guided them indirectly; his role was to encourage, support, and challenge. That is why cooperative learning was key to my sense-making task. Seven lessons were examined; there were more. Sticking with the library metaphor, his lessons would fill several shelves. As each new lesson was added, the shelves would get heavier and heavier. What held them up? Ed would need a stronger and stronger shelf, a structure or undergirding, to support all these lessons and their preparation. What was that support? Specifically, what held up Ed's leadership? It was another leadership process and my next topic.

Process: Time on the Job

Ed worked hard. Choosing where and how he would spend his time may have been his most challenging leadership decision. His job would always need more effort, more hours at work, and more hours thinking about work. Ed knew this and accepted it. This examination of his time at work has three components: a compilation of hours observed, a discussion of "non-billable" time, and Ed's time management.

Quantitative Work

I observed Ed full-time for sixteen days. (I also observed him at several superintendent functions and made after-the-fact notes, but on these occasions, my focus was elsewhere, leaving the data incomplete and uncounted.) During my regular observations, his average workday was nine hours, fifty-two minutes. Forty-four percent (seven) of his days were longer than ten hours. Ed started a little earlier and ended a little later than the official day, but other professional and hourly staff also worked longer than the official workday. On ten observation days, Ed went home slightly before 17:00 hours, but on five of these, his daytime work was extended by evening meetings. Regular board meetings, twice monthly, started at 19:00 hours and ended between 21:30 hours or 22:00 hours. They added two-and-a-half hours, and more, to his day. Officially he had an hour for lunch, and when his day permitted it, he enjoyed lunch at home. Home was but a short drive into the countryside, fifteen to twenty minutes both ways.

While there was a consistent start time to his workday, the ending time varied. The official end of the day was 17:00 hours, but events would change that. If someone needed to chat and dropped by late to catch him, Ed stayed and went home later. Principal James Thorborn counted on that and knew that if he needed a ten- to fifteen-minute conversation, he could phone or come directly to the district office between 16:45 and 17:10. Ed willingly put in extra time if someone needed his attention, direction, or support.

Did Ed know how much he worked? Probably not. His references to time were underplayed, immaterial, unimportant. He talked about short board meetings, but his numbers were an underestimate. He told Agnes Cameron, a community volunteer on the Student Accommodation Committee, to expect two or three meetings, but she had gone into her fifth meeting and expected more. If a task was taking longer than expected, Ed's solution was to work more. He did not count the heavy time demands or resent any extra work time because he expected to take the time that the job required. His focus was on doing his best for the Wapiti Falls Consolidated School District. Appendix E: "Observation Dates with Time Observed" provides all the details available.

Other Work

Ed also took work home and did qualitative tasks there and elsewhere. How much of his work was "off the clock"? At work, I could observe his work and count the time spent there. At home, or otherwise away from the district, times were unknown and uncounted. Ed admitted to working at home for an average five to six hours per weekend. No mention was made of the weekdays when work was taken home, some probably due to the extra demands of carrying me, his "shadow," everywhere except on bathroom breaks. No attempt was made to include time needed to unwind or to think and plot. Some work at home could have been counted, theoretically, but was not. Some experiences, like thinking, setting priorities, and managing innumerable details, were qualitative and uncountable. These could occur anywhere. For example, some deep thinking took place at the office, when he "disappeared," and some took place elsewhere. Quantifying Ed's total work time, including his "non-billable" time and his qualitative time, would produce speculative, fuzzy numbers. At some point the exercise of determining how hard Ed worked becomes meaningless and useless. In contrast, a conclusion that Ed worked hard whether on or off the clock would be accurate and informative.

Time Management

Ed's time management involved several practices. On a day-to-day basis, he kept his workday relatively open. "Every day has got spaces in it. I deliberately try not to schedule my day so tightly that I can't respond to what happens during the day." He used unscheduled space to "hit the phones or get out to a school, or whatever is going on, or meet with the guys here." He also had a mental clock of sorts that kept him on time, even early for events. It was a clock "of sorts," because he did not bother to track extra hours. I thought that Ed had two strategies for managing time. First, be on time. Second, take all the time needed to do it right.

It was not difficult for Ed to stay busy. He said that June was not bad because the year was winding down. He explained: There were fewer meetings. Principals stayed close to their schools and concentrated on finishing off existing tasks while avoiding new jobs. They called on Ed only if they needed help to finish off jobs, and therefore new issues were seldom brought into play. Ed said that, but I did not see less work. Instead, I saw him working hard to solve his staffing "puzzle," to attend year-end activities, to plan for next year, and to put out fires. Ed also thought that fall was easy because there were no major hitches. Again, I saw him being just as busy, helping new staff settle in, managing the new middle school division, dealing with a committee that sucked up his workday with a series of new directions that required additional off-the-clock tasks. In looking back, I saw him sit still—not actively engaged in work—just once. That was the time after a school reported on a possible sexual harassment matter. Ed explained that he did not want to start something for fear of missing a return call. When it came, he had it timed, "Thirteen minutes." By quantifying the wait time, he had signified its importance.

Ed was also ambitious regarding his time, or was it being frugal? Or both? Last year, he and deputy superintendent Don Howard had led their district's strategic planning initiative. While many organizations hired external consultants for this task, after investigating the process, they concluded that (according to Don):

> "We can do that stuff on our own. So that is what we did. Ed took it on. We didn't pay any high-priced consultant or anything and [...] the ownership is ours [...] Nobody can blame anything on an outside consultant that didn't know anything about our school district. And I think that the end result will be even more positive."

They could do it and they did. Outgoing chair Margaret O'Connell understood exactly why they had taken on the strategic planning process rather than farming it out. Doing it internally had saved money; the amount was equal to half a teacher salary for a year. Their extra duty had put an additional one-half of a teacher in the classroom—or in these times of cuts—their extra work duty kept half a teacher in the classroom?

What was the effect of all this work on Ed? Ed did not talk about his time on the job, but those I interviewed did. Several colleagues commented that there were few signs of fatigue. His retiring chair was not one of them. She thought Ed was tired, "but he doesn't, you never see him standing around yawning, and he doesn't show expressions of tiredness."

Several people thought Ed avoided the stress of overwork by unwinding at home and doing family things on the weekend. A former chairperson spoke of Ed having "two lives," that he kept his professional and personal roles apart better than other superintendents she had worked with. His wife Marie equivocated. She knew that Ed tried to separate home and work, but she saw him bringing work home, and she knew that his thoughts were sometimes at work. Nevertheless, they both made the effort. I noted during the lunches I spent with them that Ed did not mention work during his lunches at home, and Marie did not ask.

At work Ed chatted about his family, about their holidays, and their hiking excursions. This light, breezy, inconsequential chit-chat made conversations work. Still, staff, trustees, and others picked up the message that Ed had limits on what he would or wanted to share. Fair enough, as people understood and agreed that there should be a distance between private and public. But was it really privacy? He surprised me sometimes because if asked, he answered. People just did not ask. I did the same: sometimes I asked, sometimes I did not.

People liked Ed and thought he worked too hard, too long, too everything. They were concerned. Again, current trustee and former chair Margaret O'Connell expressed concern: "The man is a workaholic. He just makes me crazy. The board has to beat on him to take time off. You say, you know you are going to burn out. You are going to get sick." By fall, she was pleased because:

> "He looks better. For a while he was looking—you know. I think that he took time off this summer and sort of regenerated, but really, last year when all those cuts were coming down and everything was going crazy…plus, you know, a couple of years ago getting a new board. I mean that has got to be a major nightmare. You get three new people on board, and who knows where they are coming from."

While Margaret O'Connell thought that Ed had regenerated with time off, his secretary, Ann Spencer, said, "I haven't seen him take more holidays."

Ed's time was absolutely required to manage his very labour-intensive leadership process with its extensive data gathering, sharing, discussing, and processing. Ed's time included the quantitative count of hours at work and elsewhere, and the qualitative fact that he was always on call—working while not necessarily being at work. Could Ed maintain this pace? Would there be a cost? So far, he had managed fine, so why were his colleagues concerned?

Summary: This Was Just Normal Leadership

Consider the totality of Ed's leadership process. Ed trusted others, trusted that they could contribute, and trusted their contributions. This view was reciprocated; the years he had spent in the district had made others trust him. Together, they focused their efforts on behalf of students. Ed had the team he wanted and needed to lead the district. His leadership process was intense. Only after collecting and sharing all the knowledge out there—only after modelling the issues through their numerous versions and incarnations, and only after a debate involving as many contributors as possible—only then was Ed satisfied that they had the best possible solution. With a workable solution on hand, and with agreement that it was the correct plan, only then would Ed act. He wrote the important memo. He finalized policy recommendations. He hired and fired staff. The total energy of the team had been utilized, and all were engaged. They were as one, and their plans were implemented, mostly to strong success.

Ed's leadership process was almost identical to his personal nature—scanning, learning, picturing, acting. The difference was that Ed's action as an individual was not and could not be what the team did. The team's decisions were not Ed's. Acting as an individual was easier than coordinating, committing, and acting as a team. Ed listened to others, modified his own views to fit what his team could tackle. Their path was not necessarily his path. The two had similar roots, but with different players, everything changed.

In summary, Ed used six leadership processes—building trust, focusing on students, scanning the environmental, coordinating their vision, building a consensus cooperatively, and taking all the time needed to do it right. These six made up normal leadership. Follow along as Ed's leadership wanders through a continuous, holistic series of events. What follows is a long look at the work of one committee.

Part IV: Normal Leadership

CHAPTER 6

The Student Accommodation Committee

In the deconstruction process used to enumerate Ed's leadership processes, the flow of interactions was lost. Here, in following all of the observed meetings of one committee, context is more likely to be preserved. It is as close to being there as my field notes and my words allow. This is reconstruction, and its goal is to put the reader in the meeting. Different narrative approaches will be used—to look at the data from slightly differently angles and to add variety. Different and additional details are provided in appendices.

The district's Student Accommodation Committee held five meetings, and a sixth meeting had been scheduled for after my period of observation. The committee's first meeting took place before observations began. There were other meetings missed. To summarize, I observed three meetings, missed two, and knew that one more had been scheduled. The three meetings observed provide a good slice of Ed's leadership. It will be analyzed through the lens of the six leadership processes.

Before examining the committee's work, consider their mandate and membership. As the committee did their work, Ed compiled and refined their report. He formally stated their mandate and started the report:

> "The Student Accommodation Committee was established by the Board of Trustees as a planning committee to review the student attendance areas for each school and to make recommendations regarding these attendance areas to the board.
>
> "The Committee has examined the student accommodation realities and needs of the district and has prepared a number of recommendations and considerations for the board...."

Committee membership consisted of seven individuals: three parents, two trustees, a community representative, and the superintendent of schools—Ed Noyce. The parents were strictly volunteers. The trustees were a bit different. On election, trustees form a board of education serving a set term—back then it was three years—and received a per diem financial allowance. Trustees are therefore not quite volunteers. Like staff, they are paid, but per diems are not quite a salary. Trustees represent their communities, so that makes them politicians. But for most, they are barely politicians. Ed Noyce was none of these; he was staff and received his normal salary. He was the only salaried member of the committee. In most school committees, staff would not be voting members of a committee. Here, in Wapiti Falls, on this committee, Ed had a vote and exercised it.

The term, "student accommodation" was a local term. The student part was clear. The "accommodation" part may have referred to the building that "accommodated" students aligned with their home's locality—that is, their attendance areas. After the first meeting, I wondered if "student accommodation committee" was a politically correct euphemism for "school closure committee." While the source of the term remained confusing, my focus was soon elsewhere.

Student Accommodation Committee Meeting 2: June 7

The Student Accommodation Committee's second meeting convened at noon on Tuesday, June 7—Ed participated in two meetings that day. He started with the "Senior Admin Retreat," left it to attend this committee's second meeting, and returned to his admin meeting following the conclusion of this committee's meeting.

This first look at context starts small; it is an overview. For a more complete view, see Appendix F: "June 7 – Tabular Account of Student Accommodation Committee Meeting 2."

Everyone was engaged and inquisitive. They were invariably polite, respectful, and courteous, even while disagreeing. Committee members were learning. On finding that there were no bad questions, they gained confidence and asked more questions. Some questioned the approach of an immensely popular government; others supported the government's overall direction while struggling with its challenging fiscal adjustments. Everyone on the committee knew that efficiency and fiscal responsibility would drive their deliberations. There was also general support for the board. Of course, board support would follow naturally, as it was the board that had appointed them. Loyalty mattered.

Members were essentially donating their time, and near the end of scheduled meeting, there was evidence that they had other places to be—jobs. One member, a trustee, already had her materials closed for ten minutes prior to the meeting's end. Still, she stayed engaged and asked at least one more question. Thankfully for her, and for everyone, the meeting was soon over.

Chair Paddy Nolan, a trustee and a lawyer, started the meeting by giving directions and proposing that the committee search for guiding principles. Nolan led by guiding and reining in what he viewed as unfocused discussion. At his request, Ed read and explained board policy; this took up a large part of the meeting. Nolan set the pace. The committee's work was demanding. Here, in its second meeting, the committee was still learning about the district and how it worked.

Nolan also answered the single tough question: When he was asked what the board wanted, he replied, the board wanted the committee's best thoughts. He added, "Don't worry about the board." "Don't worry" was an expression of hope, as he did not know what the board ultimately wanted. Neither did the board, as they were open to persuasion. The work of this committee work was exploratory, open to different ideas. Nolan suggested that Ed would do further research over the summer. He was correct there. Nolan was used to being in control.

Agnes Cameron was a committee star. She was the community representative, had formerly been on the board, and was its chair when Ed was hired as a principal some eighteen years earlier. Her smarts and experience showed. Agnes and Ed knew each other, trusted each other, and worked well together. Beyond being helpful and supportive of everyone, Agnes asked the obvious questions and reached the obvious conclusions. She was an informal leader. She also had a stake in the game; the committee would eventually review a contested policy from her past.

Ed was the committee's expert, a resource who could explain policy, share history, and introduce further discussion topics, all while taking detailed notes in his role as the committee secretary. The new and descriptive terminology he used—slippage, crossovers, hot spots—were soon adopted by others. (See Appendix C: "A District Lexicon" for terms Ed used.) He was invariably polite, never interrupted, never contradicted. He answered their questions and supplied the facts when so requested. It might seem that Ed led the members, had them discuss what he thought they should discuss. I saw it differently. He recorded the committee's discussion from their previous meeting, and he presented related factual materials. He kept the committee on track by giving them ideas, and then he sat back and let the committee discuss whatever—until they asked for help or stumbled.

Committee members were involved. Discussion was largely unattributed because of the pace, because of my singular focus on Ed, and because I lacked familiarity with the people and issues. Committee members would become more focused as they learned, and my focus expanded as I learned about them.

The meeting ended after eighty-five minutes, but Ed's pace did not slow. After the meeting, Ed went directly to his office. Bill Bersche, assistant superintendent of business services, was soon there. He dropped by to advise Ed that a provincial fact-gathering meeting was being hosted in their board offices. Bill was going to drop in on them before he returned to the "Senior Admin Retreat." Like Ed, Bill had been working over lunch. Ed acknowledged Bill's comment, continued his work briefly, and was about to leave when another guest dropped by. It was brief, only a greeting. Ed needed to be back at the "Admin Retreat" at Ormand Mitchell High School, but before leaving, he also took the time to pop into the meeting that Bill had mentioned. The drop-in visitors and "putting in an appearance" were typical ceremonial parts of Ed's job. This day, and many others, consisted of meeting after meeting.

In his vehicle, Ed discovered that he was not done with the board committee meeting as I had questions, follow-up questions. Was the committee feeling their way, learning about their task? Ed thought so, at least partially. He believed that a consensus was starting to develop. He believed that the old principles were still workable. Plus, he thought that the committee was realizing how complicated their task was.

I missed the third meeting of this committee but made it to the fourth meeting.

Student Accommodation Committee Meeting 4: September 12

It was late afternoon, Monday, September 12, and the Student Accommodation Committee meeting was about to start. Earlier, while I was interviewing staff, Ed was working on his report, finalizing it. On my return, I found him making copies for the committee and for me.

His report was labelled "Draft." At seventeen pages it was already lengthy, and it would no doubt grow today. Some old content was also revised. It was entitled "Report and Recommendations," and as previously shared, it began by listing committee members and the mandate. This was followed by six pages of charts on student enrollment numbers aligned next to building capacity. The enrollment data was actual enrollment versus departmental standards. Provincially, the department thought the district had over-built, but over the years, the district grew, and more students gradually occupied the overbuilt space. Consequently, while capacity rates had improved, the buildings were still under-utilized according to provincial expectations. Since under-utilization affected provincial capital grants—building grants—the charts provided important information. Next, the report stated the principles behind student attendance areas. The draft report ended with a list of the committee's proposed revisions and recommendations.

Where the excerpt above from committee meeting 2 focused on the actors and issues, the record of committee meeting 4 is a mix of reporting styles. It begins with a summary of dialogue, and then switches to the condensed account of Table 1. This table lists the speakers, provides a brief record of the topic each raised, and gives Ed's reply, if he offered one. The committee had had a third meeting that I missed. With another meeting behind them, I found that the actors had figured out what they valued and had become more adept at stating their significant issues. They had thought more about these matters and their values were cleaner and more concise. Sides took shape, and committee decisions were foreshadowed.

At 16:05 hours, chair Paddy Nolan began by setting a meeting deadline, 18:00 hours. He flipped through the meeting package and then called for specific agenda items. Members contributed their thoughts. He listened and as he did so, he forewarned them, do not expect agreement on everything.

Nolan had issued a challenge, and parent John Cashel accepted it; he spoke up in agreement—there would be no unanimity.

Additional agenda items were identified.

Chair Nolan added one more item, excess student space. As the list of discussion topics grew, Nolan commented, all of them needed to be dealt with. He turned to Rex Lynch and said, "I know that you won't agree."

Rex Lynch responded, "I am not sure about that." Nolan and Lynch were talking about "excess" student capacity. Both knew that the board's solution, applied just that spring, to excess student space was wiping a school off the books—closing it.

On this occasion, Paddy Nolan was determined and abrupt. He alternated between encouragement—"Good work, team," and "Great work done there, Ed"—and admonishment—"don't just 'rubber stamp' Ed's report."

More discussion topics were added: Viewfield School enrollment, French immersion, Windfall School.

After spending some time identifying topics, the committee was ready to tackle the issues in detail. Agnes Cameron began by asking to look at Principle C., the process followed when students moved between schools.

Ed started this discussion, briefly explaining it, applying it, justifying it. He continued until nods said they understood—for now. Further questions would come when the policy was applied.

Still, a few more discussion items were added to their list. To get to this point, the committee had taken approximately one-half of the two hours allotted for their meeting. Finally, they were ready to start serious discussion of each item. Discussion returned to Principle C.

So far, the committee had simply built their agenda. It looked like Ed's senior admin meeting, but slower, understandable as its players, for the most part, lacked educational expertise and experience.

"Principle C: Students living in close proximity to a school should be permitted to attend that school." The chair led the restart of this discussion; Nolan asked, "What does 'close proximity' mean? When did exclusion take effect?" Exclusion was not mentioned in the policy; it was simply the negative of "should be permitted." Chair Nolan was, after all, a lawyer.

Ed replied, adding still more detail.

Members were involved; Gwen Ramots, Paddy Nolan, Agnes Cameron, Karen Oliver, and John Cashel all spoke.

The chair said that he was hearing agreement on some changes.

Ed could hear agreement and could see it from member reactions, and so he spoke up; he would rewrite the principles considering the discussion. The chair agreed, "Okay, we will see it next round."

There were many points made. Many positions were taken. But discussion rambled. I looked for another way to present data and created a table. As discussed, Table 1 condenses the subsequent discussion issues but does not preserve the order of discussion. It lists the speaker, states his or her issues, and is followed Ed's reaction.

Table 1: September 12 – Issues Discussed in Student Accommodation Committee Meeting 4

Initiated discussion:	Issue:	Ed's response, if any:
Ed	School enrollment figures versus official school capacity.	
	Average class size should be equitable within the district's divisions: elementary, middle, and high school.	
	The report's "alternative 3" had errors in the numbers. Ed apologized; he had not double checked the numbers before presenting them.	
Paddy	Promoted single-track for French immersion school (six references).	Single enrollment track would lead to student loss as parents would pull their kids out.
	Abandoned a vote, explained it colourfully—the committee had "gassed that move." Generally, Paddy played along with group and accepted Ed's gentle teasing. (Playful was the opposite of his earlier aggressive stance. Had he seen that his aggression was counter-productive?)	Humorously repeated chair's term, "gassed."
	Wanted to vote on school closure but saw that the committee was not ready and did not pursue it.	
	Acknowledged, if more provincial funds were coming, then preserving the status quo was okay.	
	Sought ideas for other efficiencies (cuts).	Fiscal efficiency could be increased by cutting staff—not that he would recommend it. This idea was left with members to discuss; they did not.
	He also complimented everyone, "Great progress" (to committee). He specifically thanked Ed.	

Agnes	Two issues were paramount: Do they recommend closing Windfall School? Do they move French immersion?	
	Why cut staff?	Hoped it would be unnecessary, that provincial equity enhancements would come through.
	Just close Windfall School and be done with it.	
	Busing was efficient.	
	Average class sizes should be equitable. (She agreed with the earlier statements made by Ed.)	
	To Paddy, I am not "Mrs. Cameron." "Call me Agnes." (Humour perhaps, but I wondered if terms "Mrs." and similar honorifics that were once respectful were now thought to be ageist. Did Agnes feel that? It also seemed that she wanted to put the "uppity" Nolan in his place.	
	Eliminate Alternative 4 (so named in Ed's package) because increasing Windfall attendance area would ultimately be inefficient. (Their search was for efficiencies.)	
Rex	What, close one school to build another?	
	Where did funding for school construction come from, and how much?	From the province, 100%. (That statement was at odds with my knowledge.)
	What is the history of school closures?	
	Suggested an Alternative 4: Solve Windfall problem by adding to attendance area.	
	Increase efficiency elsewhere.	
	French is elitist.	
	Promote small schools as a popular alternative.	
	Doubted veracity of saving estimates.	Explained cost-saving estimates by doing one estimate.
	Inquired about pupil–teacher ratios.	
	What about Dusk, another small school?	

	Was there still a north–south split?	
	How about creating charter schools to reopen closed schools? (Educational reformer Dr. Weinard had proposed the creation of what was essentially a charter school.)	While Dr. Weinard wanted an existing, operating new school, that would cut nothing and therefore save nothing.
	Why would the costs of charter schools be exorbitant?	Charter school would draw students from an existing school, lowering school and district efficiencies. Costs would be exorbitant, and therefore not a solution.
	Edmonton looked at school closure at less than fifteen pupils per classroom.	
John	Would school closure solve their space and funding issues?	
	How would consolidating programs help students?	
	A consensus was thought to be developing. (For me, that seemed to be more hope than reality.)	
	What about a survey?	Survey? Was there one?
	If staff were cut, how did that affect the individual who was cut?	Make cuts, not by cutting jobs, but by not replacing staff who resigned or were fired. Administration needed flexibility.
	North–south "split" was less now than in past?	Ed said nothing. Enrollment in his report showed excess capacity north of the river.
Karen	Why do we need more provincial money?	District's potential income was lower than other districts. In effect, Wapiti Falls was a financially poor educational district. (Some on the committee seemed not to know that they were poorer than their neighbours.)
	Deal with problem of French immersion.	
	Is closing a school fair?	

Gwen (a trustee)	Capacity? But we built a new school, and it did not affect equity or provincial funding.	
	Averages not always fair. People distrust averages.	Yes, mid-year adjustments to attain "averages" could well create "gales of laughter."
	What is the "glue," or the appeal of French immersion?	
Dale	My district, Beaver Landing, currently had classes of less than fifteen students and schools of less than twenty-three students. (Discussion with Rex after meeting just finished.)	

At 18:02 hours, there was general agreement that they would need another meeting. Dates were explored, and a meeting was set for noon, September 22. Ed stated that, as the work was of high priority, he would work on it over the weekend. The day ended with committee members trading chit-chat. Later, when we were alone, Ed and I exchanged similar sentiments; it had been a good meeting. Ed left for home at approximately 18:30 hours.

Analysis: Student Accommodation Committee Meeting 4: September 12

Table 1 provided space for Ed's reply to every issue raised, but Ed did not respond to every item brought up. The committee was not his. He understood that his role was to help, not lead. This chart made no attempt to keep up with the voluminous discussion between volunteer committee members. Extensive topics are depicted, but the chart did not come close to capturing the wealth of detail provided. I truncated it, and yet it is still long. Typically, conversations meander and discussions are unfocused, more so perhaps when topics are complicated and dense. I understood that to keep up every participant had to pay attention. Each did that; this group was seriously attentive..

Overall, discussion was lively and cordial with members interrupting, laughing, and teasing. They were comfortable offering their comments, even in disagreement. Questions raised by the group were dealt with in group discussion. In response to one query, responses were forthcoming from five of six committee members. As an overview, I found that this table of "who said what" was informative.

Ed initiated two discussion items, offered one apology, and answered ten questions. He also teased the chair at least once. (Previously—in his extensive discussion of Principle C and before the table was started—he also made one additional statement in support of equity within similar grade-level divisions.) In general, Ed was not involved unless he felt that the committee needed explanation, or to advise that he would research something for their next meeting.

As chair, Paddy Nolan was in position to make numerous contributions; he made seven. He said more on the topic of saving money, primarily through his preferred strategy of consolidation—that is, making one school a "single-track" French immersion school rather than keeping the existing two dual-track schools—French and English. This was an important issue, and Ed's three-part reply reflected its importance. He said that parents and students would disagree with that consolidation, that they would find it inconvenient, and that students would leave the program. Altogether, the net effect of a single "single-track" French immersion school would be lower enrollments. Nolan mentioned consolidation of French immersion six times. As chair, he decided when the committee was ready to move on. Interesting, too, that he started the meeting by challenging small school supporters and then backed off, letting Ed tease him and even laughing at himself.

Agnes Cameron made seven contributions; one question drew Ed's reply. She responded to committee members easily, agreeing with them or offering polite but firm challenges to their positions. Her views were clear and insightful. She kept her mood and tone light. She also declared that she was their equal, and not the "senior" member.

Rex Lynch did not speak to heavily discussed Principle C. Perhaps he was saving himself for later challenges. Perhaps he smarted from the chairmen's early call out on his views—"I know you won't agree." While wanting to avoid a confrontation, Rex Lynch was a small school supporter; that is, he wanted to keep the small enrollment schools open, if at all possible. In my experience, many small school supporters were also fiscally conservative; they sought cuts anywhere but in their school. These folks wanted it both ways and were often challenging. Rex fit that mold.

John Cashel made six contributions; his concerns were about schools, students, and staff. He wanted, basically, to preserve things the way they were. Ed spoke on two of John's comments and seemed surprised when John talked about a survey.

Karen made three contributions; Ed replied to one.

Gwen, the trustee, had only three insertions; she looked for fairness and sought to understand funding. She seemed not to understand the math supporting school construction. Ed left it at that. He worked with her on the board and knew that her strengths and interests were elsewhere.

I found the agenda building process long and convoluted. To make use of my time, I constructed the chart seen in Appendix G: "September 12 – Notes on Seating Plans Relative to Accommodation Committee Meeting 4." In other life experiences, I found that where people sat—their proximity to each other, the empty space in the room, the person they sat next to or faced—affected interactions. Further comments are shared in the above-named appendix.

Student Accommodation Committee Meeting 5: September 22nd

The Student Accommodation Committee meeting 5, planned for September 22, was changed to Monday, September 26. Neither day suited my own work schedule, and as a result, I missed this meeting. The minutes showed considerable action: adding a recommendation, approving five others, and referring three recommendations for further study. They agreed to a luncheon meeting on October 5. That one I could and did attend. It would be my last full day in the district.

Student Accommodation Committee Meeting 6: October 5

A critical part to this event happened before the meeting when Ed and a fellow committee member shared their concerns about the committee's current direction. As well, I had also been away for a few days, and Ed gave me an update. I start there.

On my arrival at shortly after 07:45 hours, October 5, Ed was finalizing his report. I had been absent for three workdays, so Ed brought me up to date on the work of the committee. "Brother Nolan," he said, had introduced another new direction. As a result, Ed had done more research and more analysis. Although this new report was "pretty tidy," he was thinking about adding another column. As was his practice, his covering memo laid out a primary concern, namely "the number of disruptions to schools…mass movement of students for the second consecutive year…." He asked me to guess the number of students moving to new schools this fall. After stalling and then guessing badly, he told me it was nearly one thousand (or nearly 13 percent of the total enrollment versus the prorated normal 9 percent). His report had not stated this number, but he had it if asked. The memo also stated that he would be "comfortable" forwarding "those recommendations which [sic] receive the endorsement of the Committee" to the full board.

After the weekly senior administrator meeting and mid-morning coffee, and after sundry other discussions, Ed returned a call to John Cashel, a parent on the committee. It was nearly 11:00 hours. Ed's initial comments revealed the gist of what would become a long discussion—mutual concerns. John was concerned that Paddy Nolan—the committee chair—had taken a new turn. Among other things, Paddy wanted special education students moved from Kananaskis Elementary. Ed agreed with John that "yanking" them out of Kananaskis would be disruptive. Asked about moving costs, Ed offered his estimates. He suggested that John "advance that" in the meeting. Then, more listening and more topics: efficiency, Ed's own "tight rope," along with his candid suggestion that he might need to "drag his heels." The discussion returned to special education matters, and Ed restated his concerns ever more dramatically, namely that moving it out of Kananaskis Elementary would "bring the wrath of God upon us from a number of directions." This back and forth continued as ever more topics were repeated and new ones popped up: the anticipation of new money from the province, French immersion, expected votes on school closure. The conversation seemed endless, and Ed began re-examining his committee tables. Finally, the conversation was over; Ed ended it with "Good stuff!" It had been a long call, well over eighteen minutes. He returned to his regular work.

By 11:50 hours Ed was in the committee room. Members already there were chatting. Paddy Nolan arrived, looked for the numbers Ed was to have had on hand, and apologized for being late. Agnes teased him. Ed left and returned with the information chair Nolan had previously looked for.

Was Ed's mind still on the matters he and John had talked about? Was that why he forgot materials he had specifically prepared for the chair?

This sixth meeting of the Student Accommodation Committee followed the patterns established in previous meetings. Instead of going directly to a summary account of conversations, I start with analysis.

Analysis: Student Accommodation Committee Meeting 6: October 5

My focus on this day's Student Accommodation Committee meeting was Ed's leadership in context. I start by considering member participation. To accomplish that, I compiled the number of times each committee member spoke. The "Find" feature of the word processor enabled me to count the entries of each participant in my field notes.

Table 2: Committee Member "Finds" in the Field Notes of Meeting 6

Paddy	John	Agnes	Rex	Karen	Gwen	Ed	Totals
48	35	29	16	12	10	42	192
25.0%	18.2%	15.1%	8.3%	6.3%	5.2%	21.9%	

While these counts did not measure the amount or the quality of discussion, it did show that everyone contributed. The chair started and carried most of the discussion. The committee's minute keeper and resource person—Ed—was the second-highest responder. The six volunteer committee members contributed 78 percent of the responses. This meant that Ed spoke on 22 percent of the discussion topics. While committee members batted ideas around and reached conclusions, Ed mostly provided technical information and direction. Overall, discussion was reasonably well balanced.

Consider now, the quality of the discussion: Members were better informed. Each had the knowledge needed to discuss and defend their positions. Rex, who had once challenged projected cost savings, now quickly made them on the go. Every member wanted to contribute and did. Together, they were prepared to make their recommendations. Ed had already endorsed their findings, stating in his working report that he was confident in the committee's work. While he was confident that their process was entirely reasonable, thorough, and fair, he disagreed with some recommendations. He and John, and occasionally Rex, voted against the majority, but that was acceptable, laudable even. Appreciating their internal differences, the committee also discussed submitting a minority report. The two dissenting parents considered it but decided not to. So did Ed, saying with some humour, "I'll get another kick at that cat" later, with the board. (See Appendix H: "October 5 – Sample Discussion from Student Accommodation Committee Meeting 6." for further detail.)

Application of Ed's Leadership Processes to the Work of the Student Accommodation Committee

The Student Accommodation Committee's work gave good insight into how the committee worked and how Ed led. Table 3 examines the six leadership processes observed.

Table 3: Ed's Leadership Processes as Observed in Student Accommodation Committee Meetings

Leadership process	Processes confirmed in Student Accommodation Committee meetings
Trust and respect	• Meetings were predictable, structured, and business-like. • Ed was consistent, respectful, and genuine. • Members were similarly polite, considerate, and respectful. • Discussion was robust, and disparate views were expressed and respected. • The chair pushed, poked, and prodded. With experience, he showed greater respect. • Committee members chatted, laughed, and congratulated each other for their work, for their accomplishments. The chair laughed at himself and allowed Ed to tease him. • Committee members recognized Ed as working hard to help them. They appreciated and trusted him.
Focus on students	• Ostensibly the committee's work was in service of students, but as students were absent, Ed reminded them to think about students. So did John. Both viewed moving students hither and thither as disruptive.
Scanning the environment	• The committee, mimicking the province's singular focus, searched for increased operational efficiencies—cost savings. This challenged the status quo. Would the existing student programming continue, or would affordability win out? • The committee, under the leadership of the chair, investigated multiple directions and weighed the benefits and costs of each. Consolidating programs and closing schools seemed best suited to meeting their perceived goal—saving money. • Simply adding in Dr. Weinard's proposed new school would take funds and resources away from existing schools. • Committee members came to understand the educational environment better because Ed shared his technical expertise and knowledge. • Ed kept the committee aware of emerging issues. For example, the district's "once in; always in" procedural rule might soon be challenged, and he outlined why.
Getting to a consensus	• Rich discussion in focused arguments. • The committee made and voted on recommendations. Their votes showed that they were split; there was no consensus. • Ed supported the committee's decisions, whatever his personal reservations. • Privately, Ed thought the committee missed the mark. I interpreted this to mean that to support political action, the board would need consensus. Trustee re-election required it. (As Ed had anticipated, the committee's plan failed in the subsequent round of board deliberation. This rejection occurred after I completed the formal process of data gathering.) • Some thought and said that Ed manipulated the topics and discussion to support his plan. This committee work showed otherwise; he was repeatedly voted down.

Slow, patient teaching	As a cooperative teacher, Ed: • Helped committee members explore a variety of issues so they could discover their best approach, their best solution. • Ensured that the issues were thoroughly discussed. To help, he listed the hot spots. • Answered questions using appropriate language, probed to see that members understood, and redirected questions back to the questioner. When asked to explain more than once, he gladly did so. Ed liked questions. • Served as their resource person, not their general. He did so by sticking to factual contributions, anticipating future questions, and sharing additional details if requested. • Shared concerns. For issues that he deemed critical, but which were not pursued, he restated his point. Then he waited patiently. Sometimes the wait and reminder worked. • Was flexible but did not waiver on his belief in fair treatment—equity—among students by grade level division. As a rational leader and strategic teacher, I thought that Ed: • Accepted that reaching a consensus was slow and inefficient, but he knew too that whatever survived, a consensus, would be the most effective approach to reach long term goals. While he did not agree with the committee's goal of saving money, he did not and would not circumvent his leadership process by being directive. • Paid a personal price. Patience did not come easily. (Hints of Ed's stress are described directly below under time utilization.) • Saw that there was no consensus on the committee and understood that the broader community would have the same concerns—a lack of consensus. In Ed's leadership model, action required consensus.
Time on task	• The three committee meetings observed took over four hours and forty-eight minutes. Extrapolated to all six committee meetings held and planned, the total committee work would involve just less than ten hours total. In the three meetings observed, Ed and his committee colleagues were busily on task. • Ed's record of the committee's work grew to reach twenty-five detailed pages—numbers, charts, and competing scenarios—and the work was not yet complete. For Ed, this was interesting, challenging work, plus there were several time-consuming extras. • As the sole researcher, Ed investigated each new direction, thought about its impact, anticipated related questions, and considered details that the committee might discover. It had him working on the project during the week and the weekends. It caused stress: he had to apologize for not checking his handout before circulating it. He forgot to present prepared materials. Privately, along with John, he was critical of the committee's directions. • Ed was preoccupied, almost undisciplined. He teased a trustee. Was it because he was comfortable or undisciplined? (I can not decide. Whatever, it was unusual.) • Asked to do more, Ed did more.

Table 3 shows that Ed's six leadership processes held; their key elements were all present. In addition to confirming the validity of the leadership processes as listed, we learned more about the nature of Ed's leadership.

While the Ed's leadership processes reflected his nature, his nature and his leadership were not always aligned. Leadership demanded Ed's patience, but being patient was personally difficult. As the committee waded through interminable discussion, seemingly going nowhere, he kept mum. He did not interfere. It was hard, but he worked at it. None of that is new.

What was new here was that we saw that his leadership processes could also conflict with his humanity. Despite his personal reservations, he left the committee alone so that they could set their own directions and reach their own conclusions. That left some on the committee, John in particular, increasingly alone, on the outside. Rex felt it too and was initially belligerent; he did not trust Ed's numbers, and he smarted when the chair declared that Rex would not agree with a specific claim. Perhaps the committee wore him down for he stopped being so vocal, but on some issues, he still voted against the majority. But not John; he kept at it. What should Ed do? He had seen this before, and I had watched it before. Ed had taken a similar approach with Jake; he left Jake alone to work out his issues. Ed could wait with Jake because there was time. Not interfering was harder with John. The committee's work was nearly done; John and Ed's time together was drawing to a close. Further, Ed agreed with John. He said that John was speaking up for the right reasons. Ed's humanity had him returning John's call before the meeting to plot. And there in his introductory notes, Ed had been there with John. During the meeting, he publicly declared that he was with John, but seeing that neither men's comments were furthering the cause, Ed stopped adding his contrarian views. His only remaining option was to vote against the majority, and he did that. But he was not done; he phoned John after the meeting and gave further support. He helped to assuage John's wounds. (To the skeptic, maybe Ed was trying to develop a relationship with a potential future trustee.)

As noted, Ed would always take in whatever personal observations were available and would process them for possible future reference. In our private, post-meeting debriefing, and in response to my questions, he spoke about two of the committee members:

Paddy Nolan, he said, was "smooth," but anticipated that Paddy would not face another trustee election. His elected official career would soon end, and his legacy would be the accomplishments of this committee, and that was not working out. I saw that while Paddy chaired the committee, he sometimes seemed unprepared. And he directed more than he guided. He did not seek Ed's thoughts or advice—just his work, which in fairness, he acknowledged. When his term was up, Paddy did not run for re-election.

Ed saw Agnes vote, as she said, "against her heart," opting instead for the calculations in her head. She had said she would, and she did. Ed said that he understood what happened, probably because he and Agnes had a shared history. Years ago, parents had forced the board's hand, had forced them to build Etzikom School. With her vote recommending school closure, that decision had come full circle. After the vote, her subtle smile and words made it clear: "This is what you call 'building in bias.'" She went into the work of this committee biased against Etzikom School. She had been right then and was right now. In her view, that school should never have been built, or that it was still in operation. It was a headache then and it still was. Ed might have agreed, if the school did not already exist, but it did, and it had to be dealt with.

Ed learned by watching, and he learned to stay silent until it mattered.

Summary of Normal Leadership in the Student Accommodation Committee

The Student Accommodation Committee investigated how their district could best accommodate current and future students. As the committee searched for and learned the pertinent facts and perspectives needed to form their recommendations, they came to trust and support each other, to value each other. In their discussions, individuals came at the committee work from different angles. Their diversity was helpful in that different views were shared and valued. They had followed Ed through his leadership process and had a report complete with recommendations and considerations, but they had not reached a consensus. The committee looked ahead and asked what was next. In sports, the appropriate metaphor would be that a new series was about to commence. This series would involve a new set of players. Reverting to real events, absent metaphor, the Wapiti Falls board would play out this new round of assessment and would make their decisions and act. At a predetermined point in time—an election—the voters would ignore or support the board's direction, or they would elect a new slate of decision-makers. Trying to figure out what they and their community supported, that is to weigh and decide on their specific values, was the board's rationale, their reason for being. How then did they act?

The committee's report was sent to the board, who would no doubt thank the committee for their work. What would they do with the report? The challenges to its adoption were steep. Ed said that the administration was already overloaded and to change that would require that the board reset its priorities. I knew that principals would be extremely interested and would worry, personally and professionally. They would not be alone. Teachers and other staff would take a stand. Parents would hear about the proposals and would challenge them. And that was only the administrative side of their recommendations. There were other considerations of other stakeholders. In summary, the committee had not considered all the ramifications. In essence, they had not thought about the political fallout.

Look to the committee's mandate ; it mentioned "attendance areas" not "school closure." School closure was blatantly political, but the committee seemed not to understand that. Ed had warned the committee that all of the suggested moves would be disruptive to schools and students. More politics. Why hadn't this committee, with its former trustee and two current trustees, dealt with the politics? Agnes raised it but backed off when Paddy told the committee what the board wanted—"independent thought"—and he added, "don't worry about the board." No one asked Ed. If asked, he likely would have helped broaden their horizon. So why hadn't he just helped it along? Would minimal help be just the guidance needed, or would a gentle nudge be interfering? Suddenly, everything became clear. "Interference." Ed did not insert himself into political matters. Politics was outside of his role.

Working within his domain, using his expertise, Ed saw the committee had not finished their work. They had come as far as they could, and still, there was no consensus. In Ed's process, action followed consensus. Without consensus, there was no action. His assessment was simple, "I don't think that it can get through the board." He was right. The board did not close schools as the committee had recommended.

Following along with these rather detailed accounts of three meetings exposed an awkward process. It moved from glacial progress to lightning quickness. (Minutes for meeting 5, show five recommendations approved, a sixth added for consideration, and three more were referred for further study.) Feelings emerged—polite, considerate, and even playful comradery—but some feelings were unresolved. It had been fun, even enjoyable work, but some on the committee would no longer involve themselves in this kind of work. They left, frustrated by the unresolved issues. Count John and Paddy in this group.

The level of detailed discussion involved in this series of meetings could not be found in the committee minutes. In minutes, there is no evidence of emotion. Minutes are straightforward and devoid of human interactions. Meetings are full of human interactions and are boring, intolerable to many good people. But meetings are important, and skills are required to make them work. Contrast the work of this committee with that of the senior administrators' meetings. When Ed and his team went about their business, Ed's leadership model was well understood. Senior administrators were confident that their process would work and stuck with the full process until done. With the Student Accommodation Committee, there was no group history, and so Ed had started out fresh. The committee progressed; it modelled Ed's leadership right up to the point where consensus was required. There, out of time, the group would dissolve with their work unfinished.

CHAPTER 7

A Newly Discovered Leadership Process: Respect Role Differentiation

As true for every chief executive officer, Ed's job was the interface between the owners and the service providers, between the bosses and the workers. In Alberta, the owners of this public enterprise, education, were represented by elected representatives called trustees. Ed's service providers were primarily teachers, but there were others, from professionals like speech therapists and psychologists, to non-professionals such as custodians, teachers' aides, and secretaries. For superintendents, the interface between political masters and working personnel was inherently challenging. Some superintendents had the scars to prove it, for they had been passed on to unsuspecting others, turfed, or retired. This set the stage for theoreticians to rush in with their explanations and theories. Consultants followed and suggested better paths for superintendents to take.

Theory and Practice: Superintendent Role Conflict

McLeod (1984: 171-190) was one of the theoreticians. He investigated the problems faced by superintendents and interpreted them in terms of power and control. Possessing a fragile power base, superintendents concentrated on containing and controlling. For many, their focus was on control, for control meant survival, and survival needs superseded those for efficiency, order, and high-quality service. "This extraordinary preoccupation with administrative control" (Ibid: 180) undermined the central purpose of school systems, namely educating students. McLeod identified three concerns: a lack of attractive career alternatives, a need for a support network, and a tendency to mix policy formulation and implementation. McLeod addressed policy and implementation. Policy formation was political and, therefore, a board function, while policy implementation was managerial. He believed that conflict followed when superintendents meddled in politics, and/or when politicians mucked about in management matters.

Consultants Zeigler, Kehoe, and Reisman (1985) had read all about the travails of superintendents in the professional literature, and they understood that superintendents feared that they had been hired to be fired, but they did not believe it. They thought such concerns were seriously exaggerated. Their research question asked just how "beleaguered" (1985: xiii) superintendents were. They looked squarely at educational decision-making and found classical politics; boards and superintendents experiencing goal disagreement. They proposed a simple solution; if superintendents accepted the educational status quo, then most conflicts would disappear. Maintaining the system as it was meant that superintendents would survive in their roles. Of course, conflicts would appear from time to time, but superintendents who relied on persuasion, bargaining, negotiating, compromising, accommodating, and collaborating would be more successful. Heavy-handed superintendents, if they stayed in the position long enough, would eventually fail.

Feilders (1982) completed a field study of Robert Alioto, a superintendent for a large American board of education. Politics was paramount to Feilders' survival. While the superintendent's role was to provide the board with expert advice, there were constraints. He was subordinate to the board because it was the board that determined policy, accepted or rejected superintendent proposals, and controlled his continued employment. Alioto understood this and consequently engaged in a continual political campaign to garner and maintain board support—political support. When his recommendations mirrored board concerns, they passed, and with passage, both his and the board's influence increased. But Alioto did "not just blindly adopt board ideas, especially if they are counter to his own…he often openly disagrees with board members who make requests…usually explicates the flaws and liabilities of a request and offers an alternate course of action, often then accepting amendments to his idea" (Feilders 1982: 71). Alioto's role varied with the setting. In public—board meetings and elsewhere—political disagreements might play out visibly and dramatically. Privately, relationships were largely unaffected. Alioto made minor decisions, participated in the development of short-term strategies, made and received requests, and participated in public ceremonies and school tours. He was instrumental in setting an organizational tone, both as a "figurehead" and as a politician.

Feilders described Alioto's profile when he was at the zenith of his career, but like others, he, too, eventually fell out of favour. In his large district, politics were central and flagrant. Canadians like to feel that we are more polite and less strident in conflict. Was it true?

In 1971, Alberta superintendents stopped being provincial employees and became employees of local boards. In this new environment, superintendents experienced the crisis of unstable employment. They were regularly fired, and that was new. It was also worrisome to government and to the superintendents. What was really happening? The government hired Downey (1976) to take stock. Through questionnaires, interviews, and observations, he found that superintendents were now dealing with role ambiguities and conflicting expectations. The "vagaries of local politics" (Downey 1976: 23) were problematic, "tearing the superintendent apart" (Downey 1976: 27). Downey stated that leaderships skills and problem-solving were critical. He offered important insights and strategies that, while helpful, did not totally solve the problem. Subsequent updates were needed, but gradually, things seemed to work out. Stability re-emerged, but superintendents still needed to take care.

Ed did not need a theoretician to understand political challenges, nor did he need to turn to a consultant for guidance. He had already been there as a deputy superintendent, had figured things out while stuck, as he was, in an ongoing battle between his board's trustees and their superintendent. Superintendent Milt Palmer was Ed's boss back then. Palmer was hired as a change agent, and he was just that. At the time, the Wapiti Falls board wanted change, and Palmer gave it to them. A large powerful man, he led large. Under his leadership the district changed and attained a solid footing. Esteem followed—from their own board, from colleagues on other boards, and from teachers and administrators in Wapiti Falls and beyond. Dynamic, forceful leadership worked…and then it did not. Ed was there from the start and described what he saw at the end:

> "Milt was openly at warfare [sic] with the board and there was no secret about that. And it was a very difficult time, and I was, I guess, confidante and supporter on both sides. I had board and trustees coming to me: how do we do this, or how do we get over this?"

Ed watched Milt Palmer's aggressive actions, his "openly rude" comments, and was "embarrassed by the things said." Ed's affability and respect for both parties allowed him to navigate these rough waters, and he learned. He learned what he did not want to do, and what he would not do.

And suddenly the battle ended. Milt Palmer retired, and Ed became the superintendent. Before taking on the role, Ed made a promise to himself: if he succeeded Palmer, he would do his best to work "with people." His words were:

> "What is important to me is that the administration of the district, not just myself, the administration of the district, offers the board what they need to keep this district moving in the right kind of direction."

Ed also had a second promise; namely that he would avoid politics. That did not seem all that hard, as he had never been political. The difference was that now, the opportunity to be overtly political occurred again and again. Milt Palmer might have started that way too, but over the years, he had become noticeably more forceful, more powerful, and more political, and it had cost him his career. Ed promised himself that he would avoid Milt Palmer's quagmire. But how? Ever the rational analyst, Ed asked himself if role separation would prevent such conflict? And he knew that if it did not prevent possible conflict, it would at least be helpful.

Administrative and Political Leadership

With his professional colleagues, Ed's work was as described—collegial and cooperative. He had the good fortune to work with good people. They kept him informed about what they were up to, and in return, he gave them a relatively free hand. Through their ongoing meetings, he knew when further direction was needed, he knew how to give subtle, almost imperceptible help, and he knew that he could normally wait events out. He could wait for his administrative team to grow. Given time, they would find solutions that would be implemented successfully. Consider Jake Harris, the assistant superintendent that spring. Until there was real damage, Jake would either get better or move to a more suitable job. (Jake was not at his personal best right then, but he had earned Ed and his colleagues' support. See Appendix J: "September 29 – Narrative Discussion on the Paragon Alternative School" for further details.) Jake moved that fall, and Ed was happy to support his replacement, Ab. As Ed found out, Ab wanted to do better. For Ab and Ed, better meant that the dodgy intern contract was gone, and regular contracts were back. Guiding, suggesting, and waiting left Ed able to expend his energy on more pressing concerns.

Ed had a successful strategy to interact with staff, but trustees were different. They were his bosses. He worked for them, and therefore he would do as they asked. He helped turn their broad goals into specific actions. The bonus was that by helping trustees—helping them meet their goals—staff and trustees could unite into a cohesive unit. We saw how he educated his Student Accommodation Committee members. Compare their early exchanges with those in the October 5 meeting. He waited for trustees to grow or depart the role. But crossing the political line between himself and trustees—going against their wishes or tinkering about in their business—that was a different matter. He had seen how it had worked out for Milt Palmer and had seen the damage that had done to the district and its people. Ed and his staff would be managerial, and his bosses would be political; that was their job. The separation served a rational purpose, and superintendent Ed Noyce would honour it. This strategy added one more arrow to Ed's quiver of leadership tactics, and that leadership process is "respect role differentiation."

Part V: Leadership in a Crisis

CHAPTER 8

Paragon Alternative School: Normal Leadership

In March 1994, Dr. Phil Weinard met with the Wapiti Falls Public District Board of Education and proposed that the district create what he called the Paragon Alternative School. The board did as asked, formally admitting this "paragon" school or this promised "model of excellence" (Merriam-Webster) but did so cautiously, approving it only "in principle." Deciding to start a new and "revolutionary" school initiated a process that required even more of Ed's leadership talents. It would be a challenge, but Ed had successfully piloted hard projects through difficult waters before. Why had the board sanctioned something so nonconforming in such a traditional province? Alberta's new status as a "have-not" province helped. Suddenly poor, all government decisions were focused on saving money.

The Premise: Alberta Desperately Needed Change

While the economy had prospered with oil, everything was suddenly topsy-turvy. Demand and prices were down, and as employment and royalties plunged, government debt increased. Some independents thought they had tax room to solve the deficit problem, but the government disagreed. Instead, they loudly declared that it was a spending problem, and, despite having the nation's lowest taxes, it was not then and never would be a tax problem. There would be only one road to prosperity and that was through balanced budgets. They cut expenses everywhere, and soon learned how well scapegoats worked. By attacking their own employees and institutions, they increased their political support. Declarations that schools were underperforming and staffed by overpaid, unionized teachers produced better than expected public support—not for schools, but for the government. So they continued shaking schools up, changing the rules as they went. New solutions were invited—informally. Even better if the new ideas came from outside their system. What was in practice now was evidently not working, so why not try something totally new? The public latched on to the concepts of charter and experimental schools. Promises to return to traditional teaching, especially as they trashed public schools, appealed to a large, vocal, conservative population. For the government, Dr. Phil Weinard's proposed "Paragon Alternative School" was perfect, as a diversion and perhaps as a possible solution.

Dr. Weinard laid out his plan in a second paper, "Proposal for a Paragon Alternative School: A Summary for Wapiti Falls Parents." It included catchy phrases like "The Cascading Educational Tiles that Count" and "Correlates of Effective Schools." His school would be staffed by teachers who agreed with "traditional" teaching methods. An independent board would be in charge, not some servile arm of a regular board of education, and there would be no union. He promised taxpayers improved results at lower costs. Plus, with his national profile, he expected private sponsors to open their wallets. Part of Weinard's appeal was his attack on the vested interests of school boards, school administrations, and schoolteachers.

> "Our local zoned public schools are in trouble…teachers are demoralized, many parents are interested in alternatives, and students increasingly fear for their safety…Educators themselves disagree on teaching methods, academic expectations, and assessment policies."

There would be no need for a central office. His crusade was well-received by the media and by folks disenchanted with most things public.

Phil Weinard needed to show the district what could be done, but perhaps more importantly, he needed a building to house his school. He wanted it in his home city of Wapiti Falls. Previously a public-school supporter, Wapiti Falls Public gave him what he was looking for.

Professional educators in the district took exception to some of what Dr. Weinard proposed, but not all of it. They had also studied the research, but they had reconciled the confusing and often contradictory findings to create a solid coherent plan. Wapiti Falls Public Schools had improved, but Dr. Weinard had not noticed. Despite their efforts, Dr. Weinard never stopped attacking them. It became personal. Some teachers were angry and spoke out, but their denunciations mostly stayed amongst themselves. Of course, there were also teachers—often struggling teachers or the tired, worn-out, desperate teachers—who were drawn to the promised return to tradition with its emphasis on phonics and discipline. And a few aspiring or overlooked principals were possible converts. These potential adherents stayed deep in the background. The teachers' union, cut out of the proposal, was no fan, but in Wapiti Falls, their involvement was minimal. They sat quietly and stayed in the backseat.

District trustees felt the general discontent, and some were invigorated by the prospect of being at the forefront of a new and promising concept. The Paragon Alternative School was approved "in principle" but with caveats—ten issues and understandings. The board's chief considerations were assurances that the project would not cost them, and that the school's parent body supported this approach. "Yes" to sponsorship; "No" to bearing any of the additional costs of operating an alternative-based, research-inspired, experimental school. This school would be semi-private.

Weinard, with approval in hand, was eager to get underway, but seemed at a loss as to how to start. He had made noise about introducing a fantastic new model of education, but in practical terms, he rested in the glow of national awards and supportive journalism. He waited and did nothing.

Now what? Ed and the board wondered why they had not heard from Dr. Weinard? Some questioned his competence.

Dr. Weinard was unconcerned. His great new school should be in Wapiti Falls, his hometown, but if not there, he was sure others would pick it up.

These winds of change involved Wapiti Falls more than other windy places. The population was traditional and conservative and disliked unions. The agent of reform lived and worked in Wapiti Falls. The government needed school reform and thought that Wapiti Falls was the perfect location. This was serious. Ed and his immediate staff understood, as did the principals, teachers, and staff in the existing schools. Dr. Weinard, though, was comfortably blasé and stayed that way until late in September, when events found him unprepared, and reaching for a lifeline.

May 26 to June 10: Paragon Alternative School

In my first four observational days, two important concerns about the "alternative" school were raised—money and communications. These are recorded in the table below:

Table 4: May 26 to June 10: Paragon Alternative School Events Summary

Date	Summary Discussion
May 26	An Alberta Education official initiated a telephone discussion on the Weinard proposal with superintendent Noyce. Dr. Weinard's plans and progress were reviewed. While he had approval, the board made it clear that they would not provide any additional funds that might be required. Dr. Weinard was okay with that; he was confident that he could attract investors. Ed still had concerns; he thought that investors were wary, and hence the Dr. Weinard commitment was "fragile at this point." Asked to keep in touch with Dr. Weinard, Ed said that he would try again. He added, Dr. Weinard did not communicate well. Ed thought Weinard was realizing "the enormity of the task" ahead.
May 27	Nothing discussed about Weinard or the Paragon Alternative School.
June 7	Nothing discussed about Weinard or the Paragon Alternative School.
June 8	During the day, nothing was discussed about Weinard or the Paragon Alternative School.
	The agenda for the regular board meeting materials included "Item 5. Paragon Alternative School:"
	An update and a two-part recommendation were included with the agenda: namely, delay staff and parent meetings to the fall, with the superintendent reporting back at the next meeting.
	That evening, the meeting was held. Trustees chatted. There were two positions—for and against the school. No one was neutral. Everyone sought greater clarity. Lacking other ideas, they adopted Ed's recommendation to delay meetings, and have Ed investigate further.
June 10	Dr. Weinard was hard to reach by phone, Ed worked on a letter to him.
	As he did so, he shared some private thoughts: Weinard lacked people skills, and his ethics were suspect. Ed's reasoning was only revealed later.

Two critical concerns were raised in these first four days of observation. First, without additional funds, there would be no Paragon Alternative School, and however crucial, Dr. Weinard was silent on funding. Second, communications would challenge Ed and his board throughout this process.

June 22: Dr. Weinard Meets with the Board

The regular board meeting day was June 22, and by morning, the meeting package was available for Ed's review. Agenda "Item 5. Paragon Alternative School" was an exact copy of that used in the meeting on June 8. The package contained two relevant documents: a short memo inviting Dr. Weinard to the meeting and a detailed procedural letter dated March 28. Coffee talk that morning was that Dr. Weinard had not replied to the invitation.

After coffee, at 15:15 hours or so, while Ed and I drove to Ormand Mitchell High School, we chatted, starting with tidbits about family, and then on issues local to my district. Ed then confided that Dr. Weinard is doing all the wrong things now, and he gave an example. In the proposed Paragon Alternative School, students could be expelled without rights to procedural fairness. Ed would not accept such practices—that is, expulsion without recourse or overview—and neither would the provincial education department. To expel a student, a district would have to demonstrate that the student had received fundamental justice—that is, provide evidence that the student had received all their due process rights.

Had Ed spoken again with Dr. Weinard? I was not sure, but clearly, he was well-informed about the school's plans. I suspected that he had read as much as he could about the school. The regular day was soon over, but the day was not done.

The regular board meeting started on time, at 19:00 hours. By 21:10, trustees had worked through much of their agenda—approved minutes from two previous meetings and heard reports from administrators and trustees. They had met with students directly—fitness award winners—and indirectly—by viewing two student projects presented via computers. Next, the board received and reviewed a technology report presented by teachers and rejected a request to abandon a future middle school site. Next up, agenda item 5. Not even half the new business items were done, and it was getting late.

While Dr. Weinard was invited to the meeting, he had not responded, but there he was, on hand and prepared. He addressed the board, cited the "spectacular" success of a private school in Baltimore. He was working with two foundations, plus the Government of Canada, and Syncrude, an oil giant. In addition, a Hamilton [Ontario] school and a school near Vancouver had both expressed interest in his model. The Vancouver-area school had parents lining up to get their kids in. He appreciated that Wapiti Falls had their challenges, but he had had no calls from trustees or subject coordinators. Dr. Weinard said that he found this "illogical." It was hard, he said, to go further without the board's support or the support of the superintendent.

Ed smiled. It seemed to be an acknowledgement to "illogical," but he stayed silent.

Dr. Weinard also admitted that he had not delivered on the promised monetary assurances, but he was confident that he could do so soon. He repeated his theme of strong interest; people would be lining up for admission to the school.

Done with the presentation, he promised to leave his materials. Ed asked for and received copies of his presentation and other materials.

The board had questions: Trustee Paddy Nolan indicated that the onus was on Dr. Weinard; he was to have presented a "real budget," not wishy-washy statements. Funding agents would expect it.

Dr. Weinard admitted his failure, but he could not do it without their support. He had a difficult task ahead.

Trustee Peter Svarich suggested a letter of board support.

Vice-chair Lydia Jacques asked whether Dr. Weinard had made this presentation before.

He said that he had, and he explained that parents could not understand the proposal from newspaper accounts. He continued, saying that getting this alternative school up was hard. It had never been done before, but the future is clear, and the future would be this type of school.

Trustee Svarich restated his suggestion; they should provide Dr. Weinard with a letter of support, confirming board "approval in principle."

Trustees made further comments. Vice-chair Jacques questioned the order of events, a parent meeting first or funding first. She thought that it needed to be funding first.

Trustee Gwen Ramots was opposed to doing anything more. She addressed Dr. Weinard, "Why should we care if you don't, if you can't get it done?"

Dr. Weinard expressed his optimism, "It will be done." Schools like this will become public policy. Surrey [B.C.] was excited about it.

Discussion continued until a consensus was reached. Despite mixed reviews, trustees formally directed Ed to provide Dr. Weinard with another letter, let him preview it, and then send out the approved copy.

Paddy Nolan repeated his concerns, but the matter was done. Ed and trustee Ramots chatted amiably. The board moved on.

They were divided. Part of the board wanted to do everything possible to help Dr. Weinard. The other part was surprised that Dr. Weinard wanted help. He had never asked for support or guidance, but now, he seemed to assume it was his due. Further, Dr. Weinard already had approval for the alternative school, knew he was to solicit funds, but had made insufficient progress to that end. The portion of the board that wanted him to succeed directed Ed to provide further help—a letter. They still had the votes and they used them.

June 23 to September 8: Paragon Alternative School

By the next morning, the normal, everyday pace returned to work. Discussions regarding the Dr. Weinard proposal have been summarized below:

Table 5: June 23 to September 8: Summary of Paragon Alternative School

Date	Summary Discussion

June 23	At discussions over morning coffee:
	     Ed thought that last night, Dr. Weinard had let a bit more humility peek out than had previously been seen.
	     Someone mentioned that Dr. Weinard got nasty in the meeting when referred to as "Phil." Weinard had corrected him; he was "Dr. Phil Weinard." And further, trustee Peter Svarich, considered by most to be a supporter, was heard referring to Weinard as a "pompous ass."
	 Later, in Ed's office, I noted that while Dr. Weinard had complained about Ed, Ed had stayed silent. Ed's private reply was that Dr. Weinard's complaint was factual, as Ed had not helped him. He added that Dr. Weinard was better last night; "before he alienated everyone." And he recalled how James Thorborn's jaw had "quivered" while in a conversation with Dr. Weinard. I formed an image of a barely controlled, terribly upset James Thorborn. Ed said that he had also challenged Dr. Weinard. I had missed that.
	 While Weinard had shared supportive letters from potential investors, Ed wondered if he had read them. They suggested improvements, and that without improvement, it seemed that they were hesitant to invest. Ed also said that contrary to what Dr. Weinard had promised, the writers thought his program would be more expensive.

August 31	The board package contained: meeting agendas regarding the alternative school proposal, September 27 (with teachers) and October 5 (with parent representatives); the board directive regarding a supportive letter for Dr. Weinard; Ed's budget projections for the proposed school; and a statement that Dr. Weinard had "commissioned" [or hired] a research designer. I thought a qualified researcher would be a good hire for Dr. Weinard; he could use professional help if he had the money to do it.

September 8 (morning only)	On returning to observations after the summer recess, Ed updated me: Dr. Weinard had financial support totalling $250,000. Ed's projected operational costs for the alternative school was $200,000 over four years. Renting an alternate facility was out—too expensive. And since the district could not provide or subsidize another building, each needed the other. If parents were excited by the proposal, and agreeable to converting an existing school to an alternative school, the proposal could work. Ed was waiting for a parent to ask what would be different in this alternative school? If asked, he had no satisfactory answer. Parents would see that what Dr. Weinard wanted to add was already there. In short, Ed did not think that the proposed school would garner strong parental support. Weinard planned on using experts to help with his presentations. Since their last encounter, Dr. Weinard had received more letters and shared them with Ed. Some proposed further improvements. Simon Fraser University was supportive, but Ed had not seen anything from Alberta universities. Maybe there were more letters, letters that Ed had not seen. Ed had made several calls to get employer permission for Dr. Weinard's choice of a presenter attendance at the upcoming meetings. While Phil Weinard thought this perspective guest was one of the "lighthouse principal for all of Canada," Ed was hearing otherwise.

September 8 (afternoon) to September 26: Paragon Alternative School

Business continued normally into the afternoon of September 8 and into the next day, as summarized below:

On September 8, at 13:58 hours, Ed met the board chair, Lydia Jacques, and the assistant superintendent of business services, Bill Bersche. Their task was to develop the agenda for the next regular board meeting. Discussed at some length were the two upcoming meetings featuring Dr. Phil Weinard and school staff, and Dr. Weinard and representative parents. Ed advised that Phil would use external presenters—guests—to help. Lydia was surprised and asked, "Why two people?" Their discussion was general, but the consensus was similar; Phil Weinard turned people off, and two guests would be better than one. Further, Dr. Weinard had requested that Ed obtain employer approval for the attendance of the Ontario principal. Ed thought that was "bizarre," but he was cooperative. Lydia asked, "What would people see in the alternative school?" Ed was quick to summarize: "Uniforms." He then asked Lydia to chair both meetings. Bill asked, "What school would they get?" Lydia had a similar question, "How would parents select a specific school?" Ed answered, "There would be individual meetings at the school. The school where a preference for the alternative school were in the majority would initiate a more intensive process." Once into the details, parents, he thought, would become "savvy" about the proposal and would begin to understand what it all means. He ended his thoughts with a dramatic flourish, "It's worth the wear and tear on the chicken." These details satisfied Lydia. Bill, however, sought further administrative details: would there be a place on the agenda for discussion? Ed agreed; teachers will need to respond. Lydia confirmed it; a discussion period would be placed on the agenda. Lydia and Ed were ready to move on to the next item. They attempted to do so, but Bill interjected; Ed's time is being "eaten up" by the alternative school project. "Phil assumes that it will just happen." The three leaders discussed this matter briefly before moving forward.

After school that same afternoon, Ed met with a classroom teacher, and then with another teacher, the teachers' union representative, Mark Cobb. After reviewing all the items on Mark's list, Ed brought up the Weinard Paragon Alternative School. They would need strong teacher representation at the meeting of September 27. Also, in preparation for the October 5 meeting, Ed had sent out invitation letters to parent councils; Mark could expect inquiries. Mark asked whether the district had verified the financial wherewithal of the alternative school sponsors.

Ed answered, "Yes." Dr. Weinard confirmed that he had one-quarter of a million dollars.

Mark questioned if Dr. Weinard had the time needed to be "proactive."

Ed thought that was a question better directed to Dr. Weinard.

It seemed that both had heard the same rumours; namely that some viewed Dr. Weinard as spending too much time on schools, leaving too little time to practise medicine. None of that mattered to Ed; it was just gossip, but as noted, gossip was everywhere and with strong participation by most everyone.

The conversation continued, with other topics reviewed, until Ed's phone rang. He took the call and paused. At this point, Mark and Ed quickly agreed that their business had been accomplished, and Ed was left alone to focus on the incoming call.

In this telephone conversation, Ed and a neighbouring superintendent talked about proofreading science exams. Each had concerns about changing departmental practices. Ed offered this extraneous comment, "The old committee reviewed the exams," and Phil Weinard might be interested in helping. It was meant to be funny, and it seemed to be heard as just that, humour. Both of them knew that despite having neither training nor experience, Phil Weinard thought of himself as a master educator.

Was Ed being snide or deep in thought or both? Whatever, something was bothering Ed, as he had both said too much and spoken in jest at the expense of another person—Dr. Weinard.

It was nearly noon on the next day, September 9, when Ed took a forwarded call, "Good morning, Dr. Weinard. Ed Noyce here."

Ed listened, then said, I will phone again. I reached a human being on the last call and left a message. No problem.

As Ed returned to listening, I guessed that Dr. Weinard had mentioned someone he knew.

Ed confirmed my conjecture when he said, "I think I know him." It was more listening, interspersed with supportive comments about using teacher presenters, summarizing with "It makes all kinds of sense." Then, presumably for good measure, he reinforced that thread of the conversation, Yes, I understand, a good positive discussion, but with assistance. It would be helpful.

With the call over, Ed admonished himself; he needed a better attitude towards Dr. Weinard.

Huh? Ed, like others, was sometimes his own harshest critic.

In the late afternoon, Ed received a call from principal Jake Harris.

This was the Jake who had made an impression on me, repeatedly. Once again, Jake had quite a bit to say. By now I knew that Jake was not a Dr. Phil Weinard fan, and he was calling because he wanted something.

Ed listened, then responded; the alternative school's board of governors could hire a principal. If this principal were an existing staff member, there would be no extra costs. If they hired externally, the additional costs would be charged to the school's budget. Dr. Weinard has a quarter of a million dollars; at least he assures us that he has. The October 5 meeting would include representatives from the parent advisory councils. It would not be all the parents. Ed opined that Phil (Weinard) was becoming more realistic, and more supportive [of the board and staff].

Ed also learned about Jake's personal strategy for the meeting. He enjoyed Jake's account of events and responded positively as Jake offered a litany of points: "Yes! Yes! Yes! Right on the button!" Their conversation went on and on. He told Jake that Phil recognized that he offended people, so he was bringing other people in. And then Ed suggested that the board might be looking for a nice, soft political way out of this alternative school program. The death knell for the proposal would be if parents say that they are not interested.

I wondered where the view that the board was tiring of the Paragon Alternative School came from. Was something said, or perhaps, was Ed reading the tea leaves? He later expressed this thought again when I interviewed him a few days later, on September 12.

The conversation then switched focus. Their talk turned to that of a former colleague. He had been fired. Who had started that thread? That, I thought, might be just the thing that Jake would fear the most.

Finally, an off-topic comment and Ed's signal that the call was almost over. Done at 16:05 hours, it had lasted a bit over ten minutes. Ed told me that Jake was "flipping out over Phil." Ed had been attentive and clearly supportive of Jake, but, as we learned later, Jake still had unvoiced concerns.

It was near the end of the day, Friday, but work continued. E-mails needed to be read and responded to. Ed and Bill chatted about events and people elsewhere, and about government policy directions. When Bill departed, Ed returned a call to a reporter. It was now quitting time, and Ed departed the office with a computer. He would be working at home for the weekend. But before leaving, he checked in at his secretary's station. There was a fax from an Ontario school board; the Ontario board had provided written approval for the upcoming attendance of Dr. Weinard's guest presenter. Another to-do list item could be checked off.

Observations from September 12 to 27 involved normal leadership; it was back to same-old, same-old. It included direct observations and notes made from my home district. My field notes are summarized in Table 6.

Table 6: September 12 to 27: Paragon Alternative School Summary Notes

Date	Summary Discussion
September 12	Note: On September 12, I interviewed Ed and two senior staff members, and attended a Student Accommodation Committee meeting. Consequently, other observational times were restricted to before 09:30 hours and after 16:00 hours. During these times, nothing was said about Weinard or the Paragon Alternative School. Two brief references to Dr. Weinard occurred during the afternoon committee meeting. First, a parent member asked Ed about the potential for a charter school in a low enrollment or closed school. Ed explained: Opening an "alternative" or charter school would require an existing school. As a new school, it would draw students out of their existing school, lowering that school's enrollment and decreasing its pupil–teacher ratios. As that school's efficiencies became "unglued," ripples would follow throughout the system. The second reference to Dr. Weinard came as the meeting was nearing its end. A date was needed for their next meeting. Ed let them know that they had to work around an already scheduled Paragon Alternative School meeting.
September 15	From my home community, I called Ed early to ask for help. He agreed to have his secretary arrange the balance of my interview schedule. This was more than I had asked. Ed told me that he had taken some heat from principals over the possibility of a charter (alternative) school coming into one of their buildings. Would they be out of a job? Ed laughed off that concern; no, he had a job for a principal. I was aware that Ed would have understated any related difficulties. It was chit-chat as Ed had no administrative openings.
September 20	Once again, I called Ed from my home: Would he share the learning styles materials with me? Yes, he agreed, and would have them ready for my pickup. I also learned that Ed, his board chair, and Dr. Weinard had met and reviewed plans for their upcoming meetings. Further, in the process of gaining permission for the Ontario school principal's participation, he developed a bit of a relationship with the HR (human resources) representative he was talking to. There he learned that this principal had philosophical differences with her board and might be fired. I was left wondering why this HR officer had shared such confidences. Was it just gossip, or was he trying to be helpful? Would Ed share this tidbit with others in Wapiti Falls? Did they need to know? All this was speculative, and I did not ask for any details. Further, I did not think it was that important, or if it was, then Ed would tell me what he wanted to tell me, or it would come out in the observations. In the end, there were no clues that this tidbit was shared.
September 22	Back in Wapiti Falls for just one full day, interviews tied me up for most of my day. Nothing about Weinard or the Paragon School was heard outside of the interviews. I attended the evening portion of a zone meeting of superintendents and I heard nothing about Dr. Weinard or the proposed school.
September 23	Attended the day portion of a zone meeting of superintendents and heard nothing about Dr. Weinard or the school.

September 27	Back in the Wapiti Falls, Ed returned a mid-morning call to Will Evans, an out-of-district principal. Evans wanted permission to attend tonight's meeting with teachers. While Evans received a "No," Ed invited him to attend the October 5 meeting with parents. Tonight, Ed told him, may have more emotion than logic. After the call, Ed said that Evans was "treating me as a long-lost friend," a friend he had met but once. When I returned from interviews, Ed talked to me about three items: • Principal Jake Harris: Jake had phoned his former superintendent, Milt Palmer, and read his prepared speech to him. Ed anticipated that tonight, at Dr. Weinard's meeting with staff, Jake would go for the "big killer question." He was a "loose cannon." Ed's hope was that Jake would follow the agenda which the board and Dr. Weinard had agreed to. • Lydia Jacques, the board chairperson, said that she considered herself to be the "swing vote" in the decision to approve the Weinard school "in principle." Lydia had told me the same thing in greater detail in our interview of September 22. • Finally, our talk turned to the Student Accommodation Committee. Ed had thought there would be fewer meetings.

Between my planned interviews and the Student Accommodation Committee meeting, I had fewer occasions to witness matters relating to Weinard or his school. From what I saw, however, I concluded that normal leadership was working fine. Ed's leadership processes were all evident, but signs of rising tension had emerged. Jake was obviously struggling with the alternative school concept, but there were others who were unsure and sought just a bit more clarification or needed a review of what was previously reviewed. Even Ed—solid, careful, unruffled Ed—revealed unacknowledged tension.

Before a further examination of events, consider what leading informants said to me about the Paragon Alternative School in their one-on-one interviews with me.

CHAPTER 9

Interviewees Speak to the Paragon Alternative School

Interviews are important for qualitative researchers. They add data that can confirm what had previously been observed and surmised, or they debunk what had been thought. Used along with other data, the formal process is called "triangulation." Creswell elaborates: "This process involves corroborating evidence from different sources to shed light on a theme or perspective" (Creswell 2013: 251). (Appendix A: "Ethics, Validity, and Reliability in Qualitative Studies" provides further details.)

In addition to providing one more datum source, interviews also reduce interruptions and therefore encourage the expression of longer, more complex thoughts. With only two participants, interviews are less complex than multi-party dialogue. But they are still conversations. Interviews were an improvement from regular dialogue, but they still present unique challenges. Complex ideas are expressed, but speakers still wander, still insert explanations in mid-thought, still fail to finish an idea. Some thoughts are communicated through the motions of hands or posture. Non-verbal nuances are of course lost and what was actually taped was all that can be remembered. Thus, I was mostly obliged to rely on their words. And to get to complete and cogent sentences, I edited what they said for length and clarity. Editing improved text management and flow, and thereby helped to preserve the thoughts of the interviewee.

Thirteen interviews were conducted that September. Ten interviewees provided useful comments about the people and issues around the Paragon Alternative School matter.

Each interview starts with my commentary, an introduction of background issues related to the interview. In all but one, I specifically asked for comments on Dr. Weinard or his Paragon Alternative School. If I thought the respondent had more information, but nothing was forthcoming, I prompted the individual to reveal more. In the end, I found the interviews interesting and productive.

Ed Noyce, Superintendent of Schools: September 12

In the privacy of a cold, empty office, Ed and I participated in a wide-ranging exit interview of nearly two-and-a-half hours. This portion of the interview focused on Dr. Weinard and the school. It also delved into something about Ed's thinking processes.

The fact was that Dr. Weinard needed a school building. The board had a soon-to-be-vacated school, but they had leased it to a private school, their competition. This building might have worked for Dr. Weinard, but that utilization was never mentioned in my time there. I found out later that it had been discussed—privately—but Dr. Weinard did not want that school and that topic did not come up again. As we saw, Ed's reaction to using a soon-to-be-closed school or a different building was neutral. He could live with either direction.

This portion of the interview starts in our discussion of that event, an administrative recommendation that lost. Rather than accepting a lessee who would open a native friendship centre, the board chose their competition, a Christian school:

> Dale: There was a switch. You supported the team's [lease] recommendation at the start, but the board went against your recommendation, and you supported [the board's choice, but] with Phil Weinard, that switch has been harder.
>
> Ed: Phil Weinard was a very hard task, because I don't think that Phil has given us a fair look. He has seen it as a parent and that's all. And the system has changed a heck of a lot since Phil's kids went through elementary school. [Still, Phil had some good ideas], so I am trying to help the board see that Phil is in fact in front of the board. I offered Phil one day of my time if he would take a day; we would tour any elementary school he wanted. I would show him, if he'd allow me to choose a school or two, the range of styles of operation and the kinds of instruction. I found his reference to direct instruction [in a board meeting before my time] to be insulting, at the least. Some very angry words with Phil [were exchanged] in front of the board that bothered me a lot, because he brought out "The Effective Schools Research" and dropped variables onto the board that did not come from "The Effective Schools Research." And I essentially called him a charlatan in front of the board for dropping in his own preferences, and attributing it to the research, when it is not in the research. He backed up, said that is not in the research, but these others are. But I have since gained a lot better understanding of Phil, as a person, as a professional, as a person with a very large ego, and as a person with a genuine desire to improve schools. And I really think what Phil wants for schools is not dramatically different from what we want for schools. The way he wants to go about it is dramatically different.
>
> We have got seven trustees, and I would say seven different responses to Phil Weinard. We had a five-to-two vote to support his proposal in principle. I have a feeling now that if we said to the board right now, don't worry about your politics with the community, where are you with Phil Weinard, we would probably have five-to-two vote to scuttle the Weinard approach. The

two trustees who would continue to support it would be the trustees who are interested in the regimentation of uniforms and kids going to school and sitting in five rows of six desks each like they did in the old days. Or the trustee that is interested in action research. That would be the trustee that wants to see us spending more of our time and resources doing properly conducted studies of changes that we have introduced to the schools. I think the majority of the board is quite fed up with it all, but they have also recognized Phil as softening—when he is talking to them—but not when he is talking to others. When he talks to the media, when he talks to groups elsewhere, I know that Wapiti Falls is mentioned by name. I mean, the man has been a catalyst, but not always a positive catalyst. So there is a lot of anger in our community. I had a phone call from a principal over the weekend who is angry that we are meeting with teachers and parents in September and October to talk about the Weinard school. He [the principal] would probably stand up and say, but this is exactly what we are doing in schools right now. What do you want that is different? And the only things that I can see that are different: #1, parent control of the school through its charter; #2, probably the use of uniforms; #3, probably the exclusive use of a phonics approach to teaching reading.

Dale: You tried to get the board to take that on [action research]?

Ed: Yes.

Dale: But it didn't work?

Ed: Nope.

Note: Ed used the Grace McCarthy teaching-learning styles inventory (1980) to better understand how people thought and reacted. Ed had thought about Dr. Weinard, put himself in Dr. Weinard's shoes, formed hypotheses about Dr. Weinard's teaching-learning style, and used it in interactions with him. As a result of such reflections, he repeatedly said that he understood Dr. Weinard better now that he did before. Ed was asked to share what the McCarthy system taught him about various individuals. Here, in a discussion of Dr. Weinard. Ed's empathy is obvious and can be confusing, as he switches in and out of what he sees as Dr. Weinard's thinking process.

Dale: Phil Weinard.

Ed: Phil Weinard has elements of a type 2—the search for data, the search for sequence, the search for pieces. But he also has elements of a type 3, the concrete side of him. This is in me.

[Briefly taking on the persona of Dr. Weinard, Ed said], "And this is what I read in this research report, and it has got to be right and I don't care if there are 397 other research reports, I believe this one. It fits into my [view] of the world."

[And then reverting back to his own analytical views, he continued], "And I think probably that he is closer to a type 3 than a type 2, but there are elements of type 2 in Phil. The sequential—the sequential certainly is common to types 2 and 3. Type 2 is abstract, and type 3 is more concrete, but there are elements in Phil of assembling the big picture from little pieces, and there are elements in Phil of "this is the way it was done when I was a kid in school [and] this is the way it is going to be now."

Ed: Some of Phil Weinard's concerns about education are really quite accurate and quite legitimate. Phil was on two of our strategic planning committees; I don't know if you were aware of that.

Dale: No.

Ed: He was on the committee. In fact, I phoned up on…

Dale: [Ed was interrupted by my reaction—laughter.] You goaded him?

Ed: No, this was after he came up with his big proposal. He was already receiving national attention, but I [thought that I] would co-opt him. I thought that we could draw him in and let him see what we are really up to and what we are really trying to accomplish. And I kind of figured that might slow him down or at least keep him onside in some way.

[So] I phoned up Phil, and said that I have got two committees that I think that you might be interested in. I would like to tell you about them and have you tell me which one you would like to be on. Committee 3 is on expectations of students. How do we get kids improving their achievement, their attendance and behaviour? It is a fairly wide-open thing. What we want is some feedback from the committee on how we as a district can establish expectations for kids and implement them in the district. The other one was committee 4, which is innovation. What the board wanted to do was to…the strategy was to…encourage innovation in the district. Phil chose innovation. He went onto that thinking [Ed assumed], "How can I get a charter school in," I suspect. "Here is how I can get parents in charge of schools," I suspect. But he heard rather quickly of all the excitement that was going on in Roger White's committee on student expectations. [He] phoned me up and asked if I minded if he could also serve on that other one. No problem; go for it. So we added him, after the fact, to Roger's committee as well, and Phil served on both of them.

Don Howard, Deputy Superintendent of Schools: September 12

Don's interview provided some technical challenges because he spoke so softly that it was hard to hear and transcribe his comments. While he was always supportive of Ed, he also disagreed with Ed's strategic response to Dr. Weinard and his school.

Don was not normally difficult to hear. Would speaking softly be his way of violating team norms, going against his boss? Or was he worried about being heard through the walls?

Dale: I think that Ed is very supportive of staff and the board. Sometimes there are conflicts on that front. I am looking at the Phil Weinard thing. How does he manage that? Maybe it is not an issue.

Don: That's a tough one. That is a good example because he doesn't have, and he knows this, he doesn't have my complete support or the coordinator's support in the decision to be cooperative with Phil Weinard. He knows that.

Dale: Yes. Jake made that real plain.

Don: But he [Jake] also knows politically in dealing with the board, that we have to. He knows.

Don: And they have made it pretty clear—and he [Ed] is not, in his own mind, he is not a Phil Weinard fan—so Ed is really…It has been difficult for him to be neutral on this one and to do what he thinks the board wants, to be honest with them. He is trying very hard to be neutral, but it was for the board. And he has made statements to make it very clear where he is at personally. When I say statements, he has made these internally, to the professional people in this office, and also to teachers, which I really wonder about in my own mind, whether he should be doing that, but he's done that. In fact, people know exactly where he sits personally, but he also says very openly that this is the direction of the board of trustees, and it is my responsibility to follow it, to do my job.

Dale: So, he has taken the high road in that, too. He has said where he is, but he has also gone where the board is.

Don: He has never said that to a trustee.

Dale: He has never said that he is not a Phil Weinard fan?

Don: He has never said it that bluntly. I don't think that there would be any doubt that our trustees realize that their superintendent is having difficulty with the directions that Phil Weinard is proposing. I don't think there is any question about that. But they also, I think, the trustees appreciate his openness to consider…

Dale: To pursue it?

Don: Yes. At times I have thought, how would I have handled that? And to be very honest with you, I don't think I would have handled it the way Ed has. I think that I would take the position that it was probably the wrong thing to do, because if you keep at it… it depends…I don't know. We are into it too far to even consider that now. And you know, I'm not sure where I would be. Eighteen months ago, I would probably say this, but, and this is really fascinating, because the end result of the decision that Ed has made—and it was his sole decision—I mean when I say that, he certainly asked for input, and we discussed things quite a bit, but he is making the decision on this. He knows that. That is the wrong word to put to it, but he realizes that it has to be his decision, and that he doesn't have the full support of everybody on it, and I don't think that he is ever going to get full support. So, he made that decision. The way that this thing will eventually turn out, in my view right now, it could be very positive for our area. Not that it is a Phil Weinard school, and I honestly hope that it doesn't turn out to be a charter school because I question—and I guess this is where the humour comes in, too. I said to Ed at our admin meeting a month ago—a couple of weeks ago—I really feel strongly that we should be pushing our trustees for this to go as an alternative public school, not as a charter school, and the consensus was "please do." Choose the opportunity. So, I did that at the last board meeting, publicly, just as my opinion. You want to try this, a different approach? Then why even consider a charter school? Why don't we spend this [money] on an alternative school? That is what people want, so we try this as an alternative school and have complete control over it. Why Dr. Weinard? If it is a good idea, why go after it without control? Anyway, the lights kind of went on around the table, and there was a fair amount of agreement. So maybe the end result of it is going to be very positive.

Bill Bersche, Assistant Superintendent of Business Services: September 12

Bill Bersche started the interview by listing his duties: "Responsibilities for financial matters, transportation, facilities, school maintenance, I guess, which is part of facilities, payroll, and benefits—in a joint responsibility with the assistant superintendent, human resources."

Bill was straightforward, no nonsense and careful—a cautious guy in charge of the district's money. He surprised me when, near the end of the interview, after we had talked about the alternative school, I asked about Ed's effectiveness. He replied—twice—without hesitation, in this short sequence:

> Dale: You have seen different superintendents, and is this how have they done it?
>
> Bill: No, they all have their own style. I think that this is the most effective. . . . Personally, I think this is more effective.

As to the Weinard school, Bill saw it through a different lens than that of his colleagues, but they were professional educators; he wasn't.

> Dale: Ed is supportive of the staff and the board. You hear good things, and he talks about good things. One of the things is that sometimes the board might go in a different direction than he would like [it] to. How is he supportive of the board and supportive of other [contradictory] things…such as when they ask about Phil Weinard? How does he handle that?
>
> Bill: I think very well. That is a particularly good example, Dale. Ed is greatly concerned; if the board could be going in a negative direction, in terms of its implications, or if its effect on the total staff is bad when he feels that the staff out there in the schools are working for the best of every student. On the other hand, he knows, and is sensitive enough to know, that education is constantly needing change. He has dealt with that and been involved in a number of those—the Effective Schools Project, working at it before Alberta Education came out with quality indicators—so from his approach he is saying that we have to look at an alternative. This Dr. Weinard school is one such alternative, and he handles it very well in terms of balancing that political football. Some part of the board wants to explore a paragon-type alternative school, and yet Ed, knowing that it has some possible negative, some "very negative" ramifications, just keeps trying to bring back the focus to the students. I guess that is one of the ways he deals with it. Number one, is it going to help education? Secondly, is it something we can afford from a fiscal and human resources [standpoint]? And he doesn't push it. There are other issues where Ed could quite clearly figure out that a certain thing would [cause damage], and the Weinard thing is probably an example. He could probably have pushed that one, knowing that it would lose on a four-to-three or five-to-two vote if he pushed it. He could say that we need a decision and we have got to plan; we can't just have this dragging on and on. But Ed tends not to work [that way]. He will keep bringing forth arguments as to why there are other alternatives that might work just as effectively, but he

leaves the final decision with the board. And so, he walks a thin line between alienating the board—and/or elements of the board—and creating problems with his own staff. It is a tough one. There are several [issues] like that.

Dale: Some superintendents don't have a good handle on the politics of their board? Does Ed?

Bill: I think we all do. Not to take away from Ed, but Ed certainly does.

James Thorborn, Principal, Ormand Mitchel High School: September 22

James Thorborn was the principal of a new high school. The year before, while serving as the principal designate, he was also Ed's executive assistant. This interview was fast and intense. There was no need for me to ask questions about Dr. Weinard. James's views simply flowed out, without solicitation.

James: You know our fiasco with the Weinard thing? I think that if we could have that back, I certainly wouldn't be going that way.

Dale: Should Ed have done something different on that?

James: I don't know. No, I think that he has tried his best. I think he had a couple of board members that were committed to go that way. I think that it will be an Achilles' heel for us up the road. Weinard is on CBC Radio this morning again. I don't think that this can do us any good. Anyway you cash this out, we can never end up looking positive on this. When Phil comes on and says that public education can't do what they are supposed to do, and then in the next breath says that he is associated with Wapiti Falls Public School District. If we were Syncrude and somebody was saying that, he would be out on his own.

Dale: Yes, he would.

James: So, I guess I am very loyal that way, and I am very family-oriented. I view myself as a company man, and I'm proud to say that. [Weinard] is not who you want in an organization.

Dale: That's hurting Ed because people know that this is the direction Ed has taken?

James: He hasn't changed. He is lucky in that way. I think that people know that it is Paddy Nolan and some of the board members who have chosen that direction. If you want just a little chink out of Ed's armour, I think that it would be facilitating the meeting of parent councils, and stuff like that. He's on that tightwire that he walks many times. You have to be careful [so] that you are not perceived by the principals in the district as undercutting their schools, and that is a fine line right now.

I said that to Don. We should set up the same kind of alternative school as Phil. Everybody has the opportunity to do so. Hillside Comp in Big Rock was offering a fine arts school as part of the high school.

Dale: Is that a magnet school? [As defined in Appendix C: "A District Lexicon," a magnet school is a school with a specialized program that attracts students to it.]

James: I would have gone out more aggressively, probably, and marketed magnet schools because you can create the same kind of thing Phil wanted to create within your own system. There is nothing that stops you from doing that. I was in Montreal and went through high school. They had uniforms. They had the whole thing. And it was just mandated in…so you know, I think that had we been nurturing that to a little higher extent, you could just have said to Windfall School, hey you know, we will let you do this, but we don't want Phil Weinard in. You go ahead. You know, the kind of thing that you were proceeding on anyways, so just take it away. But we are caught, and it is just unfortunate that Phil lives in our community. He was a parent at one of the schools when I was at W. C. Raley School, actually. He wrote me—I wish I would have [sic] kept the letters actually—but it was one of those things that got lost in the file.

Margaret O'Connell, Trustee and Former Chair: September 22

Margaret O'Connell was the chair of the board when the Weinard Paragon Alternative School was accepted "in principle." She started the discussion about the alternative school proposal by noting how hard Ed worked:

Margaret: It irritates the heck out of me that he has been doing all this stuff for this Weinard school. Weinard was supposed to make up the darn budget. Who makes up the budget for the school? Ed does. I mean, it is ridiculous. I am going to start billing Weinard for Ed's time, or else hire somebody to take over some of this stuff and bill it to Weinard.

Dale: You know where Ed stands on the issues. You know that Phil Weinard's school, that he would rather not have it.

Margaret: Hmm. I think in some ways, he thinks that it is a good thing. Let's do it, but on the other hand, it's like this is the wrong time. There are too many other things flying around to be spending time on this.

Dale: Would there be a right time?

Margaret: When I first came on the board, we had lots of money.

Lydia Jacques, Chair: September 22

Lydia was the vice-chair when the Weinard school proposal was accepted in principle. She said that she eventually came to cast the deciding vote approving it and explained why.

Lydia: The strategic plan, I think was excellent, and I really support that, getting parents involved. Things are working very well, especially in the area of bringing parents in and getting more community involvement, and in our business partnerships.

Dale: Okay. I am thinking of the Phil Weinard school; it comes up very often.

Lydia Yes. I wish it wasn't so often.

Dale: That is a frustration in the system?

Lydia: Well, Weinard is a big frustration in that you have somebody criticizing public education who is a public school taxpayer. Regardless of whether he names Wapiti Falls Public, it is Wapiti Falls Public that he is defiling, as he has done on several occasions. Offers have been made to come into the school to see what is going on. Come in, with no prior knowledge given to the school. He has never done that. So, he is a critic from afar, and that I find extremely frustrating. I am not in education, I haven't read all the data that he has read, and all the educational literature and research that he is talking about, but I hear from others that the research he talks about was from 1984, which doesn't make it old, but he keeps talking about "effective schools." I understand that before I was on the board, "effective schools" came in, that it was a big thing, and all our schools were given in-service presentations on it. So, all our schools basically run on the theory of effective schools. So, it is very frustrating when you have someone like that who has a sort of…has a very narrow view. One objective of mine is to be open to looking at what is going on.

Dale: Dr. Weinard is not supportive of the board?

Lydia: No. I would say that he isn't. He wants to approach it in a confrontational…sort of an aggressive manner rather than how can we work together to make things better?

Dale: Your board isn't really clear on what they should do with all this. They've struggled with this.

Lydia: Yeah, very much. They have struggled, and I was the one who split the vote and that was tough. I changed my mind and decided that I would support it.

Dale: Why?

Lydia: A couple of reasons…

Dale: That's okay. You don't need to tell me.

Lydia: Yeah. That's okay.

Dale: Okay.

Lydia: I mean, you are not going to phone up the *Wapiti Falls Cascade* [newspaper] tomorrow and write a story.

Dale: No, I'm not.

Lydia: That's fine then. No, a couple of reasons were because I thought this, it cuts into community pride, but if some want an alternative education, then let's put it to the public and see if that is indeed the case. That was one reason, and the second kind of ties in on the first. I would like to put it to bed, either it is a go or it's not a go, and let's get on with our lives. But the last four years having Phil Weinard's constant criticism is not appreciated.

And at the same time as that meeting was going on, my sister was diagnosed with breast cancer. I was sitting at the meeting, hurrying to phone, to find out if she was having a CAT scan that day, to find out if there was cancer anywhere else. In this state of mind, I thought that on the whole scheme of life, if people want this, then what is the big deal here? In terms of being a trustee, I don't think that I know everything about education and about what's best, and I am open enough to listen to others. And so that is another reason. I thought, fine, let's put it to the public and let the public decide.

Dale: How is your sister doing?

Lydia: She is doing fine now but it was scary at the time. Well, I mean she is still not out of the woods, because it's…

Dale: That's good.

Lydia: Yeah, I think so.

Dale: Ed has done what he needed to do for the board? As a trustee, vice-chair, [and] chair, are you satisfied?

Lydia: Yes. I am sure Ed would prefer that this thing would just go away and bury itself and had never reared its ugly head. It would make his job a lot easier. And it is, or it can be viewed as, a criticism. It is not on our minds, but the public could view it as such. If the board supports this, they obviously don't think that our own schools are good enough, that kind of idea. That would be pretty tough to swallow, but Ed doesn't see it that way at all—at least in my impression, and he says that. He has balanced the demands quite well. I'm sure it is not something that he relishes doing. I know that the only complaint from some is that he spends too much time on it. On the other hand, he is there to protect the board's interests. It does take some time. We've put it to Weinard that if this thing goes ahead, then we would have to hire somebody else [to do all these extras].

Dale: I would like to come to the meeting next time. I am hoping to. I am near the end of my time here, and I am hoping to see that meeting, the public meeting, and then the board meeting should be exciting.

Lydia: [Laughter.]

Dale: And if I get my druthers, I would like to have it when the parents, school council people show, because it is going to be…

Lydia: On the fifth. And from what I know, the staff meeting is going to be gruesome. There are some staff that are in favour of this, and—oh, that was the other reason why I voted in favour of it. It is because a committee, the Curricular Strategies Committee on student conduct and behaviour, said we should be looking at something like this, at alternatives. So, taking all those factors together, we should have a look at it.

Dale: So, if I were to describe it politically, it is that people are telling you that we need to face the issue. Is that how you see that?

Lydia: Hmm. Well I don't feel political pressure from parents. I am just open-minded enough [to see] that if this is going to help students or increase their achievement, then maybe we should open up. I don't actually feel pressured. No, I don't feel political pressures.

Herb Bondar, Student Services Coordinator: September 27

Herb's brief comments on the Weinard school proposal focused on one staff member: his friend, Jake Harris.

> Herb: Are you getting your little thing done yet?
>
> Dale: Well, no. I am just about wrapping up. How about you? Have you got your school year all figured out, so you can golf more?
>
> Herb: No, I have got this goddamn meeting with Weinard tonight. [Laughter.] Jake will give a little speech.
>
> Dale: Will he speak really well, or will he look to score a lot of points?
>
> Herb: He will do well. He will do well. He's very good when it comes to public speaking. He is articulate, to the point, and he will have reflected on the issues. And he is not scared to challenge Phil point-blank. He won't waffle; let's put it that way.
>
> Dale: He is a believer [in public education]?
>
> Herb: You betcha! Totally.

Marie Noyce, Ed's Spouse: September 28

I interviewed Marie in their acreage home.

> Dale: The Phil Weinard issue, that has taken lots of thought and energy.
>
> Marie: Yes. I don't know how much actual time Ed has spent on it. I know that it's kind of on his mind a bit. What's really worrying isn't Phil Weinard himself, it's the whole idea that our present education system—not that it can't be improved, things can always be improved—but under the present political system, the education system is being allowed to just shatter. You can see those little church schools everywhere, and now if they go into charter schools, charter schools will be everywhere. And some will emerge as very good schools, but what happens to the kids that are stuck in a really poor quality, little church school? And there are some around where they do American correspondence courses—for crying out loud—to educate Alberta kids. I have nothing against America, but this fragmentation, it is kind of

blowing apart…I think the poorest students are going to be left behind. You wonder if the public school system is allowed to disintegrate, and it's a long ways from disintegrating yet, but if it is allowed to disintegrate, are we going back to a system where the more you can pay, the better the education? That would really be a shame because there are really good brains among poor people too.

I don't know if this fragmentation can be stopped. I don't think that it is Phil Weinard's fault. That is not the main issue. It is out in the open, and he is the one pushing. And he hasn't got just bad ideas. He's trying to help but…

Dale: He's trying to help?

Marie: Yes. It is too bad that he doesn't spend as much time on his medical practice but…[laughter]…and sometimes an outsider sees things that an insider doesn't see, because you don't see the forest for the trees or whatever, but his idea is fragmenting education. Education is being blasted everywhere, and I really don't think it is as bad as they are saying. Maybe I don't see it because I'm kind of isolated, but when you look at the kids that are graduating these days from high schools. Those kids have learned a lot. They are good kids. You are always going to have the 5 percent of bad ones, and [people are] blaming education for everything under the sun. The teachers are bad. The education system is bad. As soon as you get the news media—they are onto education now—they just tend to try to destroy things rather than make it better…

But I think it is not Phil Weinard that is important, it is the idea…Well, of course, he is wanting to go back to the way it was when he went to school, where the teacher is an authority figure, and everybody sits in straight rows, and they memorize their work, and so on. I don't think he has updated his idea of what a school is…

You know I've only met Phil once or twice. We had breakfast with him one day out in Vancouver, he and his wife. I just get the impression that he is kind of longing for the days, the good old days, and of course everybody wants the good old days, but sometimes the good old days weren't perfect, either.

Ann Spencer, Secretary to the Superintendent: September 28

In her role, Ann spent considerable time with Ed and was aware of his issues, his concerns, and his general well-being.

Dale: How is the Phil Weinard stuff [with all its criticism]?

Ann: It's been very difficult for Ed because he is so proud of his district and everything that been accomplished here. He is proud of his teachers and the students.

Dale: Did you see the finished copy of his speech last night to the Weinard meeting [with staff] the night before?

Ann: Not the finished copy.

Dale: Do I ever get to see "Ed Noyce" in his work [the person, not his public face]? It's mostly the district, isn't it?

Ann: That's right.

Dale: That is a strength of character? Is that it?

Ann: I think so. Although, perhaps sometimes, somewhat to his detriment.

Dale: I said that you need to blow your horn more if you want attention. It's pretty quiet here.

Ann: Yes. And he keeps it that way. It was an extremely hard thing for him to do last night, standing up publicly to compliment the district and compliment the teaching staff.

Dale: Has the job taken a toll on Ed?

Ann: I would say so. Especially in the last year or two.

Dale: The thing with Phil Weinard, Ed's out there on his own, isn't he? Because there is a lot of things, like the board has taken a stance that the staff doesn't like, that put him out on his own.

Ann: That's about right.

Dale: Does he feel that?

Ann: Oh definitely, yes. He is trying to work for two masters and…I mean it is very difficult.

Dale: Lonely?

Ann: Yes.

Dale: What does Ed react to? What are some things that are upsetting to him?

Ann: Well, certainly some of the parent demands. Frustrations with the board. You know, they don't seem to understand the real problem.

And I think, well right now, like the things that Phil Weinard is saying about the district, that type of thing certainly does get him upset.

Dale: Is the Accommodations Committee upsetting him?

Ann: Oh, yes, that is another thing.

Ab Digby, Assistant Superintendent of Human Resources: September 29

Of all the central office staff, Ab was the closest to classroom teachers, closest to their mood and their feelings. He had worked directly with them for years as a curriculum consultant, only becoming an assistant superintendent in this new school term. Early in the interview, Ab identified a major source of his, and the teachers', frustrations—namely, the board and their decision to approve the Weinard alternative school. This was very fresh, as staff had heard Phil Weinard's pitch promoting the school just two days earlier. Asked to comment on the system's goals, accomplishments, and frustrations, Ab gave a lengthy response with numerous insights:

Dale: What are the goals, accomplishments, frustrations of the Wapiti Falls, the district?

Ab: I think our major achievement in Wapiti Falls Public is that we have good quality leadership, top to down. We have good principals—effective principals—and we generally have a very good staff. It shows up. I think that our major accomplishment is that we are providing, despite what one individual out there might be saying, a good quality education for our children…

Frustrations. The major one right now is the alternative school proposal, that's from my point of view. It is having an adverse effect on staff morale with most of our teachers, and particularly our elementary teachers, because they feel that the board…I think that the board has let them down in supporting this alternative. They are reading it as they are not doing a good enough job. One person, who is not an educator, may have convinced the board that we are not doing a good job. I think teachers are feeling a bit ill, whether the project goes through or not. It is something that is going to take a little while to heal, for these teachers to trust them [the board]. I think that we will see some of that in our dealings with staff in the next while. So that is a major frustration.

Dale: Is Ed seen as taking the right way with this, or is there questions on this direction? What is your view?

Ab: I think there is a…I think that it's Ed's nature, that he wants it to play itself out in the natural way. And he is saying that the board has made a commitment to do this, and I'm an employee of the board. I represent the board, and therefore I have to deal with this. I am supporting the board's decision, whether it is my personal belief or not, and so he has gone that way with it. Sometimes he's a little frustrated. Personally, I think it is more nails being guided into his coffin….

Maybe if Phil kills it himself, then the public will know that he can't come back to us and say well, you killed this for us. I think that is where Ed is coming from, and maybe that is where he is wiser than I am. I don't have the patience for that. Maybe I would rather be out there saying, well here are all the things wrong with what you've done, and so on, and so forth.

Since this idea has no merit, we should make no effort.

Dale: What did you think of last night's meeting? The in camera portion—starting your own research school [for action research]?

Ab: Well, I was very pleased with the reaction of some of the trustees. I mean some of them didn't surprise me, but there were a couple of them that I was pleased to hear saying so, because it seems to me that they are finally seeing that this isn't all wine and roses, that there are going to be problems with it.

They are also seeing the effect on our staff, from the meeting the night before and the reaction of our staff to the proposal. The board is saying, maybe we have made a mistake here, but they are in a situation now where I think that they have to see it through, one way or another. And if there is a school out there that is interested in this, they're going to have to go and talk to them, and make sure that the support is there. And if the support is there [for that school], I don't think that they will have any choice but to set up the alternative school. I would rather they went with what Don brought up last night. It's something that I've advocated all along. There are some merits in some of the things that Phil is saying, so why don't we incorporate it into our district?

We have a strategic plan, and all of those things are incorporated into it. The research that he quotes bothers me because I can find research on any topic that I want, that backs any belief that I have.

Whether I am right or wrong. I can go back through *Reading Teacher* and find numerous articles that support phonics. I could find just as many articles that support whole language, and I could find just as many articles that support an eclectic approach to teaching. Teachers read these, so they are aware of all the points. One of Phil's arguments that I find hard to understand is where he is coming from? He always seems to say that teachers are kept in the dark about the research, and about what is out there.

Dale: He's offensive? Isn't he?

Ab: Yeah, I find him offensive. I think that most teachers do. Unfortunately, I don't know if the parents will find him offensive.

Dale: People are worried about that, and how Ed is doing this. Ed seems to think that since he knows where things are going, parents will too? There are some nervous teachers out there.

Ab: Oh, there are. Absolutely. I know they are. Principals are nervous because some of them aren't sure where their parent associations are going to come from, or [where] the parent councils are going to come from. They are nervous that maybe one or two parents in the school who are in favour of this approach will be at the meeting and will speak in favour of it.

Dale: Jake Harris is worked up.

Ab: Very. I think not so much as he was at the beginning. Jake was very worried when this first started, and being new at the school, that it might turn out to be his school, and he would be the principal without a school. He knows that there is no way Phil Weinard would select him as the principal. Not because Jake couldn't do a good job of it, because that would wrong. They don't see eye-to-eye.

Interview Summary

The interviews offered helpful information. Overall, the professional staff did not like Dr. Weinard. Only three interviewees—one trustee, Ed's spouse, and the assistant superintendent of business services—did not question Ed's course of facilitation. Deputy superintendent Don Howard disagreed with Ed's strategy, but kept very quiet about it—literally; his interview comments were almost a whisper. Everyone gave Ed considerable latitude in his approach to Dr. Weinard, those who disagreed, as well as those who accepted it. The new assistant superintendent, Ab, had great insights, Ed "wants it to play itself out in the natural way." And Bill, the business services assistant superintendent, having worked with four superintendents, volunteered his assessment—Ed was the most effective of the four.

I was surprised with one specific aspect of the alternative school journey. I interviewed Ab on September 29, and he mentioned an event from the board meeting of September 28, referring to it as "what Don brought up last night." Ab said that he had advocated this for a long time. James Thorborn said similar things in his interview of September 22. Don said on September 4 that he had brought it up before. I had heard Ed suggest the same process much earlier. In this very permeable system, it was impossible to track down the source of ideas as most everything had previously been shared. Ed liked it that way; joint ownership of ideas and responses was superior to individual ownership. With Ed's consensual leadership, everyone owned the decisions eventually reached, and they were committed to making them work.

CHAPTER 10

September 27 to October 5: Tensions Increase

Ed had taken the lead in setting out an orderly process for the establishment of the Paragon Alternative School as proposed by educational crusader Dr. Phil Weinard. Ab Digby thought that Ed wanted the process to play out. He was right, and to get there, Ed had nurtured it—working with Dr. Weinard to have him explain his proposal to the board, earning Dr. Weinard's agreement on a suitable "go-forward" response of 85 percent parent support, setting out a suitable budget for the proposed school, and helping Dr. Weinard arrange for guest presenters. In other words, Ed took on any task that would move the process forward. Now, they had arrived at the meeting stage. Two meetings were planned. In the first meeting, Dr. Weinard would explain the process to district teachers and answer their questions. In the second meeting, Dr. Weinard would try to win over enough parents to reach the next phase in the school incorporation process. The teacher meeting was to produce goodwill, for goodwill would help, but it was not required. The meeting with parents, however, was critical.

If Dr. Weinard succeeded with parents, the proposal would move from the district level to an individual school. On the other hand, using assistant superintendent Digby's words, "if Phil kills it himself," the quest would end, and with it, what might have become the district's crisis of confidence would also end. Some watched Ed work his process, others stated that they would have done things differently. How so. His staff were uncomfortable with the process. (Ab had even talked about it as nails in Ed's coffin.) The board remained divided, and politicians, on seeing a failure, seldom blamed themselves. Some trustees wondered out loud if it was taking too much of Ed's time. It was clearly Ed's process and if it failed, confidence in the process—confidence in Ed—would fall. And these were all problems before any school was established. If created, think of all the unknowns of turning an esoteric theoretical construct into an instructional model, a working school. These two upcoming meetings would pull at the heart of the district. Tensions increased.

September 27: Paragon Alternative School Meeting with Staff

The evening meeting of September 27 capped off a long and challenging day. It began with expulsion hearings when the Walter MacEwan High School administration had requested the formal removal of several students from their school. We followed that process earlier in this study. Then there were requests from the media and the curious, spectators who wanted to catch the anticipated fireworks. Interviews took me away from what Ed would no doubt identify as a typical day, but then, Ed viewed every day as normal—same-old, same-old. He seemed to have set aside no time to prepare, to plot with his colleagues, or to relax. Where others might have jumped in, shuffled events, second-guessed themselves, Ed waited. Why would he interfere? All the focus would be on Dr. Weinard. It was Dr. Weinard's opportunity to succeed with teachers or to fail, not Ed's.

That evening, Trustee Svarich and I arrived at district offices at about the same time. We were early and had ample time to walk the short distance to Celebration Hall. We exchanged polite, awkward chat-chat. I'd seen enough of his body language to know that he was not sure what to make of me, of my role and my loyalties. Fair enough—we seemed to both question where the other stood. Inside the district, Svarich was viewed as a supporter of Dr. Weinard. Outside the district, at joint trustee-superintendent functions, trustee Svarich was friendly, talkative, open, almost gushy, but on our short walk, he seemed tongue-tied. Ed too had noticed the difference in his inside/outside personas. We had chatted about it. It seemed to me that two camps were forming, those for Dr. Weinard's proposal and those against it. It seemed that all knew where Peter Svarich was camped. Soon, we arrived at the hall and went our separate ways.

Celebration Hall was a repurposed World War II military installation, the smaller half of the larger Remembrance Centre. Although renovated, it looked old. With an external skeleton—steel supports visible on the outside—it had a unique look. It was probably an old hangar. The siding needed fresh paint. Inside was pleasant, but again, old. An overhead projector was centred in the hall's large room, a physical and symbolic obstacle between two combatants, the establishment board versus the upstart reformer. Superintendent Ed Noyce sat on one side, beside the podium, and next to him, board chair Lydia Jacques. Dr. Phil Weinard and his two guest educators sat on the other side. The presenters of both teams sat facing their audience, at their level, exposed. While the meeting was closed to the media, Dr. Weinard had arranged for videotaping. His camera was near the back, centred, like the projector. Behind the camera, near the entrance, a coffee urn perked away. Most people were sitting on the folding chairs at 19:00 hours, the scheduled start time.

At 19:03, chair Lydia Jacques stood and addressed her audience. They were mostly teachers and administrators from the district's schools. The full board was there; the chair at the front and the other six trustees scattered in the audience. Various district office staff were in attendance.

Chair Jacques talked about their district and its strategic plan, and about the alternative school's "approval-in-principle." Trustees, she noted, voted both for and against the project. She said that the vote had not been a criticism of schools or staff; the vote had been to find ways to improve education. School improvement was the issue here, and the full board was there to listen and reflect. She listed the board's commitments. It sounded like they might have been pulled from their mission statement. She stressed a key element for her; it was that the district earn the support of staff and students. Usually a clear speaker, Lydia struggled, stumbled, wavered. She was uncomfortable. She reviewed the agenda and promised time for questions after the presentations. She introduced superintendent Ed Noyce and sat.

Superintendent Noyce stood, walked to the podium, and read a prepared speech. He spoke of district history. He recognized the ongoing need for change and mentioned the change processes initiated in recent years. This alternative school, he said, would have a research component and would need to be done well. Finally, he invited "responses, professional responses." It had not been an exciting talk, but the audience was not there to listen to him. They were polite, but really, they were waiting to ask questions directly to the would-be school reformer, Dr. Phil Weinard. This portion of the meeting was brief.

Dr. Weinard stood, eager. He declared that Wapiti Falls was a good district, but what he had on offer was so much more powerful. "Overwhelming power." He pitched fear—fear of social disruption. Fear for the profession of teaching. Fear of the alarming downward "trend lines" of public school education. People listened, but there were whispers. Not everyone was going to be polite. Dr. Weinard cited the "phenomenal" results achieved in other schools, schools led by people like his first guest, Willis Hislop, a public school principal from Calgary.

Willis Hislop stood before his audience and opened up, and his vision spilled out. He called himself an "old jock." He was also a showman, and people listened. He admitted, "I don't know what the deal is here," but he did know that it made a difference when he hired who he wanted to hire, when he used a student contract, and when his staff were enthusiastic. Describing his first staff meeting at his current school, he drew laughs when he admitted serving beer and hamburgers, and again when he said that he had bought a staff barbeque from school funds that he was not sure he had. He gave other illustrations of the autonomy he enjoyed as a principal, and he described the positive turnaround of students. These results, he claimed, occurred because of his leadership. "I think that is what Phil is talking about." Willis was loose. Later, I heard a different personal description: "buffoon." No one would describe the next speaker as loose.

Dr. Patrick Mallet, a deputy superintendent from suburban British Columbia—a district adjacent to metro Vancouver—was enthusiastic and aggressive. He talked of dismissing bad teachers, of professional actions overriding political connections, of schools where principals could do what they needed to do. His message was two-pronged: schools needed autonomy to do what needed doing, and schools needed parents able to make choices about their child's education. "Create choices," he admonished attendees, "real choices." In his school, there was no beer; teachers were role models. The contrast to Dr. Weinard's first guest was not lost on the audience. But again, they turned restless as he showed overheads describing the notable failures of American schools over the previous ten years.

Where Willis Hislop was casual, Dr. Mallet was formal. He hectored. He bored his audience with noise.

Finally, at 20:40 hours, well over an hour into Dr. Weinard's team presentation, board chair Lydia Jacques asked for questions. Jake Harris, the "loose cannon" principal and a former assistant superintendent, was first up. He started; all teaching was direct. The leadership was strong in the district, "downtown and in schools." Schools were open here. His strongest objection was having a private school within a public system. That would be "unconscionable."

Jake Harris spoke with conviction. He had revised his speech, omitted some of the statements reportedly tested on colleagues, past and present. Those had been shared extensively, so the insiders knew that he had changed things up.

Dr. Weinard rose, claimed that Wapiti Falls would not be impressed with their students' test results relative to other districts with the same "socio-economic" profile. He challenged teachers to take up the challenge, to accept what he was offering.

Questions continued, and so did the audience's side conversations. Dr. Weinard plodded on, stressed "stunning results," and in his enthusiasm, he interrupted others. He challenged teachers to read the research, the findings he had cited.

Wapiti Falls principal Charles Kanouse accepted that challenge and turned it into a wager. If he could demonstrate that he knew the research, would Dr. Weinard then accept a counterchallenge, namely a visit to his school? Dr. Weinard accepted without hesitation. Then Charles Kanouse admitted that he had already read it and proved it with salient quotes. Now, having met Dr. Weinard's challenge, he tried pinning Dr. Weinard down. Kanouse suggested Thursday for Dr. Weinard's visit, two days hence. Clearly outmanoeuvred, Dr. Weinard backed away. Rather than considering other, more suitable dates, he redirected the conversation; he changed the focus. His new concern was about measuring variables.

Ed Noyce sat, impressively still. His former board chair, Margaret O'Connell, was not still. She looked around, saw that the audience was stirring. The audience's questions continued.

Dr. Mallet butted in, several times. He was here out of the goodness of his heart. In British Columbia, he was involved with thirty-nine school districts.

Mallet was impolite, seemingly on a mission. I wondered, was he working for free tonight? I also wondered if others in the audience shared my skepticism. They were restless.

Teachers, he said, typically have a negative reaction to change. To illustrate, the teachers he had worked with were opposed to the introduction of an International Baccalaureate program. His audience called him out on that, informed him that their district already had this program, and that no one had fought its introduction.

By now, the audience could see that Dr. Weinard's guests had not coordinated their presentations or learned about the district they were presenting in. If this evening had not been carefully thought out, what other detail in this grand reform proposal would not have been considered?

Herb Bondar directed a question to Dr. Mallet: are private schools better? Dr. Mallet responded, he did not think so, but choice was what was important. He bragged; his school in Abbotsford had attracted students away from a private school.

A lady stood to ask her question. In fifteen years of teaching, she had seen all that Dr. Weinard was proposing. None of it was new. So how would it work here? What were the logistics and comparable research findings?

Dr. Weinard's answer: the results would be better, and it would be cheaper. We will not need a central office.

She continued, what is it about your school that would make a difference?

It was its autonomy, Dr. Weinard stressed, and he read from his prepared materials.

Unsolicited comments came; questions about the research design, and about comparing his proposed school to a public school.

A retired district teacher and school administrator stood. He was a polished speaker and it showed. He liked innovation. Any innovation could show good results, but innovation was not the answer for all schools.

Phil Weinard became defensive, defiant. He was doing this for public education. It was hard work.

Another principal, Gavin Emerson, noted that the Weinard alternative school program was prescriptive, and asked, would that be best?

Two teachers got up and left. Both walked past Ed to a single-door exit; one patted him on the back. It was support. Interesting, as the usual exit, the main exit, was to the rear, but they chose a side exit. It was closest to the speakers and visible to all.

Dr. Weinard noted that to initiate this proposal, he would need strong parent support, 85 percent of parents within a school. No one took it up; they were not there as parents. But some were parents, and none showed any enthusiasm for his proposal.

A teacher asked, do parents want this? They can already move to the school of their choice, can't they?

Ed nodded in agreement. She did not pursue it further.

Another person rose. She qualified her question before asking it, admitted that it was late, and she may be getting dull, but who would be the researcher? Discussion continued.

I did not hear an answer but thought that it was too early for Dr. Weinard to have hired staff? Maybe this question was about administrative details, about planning. Was Dr. Weinard more of an idea person and not a detail person?

Trustee Paddy Nolan stood; he left but used the exit to the audience's rear. Unnoticed? Not likely.

Soon, chairperson Jacques was thanking people for attending. It was 21:43 hours. She asked that the audience share their thoughts with her. Gracious, unsure perhaps, she asked, was the district an impediment to getting this school going?

There was no answer. I thought it was obvious that Lydia Jacques was committed to improving schools.

The meeting was over—21:55 hours—and Ed chatted with various attendees. Ab Digby, assistant superintendent, believed that Phil (Weinard) had not earned any friends tonight. Still, he cautioned, Dr. Weinard would earn the support of parents, the audience for the next meeting. Ed asked for my views. I agreed; Dr. Weinard had upset his audience. Ed's conclusion was similar, and he marvelled that the speakers had not coordinated their approach. They had simply shown up.

Chairs were stacked and removed from the meeting space. Ruth Thompson, the assistant secretary-treasurer, and I chatted. She talked about some of the topics Jake had explored earlier, at the principals' meeting. He had definitely cooled down tonight.

Reports on an earlier version of Jake's speech had previously been delivered to me, three times, and the last two accounts had come from central office staff.

Mrs. Weinard struggled to put away their materials. She had expected one hundred fifty people, but there were probably only one hundred in attendance. Consequentially, she had a quantity of documents that she needed to pack up, to take home. She declined my offer of help.

Work and observations continued between the two critical meetings with Dr. Weinard: the district's business proceeded normally. Teachers, administrators, and others did their jobs. Ed shared his assessment of Dr. Weinard's progress—namely that it was proceeding as he had thought it would, as it should. Once again, a table summarizes salient features and thus avoids the longueur of a full account. Whereas the three previous tables summarized discussion by dates, Table 7 identifies the principal speaker and date before highlighting the discussion.

Table 7: September 28 to October 2: Paragon Alternative School Discussion Notes

Subject	Date	Action

Ed	Sept. 28	In an early morning meeting with Dale:
		    When asked, Ed did not think an 85 percent level of parent support was possible, but Dr. Weinard did.
		    Dr. Weinard's exemplars or variables did not include principal leadership, while most experts did. (As Ed had previously noted, Dr. Weinard added variables that he valued and omitted variables he did not value. Dr. Weinard thereby committed both errors of commission and omission.)
		With the senior admin team, during a discussion of last night's meeting with staff and Dr. Weinard:
		    Ed started the discussion by setting the tone, "It was all going according to script." Principals would be comfortable picking their staff but uncomfortable with the possibility that parent advisory councils might pick principals.
		    Ed's body language showed his involvement—good eye contact, inviting hand gestures, leaning in and out. He was playful. On the other hand, there was some sarcasm, which I interpreted as nerves.
		That afternoon, in a telephone conversation with his chair, Lydia Jacques:
		    Reviewed the meeting, namely that it went well. Promised elaboration of a win/win approach for board and Dr. Weinard. It would be presented that night.
		At 15:45 hours with principal Charles Kanouse:
		    After exchanging small talk on the day's events, Ed's parting comment was, "Thanks, Charles. I appreciated your comments last night."
		Later that afternoon, with Dale, advised that a presentation scheduled for tonight's board meeting had been reworked and improved.

		In the post-meeting debriefing, Ed mused on the comments he had made to trustee Hardy that night. In tempering trustee Hardy's enthusiasm with the reality of their fiscal limitations, Ed's frustration escaped in what he called his unacceptably "sharp" comments.
Senior Admin Team	Sept. 28	Wide-ranging discussion on the qualities of the speakers and staff reactions: Weinard's preferred American texts. Don Howard, deputy superintendent, proposed that the board co-opt Dr. Weinard's agenda. Despite a positive reaction, other topics were raised and discussed. Ab Digby, assistant superintendent human resources, gave a history on the district's centralized text program and its purpose. Initiated to facilitate student movement between schools, he described its impact as good for students and teachers. Don brought the discussion back to co-opting Dr. Weinard's proposal—the possible win/win scenario he had suggested earlier. Further discussion followed. Don viewed its critical advantage was that the board would "have control over it." The team agreed that it was time to bring the proposal to the board. Discussion on other topics continued.
Jake Harris	Sept. 28	In the mid-afternoon, Jake called Ed: Jake discussed his ongoing concerns, namely that the alternative school program would come to his school. Ed listened and offered reassurances, including his assessment that Dr. Weinard would not get his school.
Trustees	Sept. 28	Regular board meeting: Numerous staff utilized a coordinated team approach to present an overview of the district's Auditory Discrimination In-Depth Program which received an enthusiastic reception. Trustees wanted to expand it. Ed cooled their enthusiasm—the board's lack of additional money, and a reallocation of funds would mean that other important programs would receive less support, money. In camera session (absent minutes and everyone external to the board. While there was no press, my presence was deemed acceptable.) Don presented an option for in-house research in cooperation with Dr. Weinard. (My interpretation was that the board was very receptive and saw its potential as an "olive branch.")
Jake Harris	Sept. 29	On my arrival before 08:00 hours, Jake Harris was already in a closed-door meeting with Ed. I learned later that: Jake's concern that he would be out of a job had intensified overnight. Ed's response, was to stick to his message, refine it, and offer more—namely, Ed's emerging theory, which was that Dr. Weinard had too much negative baggage to make the alternative school work here. Nevertheless, he would continue to bad-mouth Wapiti Falls and Ed. (Further details on why Jake receives frequent mention is discussed in two appendices, Appendices J and K.)

Ed	Sept. 29	Investigation of achievement tests results and socio-economic status:
		    Checked and rechecked his facts in a phone call with Dr. Arnold Toth and then in a conversation with Dr. Weinard. Ed was triangulating the statements by Drs. Toth and Weinard, relative to provincial achievement test results.
		Ed's morning was ultra-busy:
		    Contacted school administrators to keep them in-the-loop, shared his concerns about principal Jake Harris, phoned a colleague in England.
		    (In my view, Ed's ceaseless activities had him taking on too much. It was uncharacteristic.)

Bill Bersche	Sept. 29	Shortly after 10:00 hours, advised Ed that: A cheque was received and deposited on behalf of the Paragon Alternative School. The donor wished to remain anonymous.

Ed	Sept. 30	Dale, from home:
		    Concerned, I phoned Ed to commiserate with him; yesterday had been difficult. He agreed.
		    I also needed to set my next observation date to accommodate my own interview for a new job. The date I proposed suited him.
		    He offered me advice for my interview. This response had me thinking, as busy as he was, he still had time for me.
		At my office at the end of the day:
		    Found a fax addressed to Dr. Weinard that Ed had copied to me. It was Ed's interpretation of district students' achievement test results. He invited Dr. Weinard to respond, writing "It is important that our Board of Trustees have the full information." This letter effectively declared Ed's limits, namely, no more unsubstantiated claims.

Dr. Weinard	Oct. 2	The *Wapiti Falls Cascade* newspaper: Published Dr. Weinard's reply to an earlier letter to the editor that criticized the alternative school proposal. He made his point and invited parents to the meeting coming up on October 5.

Table 7 summarized events over four days but did so at the expense of temporal order. Appendices for these four days preserve the correct order and add further details. These appendices are:

- Appendix I: "September 28 – Narrative Discussion on the Paragon Alternative School"
- Appendix J: "September 29 – Narrative Discussion on the Paragon Alternative School"
- Appendix K: "September 30 and October 2 – Narrative Discussion on the Paragon Alternative School."

October 5: The Three Letter Campaign

Upon my arrival at district offices, 07:45 hours on October 5, and after exchanging greetings with the receptionist, I went to a small committee room, and got out my things in preparation for this long and important day. Ed came in soon after. It was a Wednesday, and as with every observation day, we started with a cup of coffee. Others had already gathered in the coffee room. Someone suggested that there were still tickets to the upcoming Rolling Stones concert and teased that Ed might like them. Having previously described his musical interests as "more tuneful," Ed said he was "not interested." As requested, I had brought materials from my home district on program evaluations and celebrations, and I returned a book he had loaned me. He passed me two letters from Dr. Weinard and asked me to review them. I glanced at them as we chatted.

This review kept me busy, listening and trying to take in the significance of two nearly identical letters. Only during later analysis, did I understand that both were responses to Ed's declarative letter of September 30.

Dr. Weinard had composed two letters—faxed letters. Ed had both. Why two nearly duplicate letters? Each looked the same, but Ed pointed out that they had different dates. Ed was not on the list to receive the letter dated September 30; his copy came from someone on the "cc" list. Ed had me start there, at the "cc" version. In it, Dr. Weinard reasserted that Wapiti Falls' test results were inferior to what they should have been given the socio-economic status of their community. He also stated that he was trying to help education, not hurt it. Next, Ed had me look at the second letter—the letter sent directly to him. It was almost identical to the "cc" version, but more personal. Dr. Weinard had added one additional point—namely, that he and Ed were both good people. He elaborated—wherever he went, he spoke highly of Ed Noyce.

I did my best to carefully reread each letter, but I could not keep up as Ed's update continued unabated. Ed had also sent a letter to Alberta Education's Dr. Arnold Toth. He candidly announced that it was intended to frustrate Dr. Toth. That I understood. Dr. Toth had supplied the ammunition that Dr. Weinard was using to attack Wapiti Falls Consolidated School District. What was this ammunition? It consisted of a study of individual school results matched to their community profile. This, in Dr. Weinard's view, showed socio-economic data linked to test results. Ed told Dr. Toth, that if Dr. Weinard had it, so should he. Ed soon had a copy, a single page report. But Ed was not finished. He had asked Dr. Toth for a socio-economic analysis for each school in Wapiti Falls—namely, school test results relative to each school's socio-economic status. Further, since students in Wapiti Falls were free to move outside their school attendance area—and move they did—what was the net impact? Ed knew that such data did not exist, he said as much, but I could see that he was on a mission.

Here, early on October 5, Ed's attention was occupied by three letters, two received and one sent out as retribution. Perhaps referencing these three items as a "campaign" is an overstatement, but whatever the label, these three documents provided important information, explicit and subtextual perspectives.

October 5: Analysis of the Three Letter Campaign

Ed's update was brief, finished in a half-hour. He was doing other business by 08:15 hours, and I had no time to think things through. These three documents were related and important, but what should I make of them? It took some thought and right then I was busy. At the time, my goal was to get a fix on Ed's current actions and thoughts. Later, when I got to it, I understood more. Understanding more required starting with a review of Alberta's Achievement Test program.

Back then, students in Grades 3, 6 and 9 wrote achievement tests each spring in language arts and mathematics. Their purpose was to assist instruction and, of course, to monitor how well teachers were doing—reassurance for an anxious public. They provided teachers and administrators with solid data but did so by supplying school and district results rather than individual scores. The results simply stated the percentage of students scoring at an acceptable standard and at the standard of excellence. This was all well and good except Dr. Weinard was using local results as a hammer to show that Wapiti Falls students were underperforming given their socio-economic status. Ed had reviewed his district and school results and was surprised with Dr. Weinard's claim. Still, he investigated and found a possibility, a single page report.

Ed had repeatedly said that he would take Dr. Weinard to task for making misleading statements, and now he had the facts to challenge him. His salvo, a letter of September 30 "Re: Achievement Test Comparisons," told Dr. Weinard that enough was enough. Note Ed's effort to obtain data verification and the unstated but underlying issues of trust.

Ed started by reviewing the process used to find the comparison data. It involved several rounds of discussion between himself and Drs. Weinard and Toth. With the data in hand, he noted that no results in the report involved schools in the Wapiti Falls Consolidated School District. He therefore stated the obvious, namely that claims linking inferior district results to "socioeconomic status cannot be made." Next, he posted local results next to provincial averages. District results were better. None of this fit, but still, none of it had stopped Dr. Weinard from disparaging comments. So, he asked Dr. Weinard, in writing, did he have the right data?

Without waiting for Dr. Weinard to reply, Ed had sufficient information to arrive at his three conclusions. He took it up:

1. There are no comparisons involving socio-economic status and Grade 9 mathematics achievement tests because the study results do not indicate socio-economic status. They simply described types of communities.
2. After reviewing school results in the each of the district's five junior high schools, he found "no cause for alarm or even concern."
3. Given our "District's Achievement Test" results, we should celebrate our accomplishments.

His letter ended by repeating of his earlier request:

> "If these statistics are not the source of your comments during the meeting with our staff, I would invite you to contact me again. It is important that our Board of Trustees have the full information."

Ed had promised to confront Dr. Weinard's extraordinary claims that district results were inferior and this missive of September 30, hit that target straight on. Would Dr. Weinard reply? (Additional details on the letter and on test results are found in Appendix K September 30 and October 2 – Narrative Discussion on the Paragon Alternative School.)

Ed had two letters but were they a reply? Could they be a diversion rather than a reply?

I had to look deeper. Dr. Weinard's two letters were summarized above, but look now at what he did not say. He made claims about the district's woeful results, ignored the legitimate results provided, and presented no alternative results. Strangely incomplete. What should Ed make of this. Ed never shared his thoughts on this, but I had enough to begin further analysis.

I condensed a longer list into three issues: First, what results was Dr. Weinard using? Second, with respect to the personal letter sent directly to Ed, why would Dr. Weinard assume that Ed would not learn the facts behind his claim of always speaking well of Ed. And third, why was no one talking about the elementary school that had outstanding achievement test results?

Consider the first issue: Ed found, investigated, and shared his findings with Dr. Weinard. He then asked Dr. Weinard if he had the correct data or if there was other data. Dr. Weinard wrote back but his reply was evasive; he neither refuted Ed's claims nor did he supply other relevant numbers. Could Dr. Weinard be mistaken? Had he taken results from the other Wapiti Falls district and assumed they were from the public district? The local Catholic district could have similar sized schools. They had both the "large urban" and "mid-size urban" schools referred to in the Grade 9 mathematics achievement test report. But these higher enrollment schools had superior results. Either district, public or Catholic, would have been satisfied with them. So why had neither party mentioned Catholic schools? I looked at the six school results again, no pattern was obvious. Nothing reflected Dr. Weinard's claim. There was not much wiggle room for interpretation, but there was some history. Dr. Weinard had committed the sins of omission and commission before. And he had never admitted a mistake. If the study that Dr. Weinard had led Ed to was his source, the only conclusion possible was that Dr. Weinard was lying once again.

Second, why send two almost identical letters? Dr. Weinard said in one letter that he spoke well of Ed when outside the district, but Ed had other reports, both verbal and televised segments, that proved otherwise. And had he forgotten that even inside the district, at the June 22 regular board meeting, he had complained of being held back because he neither the support of the board or its superintendent? Was that not publicly pointing fingers?

So again, why two letters? Was Dr. Weinard stressed? Was he feeling the same tension that gripped others in the district? Did he worry about being publicly exposed for making claims without supportive data, for using data questionably, for relying on suspect interpretations, or for ethics that were, at best, shoddy? Had his proposal created a crisis at both ends of the quest?

Or had Ed held back? If he had asked Dr. Weinard to provide numbers he did not have, would Dr. Weinard simply change tactics? Dr. Weinard did that in a meeting with teachers; he switched things up by answering questions not asked or he started a new topic. With a switch, perhaps Dr. Weinard's quest of some four-plus years, could be restarted, reinvigorated. But by not forcing this issue, there would be no reason for delay. And so, Dr. Weinard would make his pitch at the parent meeting, confident that parents would want their kids in his model school.

That fit Ed's plan. He needed parents to decide on the fate of the Paragon Alternative School in Wapiti Falls. Ed wanted Dr. Weinard to finish what he had started. That made "all kinds of sense."

Third, I wondered why, in all this hubbub about achievement tests, no one looked to the one Wapiti Falls district school with extraordinary results. It was a larger elementary school, and 100 percent of their Grade 6 students had achieved at the satisfactory score level. And if any school in the district had a lower socio-economic status than average, Goodwater School would be it. Located in an older area of Wapiti Falls, this school's attendance area was less affluent. It had a mix of rental properties—older, smaller properties, and apartments—as well as less expensive, older, owner-occupied homes. These students would likely change schools more than those from other areas. And yet Goodwater School was so successful that it attracted students from the district's upscale communities. It could have been a "magnet school," except that the district did not compare schools or brag. The district did not even mention it except in passing. Why not use these results as bragging rights for that school, for the entire district?

Under Ed's leadership, the district's achievement test results would never become a system to rate individual schools or teachers. But others had used them in just that way. The weekly magazine *Our Alberta* had made the unauthorized release of individual schools' achievement test results, school by school, and province-wide, one of their signature achievements, their cause célèbre, a highlight in their annual report on education.

My conclusion was straight forward: First, Dr. Weinard did not have the facts he claimed to have. Second, Ed did not want Dr. Weinard to weasel out of his spurious claim by changing tactics. Third, while district results were satisfactory or better, they would not be used as tools to promote schools or the district. So much for achievement tests and Dr. Weinard's claims of local results that would dismay local residents. Look now to Dr. Toth's department and Ed's aggressive written request.

Dr. Toth oversaw the achievement test program, and while he supported their instructional purposes, he had silently watched as the tests morphed into a competition between schools. The Fraser Institute, a policy think tank, and the weekly magazine, *Our Alberta*, both published the "unauthorized" results, which included their well-known rightward tilt. The teachers' union complained that these reports were less about rating schools and more about rating teachers, but Dr. Arnold Toth watched this process silently. No one in Alberta Education seemed to care.

Ed had alluded to what he viewed as menacing practices perpetrated by Dr. Toth and his departmental colleagues—namely, that they were under the spell of their boss, Dr. Giuseppe Garibaldi, the deputy minister of education. Why was that a problem? Like Ed, the deputy was a professional educator, and like Ed, he served two masters, educational and political. But unlike Ed, Dr. Garibaldi leaned political. Political expediency drove his actions. It was all too much for Ed. And Dr. Toth was not a solitary minion of the deputy; Ed saw ever more Alberta Education staff mimicking their boss's attitudes and leadership style.

So why did Ed send the letter? In my view, Ed was poking Alberta Education in the eye. Having sent it, he felt good; he was beyond caring what Dr. Toth and others thought. Ed valued principled and ethical behaviour.

Here we have two incidents: a letter-writing Dr. Weinard and a letter-receiving Dr. Toth. Dr. Weinard was unethical and unpredictable, and Dr. Toth's ethics appeared to be malleable. Ed found both troubling. Ed, while visibly in full control, inside he showed his anger. He was mad. A "poke in the eye," from Ed? He revealed his feelings here, obliquely. After considerable reflection, I could only conclude that Ed's logic was not in perfect working order.

October 5: The Regular Workday

Ed's update at 07:45 hours started another typical day; it was busy normal. Following the update, Ab Digby dropped by the office with a video. Made in Saskatoon, a larger city in our neighbouring province, he described the video as refuting Dr. Weinard's guiding principles.

The senior admin meeting would start soon, around 08:15 hours. It began with their usual roundtable discussion of issues and updates. Each administrator reviewed their items and the round table discussion began. It was the normal cycle of business. When it was Ed's turn, maybe a half-hour into the meeting, he started by telling the team that Dr. Arnold Toth would not be eager to take calls from Wapiti Falls Consolidated. He explained why, in depth. Left unsaid, I knew that Ed's missive was more than an oblique request for more care and help. His letter would ramp up tensions. Increasing tension was not Ed's typical leadership initiative, but there it was.

Ruth Thompson, assistant secretary-treasurer, asked Ed if there had been any response from Phil Weinard. Everyone seemed to know that there had been, and Ed confirmed it. He spoke about the two Weinard letters and promised them copies.

Private matters were being shared, another surprise for me. Was there an operational distinction to this openness? Maybe if it was business, it was not personal or private.

The team discussed parental choices in schools. Ed suggested that Calgary might soon be the first-ever setting for a private school in the Dr. Weinard mould; Weinard was now optimistic about that possibility. Ed's team of senior administrators was fully engaged. They discussed the meeting that evening, possible trustee reaction, and charter schools. Twists on old topics were worked over: was Dr. Weinard really proposing a "charter" school or an "alternative" school? How would site-based management affect schools? Someone asked, "Hasn't the province co-opted this aspect of the Weinard agenda—the local 'school-based control' agenda? Did the district need their principals to 'declare allegiance'?"

This last reference may have been a shot at a local principal, but who? Jake Harris's name was mentioned, not as a convert, but as a thorn. They wondered about his coming antics, but in his encounter with Dr. Weinard a week earlier, he had been reasonable—not fanatical. Some teachers were expected to be in attendance tonight. There as both teachers and parents, Ed hoped that they would not take over from other parents. Ruth lightened the mood; her vision had the parties asking for forgiveness—crossing themselves and saying their prayers. Cute, a Catholic vision cited in a nominally Protestant district.

It was now 09:51 hours, about an hour on this single alternate school issue, and they were nearly done. Logistics for the meeting tonight were reviewed—coffee, sign-in sheets, and more. Ed indicated that one community, Cheyenne, was keen on the concept and would have two people at the meeting. Then the meeting was over, and Ed and I were left alone.

Ed sat quietly, but I thought he wanted to talk. Maybe it would be background chatter hiding the real conversation going on in his thoughts. We chatted about events outside the district, and about politicians, and then about the personal growth he saw in his administrative team.

There were soon a couple of calls. One was from the *Calgary Mercury*. When it ended, Ed admitted that he had tried not to say too much. (He had succeeded.) Another was from his official liaison contact at Alberta Education, Sharon. She was new to this area, so Ed brought her up to speed: Their conversation soon came around to Dr. Phil Weinard. His board supported the Paragon Alternative School "in principle." Dr. Weinard was currently working to obtain community support. Phil Weinard, Ed told her, was a "very interesting person." That portion of the exchange was finished, and Ed listened, then agreed, that is "very significant, Sharon." Shortly, Ed was saying, tonight, Dr. Weinard will be on his "apple box." Ed confirmed that she had the phone number for Walter MacEwan High School, and the call ended. It had started with a question about a recent student expulsion at Walter MacEwan High School but ended up focusing on Dr. Phil Weinard.

There was a brief break from the alternative school business when Ed went to his secretary. There he reviewed the material intended for the Accommodation Committee's noon meeting. He returned and did some work but soon he was on the way to coffee. On his return, he checked the room where the evening meeting would take place. He rearranged chairs to leave space for an overhead projector. When he left to get lens cleaner, I worked on the mirror. He returned, said that my efforts to clean the mirror would not help. What mattered was screen position, the proper focus. (So why, I thought, had he fetched lens cleaner?)

Everyday work continued. Soon it was 11:50 hours, and Ed went to the room where the Accommodation Committee would meet. Members were gathering and chatting. Comments about the Weinard school proposal were heard. Ed told them that he had challenged Dr. Weinard's claim that Wapiti Falls students had not done well on provincial achievement exams. District students, he said, had exceeded average provincial scores. He waited, nibbled on a few sandwiches. Conversations continued. Someone indicated education was in a mess. The chair of the committee arrived and soon had the members on task.

After the committee meeting ended, about 13:50 hours, Ed went on to other jobs: a meeting in a downtown office, a discussion of finances, drafting student expulsion letters, a TV interview, a long supportive call to a discouraged member of the Accommodations Committee, a call to the union representative to set up another meeting. Finally, he told me that his day was about done. By 16:19, he was out of his office, but I knew he was still there, somewhere. Another ten to twenty minutes passed, and his car was no longer in the parking lot. Now, he was really gone.

The *Edmonton Diary* anticipated the results of the meeting that evening by declaring that the alternative school was almost there. The article continued, advising readers that Weinard will pitch the idea to Wapiti Falls school councils tonight. Last week, he pitched the idea to the district's teachers and had received about thirty calls of support. Tonight's meeting would be crucial. As an aid, they offered a special block insert telling readers what they needed to know about "Charter" schools.

The reported "thirty calls of support" was a surprising detail, something unknown to the district or their staff. Then again, why would supporters contact the Wapiti Falls School District? Another question came to mind about the calls of support: were they from parents or backers? Dr. Weinard had many vocal moral and financial supporters.

CHAPTER 11

October 5, Crisis—Trust the Parents

To get his school, Dr. Weinard had to persuade parents that his school would deliver a better education than that offered by Wapiti Falls Public. Presentations that night would make all the difference. He knew it and was prepared. Confident that his product and his presentation were superior, he would persuade parents to switch schools. The district knew it was important, too. They had reserved their most prestigious space available for this meeting, and that space was the boardroom of the Wapiti Falls Consolidated School District #1. To arrive there, parents would walk past photographs of each district school, an entire wall of the schools that they had gone to, or that their children had attended or were attending now. The district's building would help do battle with Dr. Weinard's reform proposal.

Board Meeting Room with Trustee Workstations.

It was a lovely fall day, and the sunlight still streamed through the north windows as I signed in at 18:40 hours. The seating configuration used for board meetings had disappeared. The semi-circle of desks, each with an executive chair, was now elsewhere, as were the rectangular tables and chairs that normally filled the public space. It was simpler now, a small head table facing rows of chairs placed widthwise across the room—theatre style. Behind the head table, Dr. Weinard had posted his research correlates.

My vantage point was towards the back, near two secretaries from the district office, and alongside Ab Digby, assistant superintendent. A lady unknown to me was on the other side. A few older couples were already there, midway between front and back. My guess was that they were from funding agencies. Trustees, other than chair Lydia Jacques, were scattered throughout the room. She was at the front. People arrived, looked into the room, and seeing that it would soon be full, entered

Boardroom with Seating for Public Meeting.

and sat. Former chair Margaret O'Connell was nearby. People looked anxious, at least the ones who asked Margaret O'Connell to quiet down. Margaret had been speaking out clearly in direct opposition to the alternative school proposal. Perhaps these folks did not want to hear what she had to say.

Lydia Jacques, board chair, opened the meeting at 19:03 hours. Her comments were like those of the week before when she stood and addressed teachers. Tonight she spoke about the format for the evening's meeting, why the vote approving the Paragon Alternative School was taken, the conditions attached to the board's "approval in principle," and the difficulty the board had had with the proposal. The board had not been unanimous with their vote of support. Again, she stressed that to open the alternative school, there must be strong parental support. If parents want this school, they had to go back to their parent advisory council (PAC) and request another meeting. Their PAC would, with the assistance of the superintendent, organize a meeting of the school's entire parent body. There, parents would discuss the proposal and vote, for or against it. If the vote reached 80 to 85 percent support, then Dr. Weinard's school expectations would be reviewed, and if still acceptable to parents, a board of governors would be selected. She promised that the full board would be at such a meeting, just as they were tonight. Lydia was succinct and sensible. Her audience listened and understood. Finished, she invited Ed Noyce, superintendent, to speak.

Ed rose and read his prepared speech. He started with compliments all around and spoke of successful changes already made. It was like his speech the previous week, except now he spoke about the ways parents would know the district: he complimented their children's teachers, the parent's role in developing the district's strategic plan, and their knowledge of the challenging shift to middle schools. He then shifted his focus to Dr. Weinard. The purpose of this meeting was to give parents the opportunity to ask their questions. If they had questions for him, he would do his best to answer. He was done and returned to his chair. The chair and superintendent had split their time about evenly, fifteen minutes for the two of them.

Dr. Weinard stood at 19:17 hours and talked about the uncharted course ahead. His purpose was not to criticize the Wapiti Falls Consolidated School District; his purpose was about doing education better. This school would not be elitist; it was just that public schools were not working. After five years of development, this proposal is a co-winner of a recent prize, selected over eight hundred other proposals. Some district staff supported his proposal. Now he needed supportive parents to initiate an alternative school; 80 percent of the parent population of a school would probably work. His confidence was obvious, and to highlight how strong the proposal was, he stated that this school would proceed with or without Wapiti Falls. He moved on to international comparisons and noted how poorly our country's students were doing. Having established the need, Dr. Weinard discussed the "educational markers that count," his research on effective schools. He discounted any possible contribution from the central office.

People were quiet and attentive; it was still early, 19:43 hours. He began introducing terminology relevant to his proposal. He referenced "phonemics" but spoke about phonics. Different words and different meanings.

Phonemics is a branch of linguistics involving phonemes or sounds, and phonics is a method of teaching reading. My untutored experience was that "phonemics" was just a more sophisticated term than phonics; it was an upscale equivalency. Whatever the distinction, I soon heard and wrote it all as phonics.

Weinard claimed that in Wapiti Falls, a student could get instruction in phonics, but only after failing. He introduced his two speakers, both educators from public boards: Beata Nilsson, an Ontario principal, and Dr. Patrick Mallet, a deputy superintendent from British Columbia. Dr. Mallet had addressed teachers in Wapiti Falls earlier, September 27. Beata Nilsson was a recruit, replacing the beer- and barbeque-loving Willis Hislop. Dr. Weinard sat down to the same silence that Lydia and Ed experienced. The first speaker, Beata, would receive a different response.

Beata Nilsson spoke softly, softly enough that people strained to hear her, but they did strain. They liked her thoughtful, egalitarian comments. As she spoke, I surveyed the audience. Esther Hoffman, chair of the Calgary Board of Education, was in attendance. (I noticed her because Ed had told me that Calgary was interested in Dr. Weinard's school concept and would likely have a trustee at the meeting. Accordingly, Ed had invited her as a district guest.)

Beata spoke about teaching, about the difficulty in reaching and maintaining a consensus. A charter school, organized on an agreed-upon focus, would start with an unanimity of direction. She connected what she did in her school to what Dr. Weinard was proposing. She complimented Dr. Weinard; she was a team player. Beata continued talking about her school, and its traditional rules and expectations. Some neighbours whispered quietly as she spoke about lining students up outside and walking them silently to their classes. In her school, students stood when an adult entered the room. There was less fighting in her school than other schools, leaving more time for teaching. She talked about her parents liking Dr. Weinard's videotape. She finished, and the audience clapped.

Dr. Patrick Mallet was up next and eager; he launched into his talk. He was here because he believed in this school. It was about parental choice within the public school system. He struck out at anecdotal report cards; they lacked accountability. And open classrooms, no one wanted them, but we got them.

Was this idea still alive? I asked the lady beside me if she knew what open classrooms were. She did; she had heard about them in college. Obviously, my neighbour was informed about education; maybe, as I soon learned, it was partly because she had a sister teaching in China. It was also obvious that she was no fan of Dr. Weinard.

Patrick Mallet went on and on. He gave examples of school failures, cited the student dropout rate. He said that it was all about caring for kids; care generated commitment, and commitment made all the difference. Mallet demonstrated some effective public speaking practices: he used short, snappy, dramatic sentences. He modulated his voice and repeated phrases for emphasis. He asked, "Who can refute these markers of educational success?" His attack continued by citing failures of the entire educational system, of jobs going unfilled while unemployment was high, and of courts where judges made decisions that robbed schools of funds due them. (It had been well publicized that school boards in his province were paying court-ordered damages to parents.) At 20:45 hours, Dr. Mallet delivered his closer, "I support this choice," but instead of quitting, he continued. He just had to talk about no-smoking policies. No one cared; this was an audience of parents with elementary-aged children—non-smokers. Then he chastised people because they did not have enough "guts" to do something. He went on a bit more and finally sat, and his audience clapped—perfunctorily and briefly. They were ready for questions.

Dr. Weinard and guests had spoken for just shy of an hour and a half. While it was 20:45 hours, no one wanted to be the first to ask a question. After a noticeable pause, a young parent asked about programs for students with disabilities and French immersion. Dr. Weinard critiqued French immersion as an elite program in the public system. Then he pulled out a report from the teachers' union titled, "Trying to Teach." Teachers, Dr. Weinard railed, want site-based decisions. The questioner sat, but he did not look happy.

The next parent identified herself as both a parent and a teacher assistant. She prefaced her two questions by criticizing their lack of time to ask questions and concluded that the evening was not well-planned. She asked her first question: what would happen to the 20 percent of parents who did not want their children in this alternative school? She continued to her second question. It was about research design; what if the group was not "typical?" In his answer, Dr. Weinard identified his target population—"middle to lower socio-economic students"—and as to students who don't want to be in the school, "dissenters," they would be elsewhere. To fill enrollment numbers, they would pull students from a waiting list. Looking around, I saw several heads expressing wonder. Dr. Weinard delivered further comments that jumped around the question, but he ended crisply, clearly. Parents should go back to their home schools and talk about it.

The third questioner returned to the theme of "high needs" students. This questioner asked, since high needs students were not in your school, where would they be? Dr. Weinard answered, the alternative school would do a good job. Beata Nilsson recognized danger, so she stood, reassured all that they would do what was best for students. It was now 20:55 hours.

Dr. Patrick Mallet stood again, ready to contribute, ready to confront the naysayers. He asked, politely, if he could speak. Recognized by the chair, he talked about disruptive students, and the need to get them out of schools. This, he explained, was a failure of public schools and the judicial system.

The fourth questioner pointed out that it would be "very hard" to get 85 percent parent support. He suggested starting smaller, a school within a school, or perhaps with Grades 1 to 3. Phil Weinard stood and agreed, "I would love this." Beata spoke about her school start-up. The parent was up again and asked for clarification, further explanation. The room was buzzing. Chair Lydia asked a question. Others were whispering. (I did my best to hear the whispers while struggling to catch the dialogue between parent and presenters.) I just made out this from the parent; her school had a small group of students doing French. Now, Dr. Phil Weinard jumped back in, involved. He had not understood before but did now. The research model, he told parents, required that the full school participate in the study. He repeated, he needed a whole school.

Harold Wilder, a member of a school parent advisory council and a professor at Wapiti Falls College, stood. He noted that there was an implicit threat in this proposal, that students cooperate or else. What would happen to those "or else" students? Dr. Weinard, assisted by Beata Nilsson, promised that they would do their best to keep students in school, to help them be successful. They would "bend over backwards" to help. More chatter emerged from the audience.

It was about 21:14 hours, and Dr. Weinard talked about his choice of a reading text. But Dr. Wilder persisted, "What is being done differently" in this proposed school relative to what Wapiti Falls School District was already doing? Not waiting for an answer, he followed with another question to the Weinard team: when was the last time you were in a Wapiti Falls school? Dr. Weinard said that he was in G. W. Smith about three years ago.

My seat neighbour explained, after that the Weinards pulled their daughter out and sent her to a private school on Vancouver Island. When she returned, her description of the difference between the schools was succinct; they had uniforms in the private school.

Meanwhile, Dr. Phil Weinard explained that a visit would not tell if they were utilizing "phonemic readiness tests."

The chatter increased. Esther Hoffman, chair of the Calgary Board of Education, left.

Gossip about her departure was in the air the next day—namely, that as she and her husband walked out, she apologized for bringing him and was afraid that he would never want to come to an educational meeting again.

Mrs. Weinard watched from the back of the room as Beata Nilsson addressed the audience. The contrast was obvious. Ms. Nilsson was engaged, loyally assisting her evening's employer. Mrs. Weinard watched and waited, impassive; she had heard much of this before, several times. At least Phil Weinard's stump phrase, the one I had heard several times on previous occasions, "stunning results," was only offered once that night.

Any number of hands were now up, people were suddenly eager to pose their questions. One was recognized and asked Dr. Weinard to clarify the contrast between his proposal and what the district was already doing. She added that she volunteered in schools; she helped kids read. She thought that an eclectic model was superior to the inflexible model Dr. Weinard was proposing.

Dr. Patrick Mallet jumped to his feet and asked what the dropout rate was in Wapiti Falls. He was ignored as more questions poured forth; some were recognized by the chair. Another parent volunteer lamented the lack of instruction in phonics.

Soon, a parent recognized by the chair had a different question. She asked, what would Dr. Weinard propose for children who read when they entered school? Dr. Weinard referred this question to Beata Nilsson. Beata talked about the ideal—parallel instruction.

Dr. Patrick Mallet returned to his question about the dropout rate. In his district, they had changed the dropout rate from 40 percent to 20 percent. He heard that it was 6 percent in Wapiti Falls and computed this to mean 30 percent over their years in high school.

Were parents doing the calculation? Was he really saying 30 percent? Would that be his announced 6 percent times five years? Who had five years of high school? Someone apparently had done similar calculations because the shout back was that means 110 percent over five years. The numbers were flying, incorrectly, when Ed stepped forward and asked to speak.

People listened. He did not want the student dropout rate to be zero; some students needed to leave school. Some also returned to school. The elementary dropout rate was zero. Ed spoke to this audience, the parents with elementary-aged children, and not to some other audience, not to the ones that might care about dropout rates.

Deputy superintendent Don Howard added his voice. He offered parents more numbers: "Wapiti Falls has a 6 percent annual dropout rate…but long term, our dropout rate is 17 percent."

Again, I silently ran the numbers and could not make them work. Could it be because some students drop in and out of school? Dr. Patrick Mallet, apparently needing the last word, responded, but I could not catch his last word. There were other comments louder than his. All these different threads were confusing.

A mother, another parent volunteer, was recognized next. She was the eighth parent questioner. I suspected that she was a former teacher. Her children's school, she said, complied with every correlate that Dr. Weinard had listed. Dr. Weinard started his reply as she elaborated. She was nearly finished when he described this as anecdotal evidence and asked, but did she see the results from CTBS, the Canadian Test of Basic Skills? She had. And she remained standing; she was going to continue. She told Dr. Weinard that he was wrong, public schools do work. Dr. Weinard insisted that this was research, not an attack on your school. Beata Nilsson came in to help. She told the audience that the focus in this school would remain steady, focused. It was the commitment of the school, and a guarantee.

The next questioner was a parent who stated that Dr. Weinard was selling parents short. Phil Weinard countered, but again the parent continued. There had been a lot of changes in the last five years. The teachers and parents compared their Grade 3 students. What research do you have, Dr. Weinard? Dr. Weinard admitted, he did not do research, but he did his homework. He had an American study, and then he rambled on about research.

An older man was up, leaving, "I can't wait any longer." Had he had enough of the meeting, or was it a bathroom break that he needed. I did not notice if he returned.

Dr. Weinard continued lecturing his audience. Dr. Mallet tried to interrupt, but Weinard continued.

Chairperson Lydia Jacques asked Beata Nilsson, what kind of phonics test do you use at your school?

Beata Nilsson replied, she did not do a phonics test. She used CTBS (Canadian Test of Basic Schools) and another test. Dr. Patrick Mallet stood and talked about a Minnesota test, and named still more tests. He was ignored. This allowed Beata Nilsson to continue. Our textbook has a higher vocabulary than others. She picked this text when she got a new school and new budget. Someone asked if she supplemented the text. She did not, but she did add some novels.

The guests began to argue amongst themselves as to whether a test of phonics awareness actually existed.

The audience was listening, figuring things out, learning that a key element in Dr. Weinard's approach might not even exist? If wrong about this, what else was he wrong about?

The next questioner prefaced his remarks with, "I am not here to argue." Should the research go forward, he asked, what was the control group? The design, he knew, needed to be good. Dr. Weinard was pleased to respond: the scholars agree, they need to match students on socio-economic levels. The research protocol needed to be tight.

Ed entered the discussion and talked about longitudinal data. He believed that the research design was the most difficult step.

Dr. Patrick Mallet was heard, "It can be done." It was 21:35 hours.

The questioner continued and asked about research design. What in this design would be different than what Wapiti Falls Consolidated was already doing? There was already a lot of parent involvement and autonomy. Dr. Weinard disagreed.

Two other questions followed in short order. A teacher asked, "Is it too much, too fast?" In the light of government cutbacks, was now the right time? Someone clapped, but that response soon died out.

Dr. Weinard said that he recognized that teachers cared. Measuring results would be disruptive, but only at the start. He stood quiet, determined, then suggested two or three more questions.

Beata Nilsson was asked to discuss the advantages of the reader she used over other readers. She answered, the series *Open Court* was consistent in its approach to reading.

Another questioner suggested that they should give teachers more credit. They could come together. It happened all the time. Beata agreed, it did, but it would be faster if we started out with the same philosophy.

Mark Cobb, teachers' union representative, was up; he stated that he had waited to get in the last question, the last word. Reading from Dr. Weinard's handouts, he asked, what do you mean that the school will be "free of the control of the teachers' union?"

Dr. Weinard advised that it meant that teachers would have to sort things out, that they would need to agree to this condition.

That was it. The chair had actually covered this in her opening remarks with her statement that collective agreements would be honoured. Perhaps the union needed to ask their question, but for parents, union matters were simply a non-issue.

At 21:40 hours, chair Lydia Jacques stood, ready to adjourn the meeting. Before doing so, she repeated the directions stated earlier; parents interested in pursuing this school needed to get back to the board, through superintendent Ed Noyce and before the end of October. If not, the proposal was dead. She closed the meeting. As the audience left, reporters entered. Professor Harold Wilder moved to sit beside Ab Digby. He and Ab talked about the changes already made in the district, about the new strategic plan, and about changes the province was expected to announce concerning the School Act. He concluded that Dr. Weinard's agenda had been "co-opted" by the province. Asked for an interview, Professor Wilder declined.

After his interview with a reporter from the *Wapiti Falls Cascade*, Ed talked quietly and privately with Dr. Patrick Mallet. It looked pleasant enough, but was it? Ed had been frustrated with comments made by Dr. Mallet in the earlier meeting with teachers. Once again, Mallet had made unfounded assumptions about the Wapiti Falls district, about their dropout rate. By 22:10 hours, Ed was on another interview, this time with the local television station.

As trustee Peter Svarich was being interviewed, one of the older men, not a parent, jostled into position to hear Peter's assessment. He left when the interviewer turned to trustee Gwen Ramots. I wondered if the gentleman had wanted to hear the thoughts of a supporter but cared not what someone who might disagree thought. Unfortunately, I was too far away to eavesdrop.

It was 22:10 hours, and the "officially" finished meeting was now really over. Most everyone was gone. Three of us remained: Ed; Ruth Thompson, the assistant secretary-treasurer; and me. I congratulated Ed on a good night's work. His reply shocked me, "It was a disaster." Factions would be fighting. They would keep "nipping away." The community was divided. Schools would compete over test results. He wondered about that. Talking to himself after the meeting, he mentioned Goodwater school results and asked, "What do schools have to do to prove themselves?"

He continued, talked about the "plants" in the meeting.

Ruth Thompson replied, she had seen no "plants."

Her interjection helped, and Ed quietly backed off. He said that he would be talking to Dr. Weinard. Weinard could not continue demoralizing staff and parents, always attacking, always divisive. Somehow, he had already arranged a meeting with Dr. Weinard, next week, at a restaurant. Ruth teased. She asked, "Who would pay?"

I thanked Ed for what he had done for me. His response, "Too bad it was all bad." He was serious.

Analysis: October 5, Crisis—Trust the Parents

This meeting was the culmination of Ed's efforts to give Dr. Weinard all the scope he needed to either sell his project or to end it in the Wapiti Falls Consolidated School District. Ed wanted parents to have the final decision; he trusted them to make the best decision about their children.

They had asked their questions. They had listened. Ed did not interfere; he interrupted twice, once to express his trust in students—even as they dropped in and out of school—and once to stress the importance of research design. The parents made their decision. They knew what they should do, and that was to turn away from Dr. Weinard's Paragon Alternative School.

Finally done, Ed's process had been hard work, and he was now paying a price. His words about a "disastrous" meeting belied my observations. He was definitely off-balance. His normal confidence was absent. I took stock. For Ed, the big picture had never been stopping Dr. Weinard; it was about offering service and Dr. Weinard might have contributed to that service. He had to be heard out. Ed's role was to implement the district's mission, "striving for excellence by providing the best curriculum, instruction and learning opportunities…for all students." But the process had flummoxed Ed—almost.

At this juncture, Ed was alone with just two supporters, Ruth Thompson and Dale. Ruth helped him change his thought processes by her outright denial of seeing "plants," and with her gentle tease about paying for lunch. Dale was reassuring—more participant than observer.

That night was the end of a long, arduous process, and the end of a long, challenging day. Ed had started the day by relating disturbing events—two letters from Dr. Weinard and his own letter of frustration sent to Dr. Toth. He had a senior admin meeting, There was good business conducted there, thoughtful business. In fact he had tested his deputy then, a lesson that informed everyone but was intended as a message of caution for Don. The meeting had started with normal leadership, but much of the attention of senior administrators soon turned to that evening's meeting. After the admin meeting, he briefly paused before taking and making calls. The Student Accommodation Committee meeting came next. That was lunch. In the afternoon, he met with a lawyer to assist a colleague and found that the colleague had changed his mind. He commiserated with a parent from the Student Accommodation Committee. Finally, he kept quiet in a meeting so that others could talk, so that parents could ask their questions and listen to the answers given. His day ended nearly alone, deserted by all but two people, a woman busy cleaning up, and Dale, who offered biased reassurance.

I had previously been in situations where people struggled with their emotions; sporting events would be a prime example. Some get high with a win. And with a loss, some plunge into despair. Ed relaxed and crashed. People get over these highs and lows, and I knew that Ed would start a new phase with a revised plan. He had already initiated it, arranging a meeting with Dr. Weinard (and I had missed seeing it being set up).

I felt a loss; my time in the district was over. I was done in Wapiti Falls, and everything had come together. I had observed Ed at work. His leadership assured me that important matters could be pursued with style and substance.

I was on the road home by 23:35 hours. Meanwhile, I suspected that Ed would be playing this meeting over and over in his thoughts.

CHAPTER 12

PostScript Events with Analysis

Ed's fears that the attacks would continue were realized in the press coverage of only one magazine, the aforementioned and conservative *Our Alberta*. Their coverage blamed everyone but Dr. Weinard for the meeting's failure. They announced that although support for the alternative school was half and half, "the nays did all the talking." Apparently, Harold Wilder Wapiti Falls College professor, was not surprised; he was quoted as saying, "The crowd is probably a little stacked." Dr. Weinard was in this camp as well; he described it as "a lot of vested interests" saying that they liked things as they were. However, even the Alberta Report recognized that the main objections came from parents. "The more vocal insisted that Wapiti Falls' system already had most of Dr. Weinard's proposal in place, with the exception of phonics." And Dr. Weinard conceded that he may have trouble finding a willing school. The magazine pointed out that despite having the funds and permission, the community was not interested in the Paragon Alternative School, a stance that they found surprising.

In contrast to *Our Alberta*, the *Wapiti Falls Cascade* headline read simply, "Parents cool; Experimental school greeted with skepticism." They quoted board chair Lydia Jacques, "'Dr. Weinard couldn't show how his alternative would be different.'" Still, she said, parents had until the end of October to express their interest. One day later, the *National Press* reporter came to the same conclusion as the local paper: "Parents unimpressed by school plan." The proposal, the paper said, was for an elementary school based on "standardized tests, phonetic language instruction and high behaviour standards." They described Phil Weinard, a well-known and vocal educational reformer, and his proposal as an "alternative school which would operate like a private school within the public system."

These later two reports described the meeting I had attended. In contrast to the *Alberta Report* article which leaned to their reader's viewpoints, the local paper and the National Press were accurate. Parents did not want the alternate school, but was it true that these "nays did all the talking?"

I rechecked the speaking times. The meeting took one hundred fifty-seven minutes. Dr. Weinard and team took just short of ninety minutes for their initial presentation—56 percent of the meeting time versus 9 percent for the chair and superintendent. The time for questions and answers took fifty-five minutes—that is, parents, Dr. Weinard and his team, and the chair, shared 35 percent of the meeting time. Clearly, Dr. Weinard and his team did most of the talking. It was just that in all this talk, they had not persuaded parents to their point of view. They did a poor job of answering the questions posed by the parents, and parents were their target audience.

The meeting was for parents, but parents only had time to ask twelve questions. Was it enough? All three print publications cited above knew the answer, even if one disagreed with the choice parents had made. The press knew that the meeting would not bring parents on board with the proposal. They were right. No parent advisory council requested further action. This proposal was dead in Wapiti Falls.

Early one November morning, Ed and I met at a conference and talked; much of it concerned Dr. Weinard's alternative school proposal. Ed was not at all optimistic about his prospects for such a school—anywhere.

Later that day, Ed and I had lunch together. Ed told me that he owed the Calgary Public superintendent, Howell Stanley, "big time." He explained that just as Dr. Weinard was about to run advertisements recruiting Wapiti Falls parents, he received a call from Calgary Public requesting a board presentation. With this news, Dr. Weinard pulled his local ads. Purportedly, the ad would have contrasted Wapiti Falls Consolidated School District results against international test scores. "International test results," that was where Dr. Weinard had made his mark originally. In his earlier work—and it required dedicated and courageous effort—Dr. Weinard had made a recognized contribution to education. And the establishment responded. Tests like Alberta's Achievement Tests came into being. Having drawn attention to achievement test results, folks in Wapiti Falls would likely pay more attention when the local paper, the Cascade, published subsequent district assessments. They would probably see that local students fared better than their provincial counterparts. How then could Dr. Weinard disparage local schools on the basis of comparison tests? That ammunition had been spent, unsuccessfully.

On November 25, the *Edmonton Diary* reported that Weinard concluded that his school proposal for Wapiti Falls was a "dead duck." What else could he say after it did not receive support of even one of the city's parent advisory councils. He was still confident, however, that it would be adopted, if not in Calgary or Edmonton, then outside the province.

Did Dr. Weinard's proposal lose because Wapiti Falls parents were unreceptive to change? Could it be that parents there just did not think outside the box? Not so. While parents did not choose Dr. Weinard's proposal for an alternative school, elsewhere in the city they were considering alternative educational choices. The *Edmonton Diary* reported that a local high school was about to put its future in the hands of parents. Parents were voting on two options:
- a traditional, academic-oriented, two-semester program, with classes of 80 minutes, or
- expanding on the experimental four-quarter Copernican system currently serving a trial run. In this system, class times doubled to 160 minutes and students could completed a course in half the usual time, 10 weeks rather than 20.

I concluded that parents were still open to new ideas, but not to Dr. Weinard. Despite years of campaigning for educational reform, he had no carry-over appeal in his own community, or in the grades he was so concerned about, the elementary grades. Could he succeed elsewhere?

In May 1995, Dr. Weinard's campaign for reform had a further setback when the *Calgary Mercury* article reported:

> "Public school officials will no longer consider a proposal by educational reformer Phil Weinard to set up an experimental school in Calgary without major changes…In response, Weinard said that he has received 'some very serious interest' from U.S. educators. 'I think the Americans are more ready to do this than are Canadians. We're a reticent bunch,' he said.

Nearly a year after Wapiti Fall's parent meeting, September 1995, Ed thought someone in New England was interested in Dr. Weinard's ideas.

This crisis had passed in the Wapiti Falls Consolidated School District #1. Judging by newspaper accounts, normal leadership had returned. Seeing Ed, I saw nothing to challenge that conclusion.

CHAPTER 13

Analysis of Paragon Alternative School Proposal

This study began in the hope that leadership, as practised by one outstanding Alberta superintendent, could be observed, described, and understood. This hope was sustained with the identification of Ed Noyce's leadership processes, insofar as a mere list can explain human activities. Then a crisis came into the district. Would his processes still work, or would Ed be forced to change his leadership?

Officially, my account ended minutes after Ed declared that Dr. Weinard's supporters would keep "nipping away." Ed was worried that the community would be divided over the issue. But my observational work was not over. I followed up from the sidelines, kept in touch, in person and through newspapers. Analysis starts with the board decision earlier that March.

In March 1994, the Wapiti Falls Consolidated School District #1 was divided when they were asked to either support or reject Dr. Weinard's Paragon Alternative School proposal. Their vote revealed the dividing line between the old-line board and the reformers. Lydia Jacques, the vice-chair of the board at that time, described the vote as she saw it. While one of the "old guard," in the end, she switched sides. Why?

In the face of a personal life/death drama, Lydia decided, rather than fight it, why not see what the people want? "I was the one who split the vote," she had said. But she was not the deciding vote. Ed was sure that the vote had passed by two, not by her single vote. Either way, the advocates for change believed that it put the board at the vanguard; they were showing leadership in approving the Paragon Alternative School "in principle." Those opposed thought the board was wrong, but they accepted it in good faith. They ardently hoped that Dr. Weinard's idea would die when exposed to teachers, parents, and the all-important financial backers. Ed's normal leadership processes continued, but now tensions within the board and within the professional staff in schools were visible. The board offered Dr. Weinard help, tried to gin up or re-energize potential backers of the Paragon Alternative School with one more letter. That vote was close, but it passed. Even the professionals on Ed's senior administrative team were tense, in disagreement with Ed, thinking of better ways to attack the crisis, but they went along with Ed because he was their boss. And why not? His track record was unblemished. We saw how Ed's quiet leadership held firm and succeeded in his work with the Student Accommodation Committee. Would this continue in a crisis?

So, what did discussions on the Paragon Alternative School look like? I undertook a rudimentary content analysis of events related to these events. Using my field notes, I examined each recorded utterance dealing with the alternate school of Ed's and his colleagues regarding the alternative school and summarized them as bullets according to their fit within Ed's seven leadership processes. In assembling the various statements, I also discovered that not every relevant statement represented a leadership process. Some comments indicated stress. I labelled these as "stressors" and made a place for their bullet statements. Additionally, other statements did not fit at all. These I called "non-conforming statements" and I added their bullet to the table. The precursor to Table 8 grew beyond recognition. While this preliminary table was too detailed to be helpful, when simplified, it became the result shown below.

Table 8: A Count of Key Leadership Processes Related to the Paragon Alternative School

Leadership Processes			
Leadership Process	Count	Leadership Process	Count
Trust and Respect	11	Focus on Students	4
Scanning the Environment	15	Getting to Consensus	6
Slow, Patient Teaching	20	Time on Task	3
Respect Role Differentiation	1		
Non-Leadership Categories			
Stressors	5	Non-conforming Statements	3

Table 8 was helpful. I saw that the discussions on the Paragon Alternative School looked like Ed's normal leadership processes, but it was different as well. When I examined leadership processes in the Student Accommodation Committee, there was no need to look beyond the seven processes. But here, in the Paragon Alternative School discussions, I needed to add categories. Ed was still consistent and predictable, but somehow leadership in a crisis was unlike what I had seen. So, where did the differences lie? Consider the table again, briefly.

In the alternative school deliberations three processes, modelling "trust and respect," "scanning the environment," and "slow, patient teaching" to incorporate new data, were the most commonly counted processes. The other processes were there as well. Good, so the processes were all present.

Now compare the two events followed in detail. Recall that with the Student Accommodation Committee there was no consensus. With the Alternative School, parents reached a consensus; they did not want a Paragon Alternative School. In Ed's leadership process, consensus led to action, but here, in the school crisis, no action was needed. The fight to establish the Paragon Alternative School was over; it lost. Under Ed's leadership process, consensus was critical. There was one more critical ingredient as well, but before detailing this missing ingredient, weigh the processes with me.

In all of the discussions and meetings, I thought the most significant leadership process was "trust and respect." In all of the meetings, participants showed the same respect that Ed led with. When a teacher pointed out that nothing was new in Dr. Weinard's proposal, she was respectful. Parents were just as respectful when asking where their high-needs students would go, or when inquiring about the research design and control group. They tolerated Dr. Weinard's obfuscations. Of course, this is simply good manners and expected everywhere, but not all meetings manage it. The whole purpose of the parent meetings was that parents could and should be trusted to make the best decisions possible about their children's education, and a decision was respectfully reached.

Trust and respect were reciprocated by everyone but Dr. Weinard. Weinard did not fit the pattern, and it stood out. I counted three non-conforming statements in compiling Table 8. He had basically two strategies: attack and ignore. He occasionally returned respect, but mostly he struck out at those who were not on board with his proposal. He sent his proposal to research agencies, and they showed the respect of responding. He ignored their suggestions. He answered different questions than those directed to him by parents. Where Ed modelled respect, Dr. Weinard displayed arrogance.

As noted, parents had only fifty-five minutes to ask their twelve questions. It turned out to be enough. They knew that they did not want Dr. Weinard running their children's school. Consequently, there was no push from any parent advisory council to discuss his proposal any further. Significantly, they also avoided the one activity that would have torn their community apart. Separating kids according to their family's wealth or socio-economic status would have been problematic for Wapiti Falls. In a community with egalitarian values, how could anyone formally label children as poorer than their playmates, and then group them accordingly. Publicly. Doing that might well have exposed a hypocritical Dr. Weinard. While he spoke of wanting a mix of children of middle to lower socio-economic backgrounds, he had previously rejected offers of the soon-to-be-closed Pawoki School located in just that type of city community. Ed thought that Dr. Weinard really wanted a better community, and a better building. When he moved his child out of Wapiti Falls, he did not choose a school based on egalitarian principles. He selected an exclusive private school, an elitist school. He was not who he said he was, or thought he was.

Ed's leadership had allowed the Weinard proposal to die of natural causes, his ideal outcome. He fervently hoped he was right before the parent meeting, and after the meeting, he was sure about their decision. Parents knew the Weinard proposal was dead. The press knew it. Dr. Weinard knew it. Everyone knew it. But before Ed could refocus—take control—signs of his stress escaped.

Recall that on September 28, the day after Dr. Weinard had met with teachers, Ab saw that teachers were not impressed, but he feared that some parents would be. Ed wondered, could that happen? Had he been right to put his trust in parents? His concerns showed up as distractions. His body language and his out-of-character comments said that his guard was down; his mind was elsewhere. He sent a carefully crafted letter that challenged a colleague in Alberta Education.

Normally, Ed diverted stress or minimized it for others, but not in the buildup to the parent meeting, and definitely not in the anticlimactic moments after the parent meeting. In my last few minutes in the district, Ed reacted forcefully—worried that his plan had missed something crucial, worried about the next step. He expressed alarm. Consequently, he received support rather than dispensed it. And even then, while stressed, he was still disciplined enough to arrange yet another meeting with Dr. Weinard.

The whole last period of dealing with the Paragon Alternative School was not normal leadership. The board's "approval in principle" had turned into a crisis. I wondered if others knew it, but I knew that Ed had felt it. For the first time, I saw his emotions clearly spill out. In crisis, leadership became emotional. But was this a crisis?

Why the Paragon Alternative School Proposal Was a Crisis

There were three competing perspectives to these events: the professional educators had theirs, the crusader/reformer Dr. Phil Weinard had his, and between them, a board of elected school leaders would choose one. These three would determine the way forward for the district, and maybe beyond the district.

I saw these events as a crisis and relied on science historian and philosopher T. S. Kuhn's model of crisis for my understanding of events in Wapiti Falls Consolidated. Kuhn detailed the progression of old science to new in his seminal book, *The Structure of Scientific Revolutions* (1970). In this book, Kuhn described challenges to established scientific principles. When a basic overarching theory kept encountering problems, and tweaks could not resolve underlying issues, tensions built until a critical mass was reached. Sides were taken. New scientists, newcomers really, often looked outside the current paradigm and proposed new, divergent, and untested theories. The older theorists, established and comfortable, continued their normal work within the existing paradigm. Their approach could be summarized as, why bother with a new approach? Typically, neither side understood the other. Usually the old paradigm proved resilient, leaving the new theories abandoned, but sometimes—occasionally—the new paradigm emerged successful. For me, this Wapiti Falls alternative school debate resembled a scientific revolution.

But there is no equivalency between establishing or not establishing a small alternative school in a hinterland community and a scientific revolution. The scale of events in Wapiti Falls was not comparable, but the process was. Both sides had their supporters, and only one side would emerge victorious.

Consider first the supporters of the alternative school headed by Dr. Weinard. He believed schools were failing. He knew the statistics; he saw that Canadian and Alberta children were unable to read as well as their peers elsewhere. Why was that? He completed an extensive study of reading and schools and discovered his answer; it was a new corrective model for schooling. His model, he claimed, would produce "stunning results." It was brand new, "never been done before."

Consider his opposition—almost everyone working within the old, existing paradigm, like those typically employed in Wapiti Falls schools. They thought Dr. Weinard had returned to old, abandoned theory. And so Weinard found resistance at every turn. He pushed harder, and the status quo adherents resisted harder.

Consider the Wapiti Falls District board. When they officially entered the debate, Ed was placed directly into the conflict. Now the conflict was political. For superintendents, political conflicts were awkward and could potentially end careers. Ed had seen that happen to his predecessor.

This was no revolution in the Kuhnian sense of competing theories doing revolutionary battle, but for Dr. Weinard and the Wapiti Falls Consolidated School District, getting a new "alternative" school up and running was a veritable crisis, a revolution.

Battles and revolutions are stressful. For the district and all those in it, their beliefs were on the line. Was it their future? Ab Digby, assistant superintendent, saw what was happening as result of the board accepting the alternative school "in principle." He worried about schools and teachers. He thought that extensive healing would be required, and that the damage done would have a long-term impact. Principals were also stressed, wondering if they would still have jobs in the near future, and if parent councils would now be selecting school principals. Jake, newly returned to the principalship, felt this most strongly, and so Ed counselled him. And Ed's senior admin team did not support his decision to cooperate with Dr. Weinard. They understood that his board, their board, had so directed him, but they did not like it. All this affected Ed.

Those closest to Ed thought that his ascendency from deputy to superintendent had changed him, "He still has his fun, but occasions are less frequent."

Now, well into this crisis, Ed was alone. Sure, he still had the official support of his professional cohorts and his political bosses, because he was their appointed leader. But the board had put him on the outside. The alternative school concept and the person leading it were both challenging. Ed heard everything, considered various workarounds, thought that he might eventually go there, but not yet. That remained a worrisome eventuality. Ed felt conflicted and alienated, and the internal stresses due to his normal leadership process allowed these feelings to grow.

Throughout the alternative school process, Ed soldiered on. He respected the process. He set it up and then he watched without interfering. In two meetings, first with staff for two hours and forty minutes, and second with parents totalling two hours and thirty-seven minutes, Ed contributed two brief speeches and offered only three short points during the question periods: with staff, he nodded his agreement to a teacher question. With parents, he talked about the student dropout rate and then about the importance of longitudinal data and research design. He also avoided inserting his views about achievement test results, and thereby resisted making achievement test results political. He wondered about that. Talking to himself after the meeting, he mentioned Goodwater School results and asked, "What do schools have to do to prove themselves?" But publicly, Ed never ventured there. His discipline held.

Considering the crisis, Ed was markedly restrained.

A Newly Recognized Process: Work/Life Balance

How did Ed manage his stresses? Several trustees thought that Ed separated work from life better than other superintendents, that his private person was separate from his public persona. He would avoid public gatherings because, in part, they always turned into the topic of work and there was no escape. Still, he learned to use work purposefully. In normal work conversations, light, breezy comments about life outside of work meant that their business was drawing to an end, and so was their conversation or their meeting. This worked because there was an invisible boundary between public and private, and no one ventured beyond it. But was it even there?

Ed was private, but if asked, he was surprisingly candid and forthright. It was as though he thought no one would be interested in his private business. When he volunteered to share Dr. Weinard's letters, letters meant for only for Ed, had he crossed a line?

I wondered, but Ed did not see it that way. How did I reconcile that? I decided that sharing was what Ed did, and if it would help others understand, then going public by sharing additional insights might well be worth it.

How did Ed stay silent, patient, private? It was in Ed's nature to be private, and this tendency followed him into his work. And because he had a plan, he knew when to talk and when to stay silent, and he knew what to say and what not to say. And Ed had the discipline to stick to his game plan. That required trust and consistency. He trusted that others would figure things out and that the team was better than any one person. Since his style of leadership had worked for him, it would continue to work. Fine, but there was still stress.

Stress was everywhere in Ed's life. His wife, Marie, would know something about Ed's stresses. She knew that Ed tried to keep work and home separate, but it did not quite work. The separation was fuzzy, situationally dependent. Marie admitted that she was bothered by schools that fragmented education with little "church schools" popping up all around them, and with the media and the public denigrating education and students. She thought education had lost some public esteem, but she would not be alone in these thoughts. Husband and wife would have talked about it, likely agreed. It bothered her, and it bothered Ed.

Ed concluded that Dr. Weinard was "doing all the wrong things now"; in effect, Dr. Weinard was sabotaging a good idea. Ed found that stressful. Despite the challenges of working with Dr. Weinard, Ed had thought that Dr. Weinard could help the board and help education; several trustees talked about Ed saying just that. And then there was his deteriorating relationship with Alberta Education. He attacked a department manager, when he really wanted the deputy to be more concerned with education than with politics. And there were all those stresses inside his district, the interminable discussions, and his glacially slow leadership process. He even wondered if he should be in a people business, and if there, should he be more forceful? Sure, he knew some of his stresses came with the job, and that his other stressors reflected his leadership processes, but so what? How did Ed manage?

For some people, work is life, but for Ed, work was part of life. Ed managed stresses by having another life, by keeping work and life vaguely compartmentalized and in balance. After all, he had a balance between the satisfying and the dissatisfying, a balance between revealing and holding back. Balance was not new to Ed. As some had said, Ed did separate his work and personal life.

I thought that Ed had managed this crisis remarkably well, but for my complete understanding, I needed a new leadership process, one currently absent from my list of seven. I had found six directly through observation. I found a seventh, respect role differentiation, when I came to understood Ed's avoidance of "insertion." Finally, while I could not see work/life balance through observations, it was there, unseen but real. I did not invent it; I simply recognized its existence.

Ed and Marie had a full life. They talked about their family, and they had old friends from work and life. They did things with each other and with all of their family and friends. They kept in touch with them. Ed could talk about their weekends away because they had a significant life outside of work. Ed's friends and colleagues understood that, but they worried about him. Was it destroying him? Ed never talked about it.

In the last hour of my last observational day, Ed imploded, briefly, and even though I had been warned, it left me dumbfounded. In the next chapter, I explore what I viewed as a related, but strange request. He asked me to expose his "scam."

CHAPTER 14

Ed's Hidden Scam

I became aware of Ed's issue with his own leadership in our interview of September 12. It was during our wrap-up, and we were trading compliments. I told him that I was impressed with the "pastoral care" observed, with the admirable "family feeling" which permeated interactions, with the fact that "you know everyone's name; you know the family." His reply was modest, almost self-deprecating:

> "Four years ago, we could meet 100 percent of our teaching staff in the mall, and I could, if my memory would work right, I could come up with a name. It may take a minute to get to it. Support staff maybe 60 to 75 percent, but right now I am thinking on professional staff I am probably about 85 percent. I want to get that back up to 100…"

And then Ed did what he often did; he turned the tables, started talking about me. I reminded him that in this interview I was to learn from him. Okay, he agreed, and we reverted to complimentary chit-chat. But something in his tone or words led me to ask, "Do you want more of this?" He replied, "I have a hard time listening to it," but then having thought about it, he let up, and gave me permission to tell the complimentary things, but only if I "expose the other side too." It was then that I heard the words, "The scam has got to come out."

What? A scam? All my observations had revealed the opposite, to the point where early on, I had sought advice. Was it possible, I had asked my faculty advisor, that I would find no issues with my subject? His answer was clear; there would be "no downside." I believed him; I still do. Hearing Ed talk of a scam, I shared my advisor's view. Ed was not swayed, "No, there is. I have hidden it well." But Ed was once again ready to move on, to change the subject. We have "a lot of similarities, Dale." There it was. Another "just like me" connection that I heard throughout my observations. Mutual identification. It was a respectful diversion, and diverted, I did not inquire further about Ed's hidden scams.

Doubts laid in Ed's heart, and he had tasked me to reveal his "scam." Worse, he was serious, and in my view "very serious." Ed Noyce, the leader and teacher, was also Ed Noyce, the introspective, abstract thinker, and this latter Ed Noyce questioned himself, questioned his motives and actions. Had I missed earlier signs? I did look, and all I found was the casual comment, at the end of a long day, near the end of the week, and as the school year wound down. He told me that he did not want to be remembered as the person who used relationships to make cuts—budget cuts and hence job cuts. Could this haunt him?

The Ed that I had observed was quietly confident, and he felt good about what he did and about where he was leading his district. I never saw him hesitate to do what he believed necessary. I could understand that on the dark days, as the crisis loomed large, Ed Noyce would question his motives and his integrity. Who would not doubt himself as he led his district, alone, into an unknown future? But he had directed me to expose all I could, and I took up the quest. I started with three tentative theories about his "scam." Then I waited, thought of more ideas. These brainstorming ideas were not all of high quality. The results became Table 9: Were There Hidden Scams? It consists of a numbered list of the ways Ed may have thought he was a scammer. Each item has a summary title, a question,. Next follows an argument sketched out to support the question asked. A counter-argument follows, a "But" statement. Finally, after weighing the two opposing arguments, I state my conclusion.

Table 9: Were There Hidden Scams?

Ed's Scam	The Counter Argument	Conclusion
1. Was Ed a self-interested manipulator?		
Ed was the powerful, visible symbol for the good things happening in the district. But he did it by bringing people together and letting them figure out what to do. Then he took credit for it. He appeared magnanimous because he oversaw everything, controlled all of it, and overpowered everyone. He was grace hiding behind manipulative control; he exploited people.		
	But: Manipulators "control or play upon by artful, unfair, or insidious means to serve one's own interest" (Webster's Ninth New Collegiate Dictionary, 1987, p. 724). Rather than controlling, Ed led by "the tapping of existing and potential motive and power bases of followers by leaders, for the purpose of achieving intended change" (Burns 1978: 448). I saw it; Ed described it: "The best work is done from bottom up. If you can get the people at the bottom saying the right things and moving [in] the right directions, the top can just sort of follow along, if it is the right direction." With Ed, self-interest was absent; it was never about him. Publicly and privately, Ed did not take credit for the good things happening throughout the district, but he did accept responsibility for the district's problems. His leadership involved teaching people, helping them understand what their best course of action was. His focus was to hold to or move "towards the middle…to try to get that stable, centre position." Hard work. Demanding work. Ed empowered others, and he did his best to send any resultant limelight closer to the source or the district's successes—to students, teachers, and schools.	
		Not manipulative. No scam.
2. Was Ed a fraudulent leader?		
It was not Ed's success; it was their success. He was the fraud; they were the success. He was at the head of the parade but was not what made the parade successful.		

	But:
	Ed led by consensus, and it was indirect. It took prolonged discussion, trust that others would eventually find and implement good solutions, and the patience needed to proceed through all of the in-between stages. He understood that if it was "the wrong direction, you have to jump in." Ed was also well aware of other paths: "I have often thought that maybe the ego should be a little bigger in a leader so that you do protect things, perhaps a bit more." Ed rejected that approach, the autocratic, directive style, because he had seen that it was less productive.
	Ed was a teacher-mentor, helping others become their better self.
	Not a fraudster. **No scam.**

3. Was Ed more devious than true leader?

Had Ed played Phil Weinard? He got Dr. Weinard on board with a parent support level of 85 percent, which he knew was unattainable.

More significantly, Ed did not think that parents would agree to an experiment involving their kids under the leadership of the inflexible, arrogant Weinard. So why bother with all that work and worry? Was it a trick, an unnecessary deception?

	But:
	Ed was simply trying to apply what he understood about how Dr. Weinard thought and worked. He invited Dr. Weinard's participation on a district planning committee. He developed a budget for Weinard's proposed school. Just how much help should he offer Dr. Weinard?
	As with others, Ed waited, let them learn, and stepped in only if harm was imminent. That was his normal teaching strategy, and we saw it repeatedly with Jake and in the lesson Ab received. But Dr. Weinard's work on the strategic planning committee had not brought Weinard new insights, and his tour of district schools had not happened—it would probably never happen. Dr. Weinard simply could not, or would not, learn.
	Ed had let others end their careers or end their relationship with the district; he let them quit.
	Ed's responsibility for Dr. Weinard had to end, and it did.
	Were there other schemes?
	Had Ed schemed to have Dr. Weinard finish what he had started, or was he simply following a board directive?
	Had he schemed to let his deputy present an option that others had thought about, and spoken about? When the deputy presented it, the board was pleased, enthusiastic even. They were coming together at last. It changed Don's somewhat tentative relationship with the board.
	Ed had spoken about Don's growth, and no doubt he would like Don to inherit the job, as Ed had inherited it from his predecessor. And Don did replace him when the time came. Had Ed schemed to make it happen?
	Strategic perhaps, but not devious. **No scam.**

4. Was Ed's decision-making faulty?

Did Ed choose the wrong path for the Paragon Alternative School assessment process? He had listened to others, analyzed everything, but disagreed with the advice received. He should have shut out Dr. Weinard, or at least tried to do that. Had he heeded the advice of others, all that work and tension would have been avoided. Yes, he did what the board wanted, but he had held back on what he thought best; he capitulated.

	But:
	In this crisis, the debate was political; it was a choice of values (Zeigler et al. 1985). The board weighed their values and the community's values. The board made their initial decision, approving the "Paragon School" and therefore Ed's focus was on how to implement their decision, to make it work. This forced Ed to find out what parents wanted for their children.
	Ed chose to trust the values of his board bosses and those of the end users, namely the children via their most committed representatives—parents. Until the parents had decided, Ed's feelings had no outlet. When the parents knew; the board would know too. Staying in limbo was stressful, but it reflected his leadership processes and his principals. He did his job.
	Trusting parents led to resolution. **No scam.**

5. Worn out, angry, and vengeful, was Ed the wrong leader for a crisis?

Had stress done Ed in? Others had thought about that. His approach was slow, hard, and lonely. How lonely? After the final meeting, at the climax of a long grueling process, Ed was left with two people, a new staff member—a woman tidying up the space—and his shadow—Dale. Here, Ed expressed the depths of his feelings—carefully. He knew that his despair would stay in the room, at least for now. He was in a safe space. Consider, too, that Ed's process required that he keep colleagues feeling good about themselves, and comfortable sharing ideas in a non-judgmental setting. He often smoothed things over, but in doing so, he suppressed his own feelings—healthy for others, but unhealthy for him (Beck 2019).

Ed had bought into a leadership model that said that success had a limited life; he thought that leaders tired, and that a once-novel methodology could eventually wear thin as followers looked for new strategies. Ed believed all this because an expert had pointed it all out. He felt used up. Was Ed's successful run at leadership about to end?

	But:
	People recover from being tired and so would Ed. He had an external and internal support network, and it was working. When I met with him after the last Weinard meeting, and again over subsequent months, he seemed fine—relaxed, chatty, and positive.
	When the crisis ended, Ed's energy and composure returned. **No scam.**

6. Had Ed anticipated every wrinkle, every angle and just pretended otherwise?

Ed seemed to have anticipated everything about issues in his district, and it all fit with his plan.

He was an outstanding teacher, but his adult "students" were not selecting their own projects. They may have thought they were, thought they were following their agenda, but really, they were simply Ed's focus group. The projects undertaken were the topics that Ed had anticipated and solved. Former trustee and chairperson, Agnes Cameron, had wondered out loud, were Ed's solutions preordained, planned out in advance? Not so, said Ed, but was that his scam?

Was his well-planned path—his scam—unravelling?

	But:
	Perfect insight is impossible, but Ed made up for it by careful planning and adapting, His board hired him for his people skills as well as for his expertise.
	As to getting others to reach his preferred solution, that suggestion would miss the mark. Reaching consensus always required adjustment. And Ed's colleagues were smart people. Discussion had them considering ideas from others, ideas they had missed, ideas that made the group decision better. This whole was larger than any individual part, including Ed's part.
	And if events changed from what Ed once thought best, he would change with it. Adjustment is not failure or fraudulent.
		Perfect or imperfect, Ed's plan worked.
		No scam.

7. Was Ed at war with Albert Education?

Ed's relationship with Alberta Education had deteriorated to onerous smog—biting and unhealthy. Ed kept hoping for fresh air, a return to the clean air of the past. Back then, Alberta Education had been better. Still, the department was nominally one of his bosses, and he wanted to please them. But now their focus seemed to be more on politics and power and less on students and education. Ed was perhaps the last superintendent to understand the change—he kept trying to persuade them—but when understanding finally came, it left him frustrated and uncomfortable.

Ed was without power or influence with the province. Was it making him feisty, batty, or both? Would he settle into a prolonged, rear-guard fight?

	But:
	Like so many things in Alberta, and specifically in Ed's district, disagreements started over money. Money had caused them to delay staffing decisions that spring, and the Student Accommodation Committee searched for ways to save money the very next fall. Fundamentally, Ed's district was poor, had been poor for years, while his neighbours were rich. Its impact was especially deleterious to his students and for students in other poor districts, so he proposed a provincial remedy and promoted it throughout the province. Some in Alberta Education agreed with Ed. and they tried to help. When this had no discernible impact, Ed changed tactics. He turned aggressive out of desperation.
	What else could Ed do? This dilemma became Ed's personal crisis and mission.
		Ed fought for his students.
		There might be a scam, but Ed was not the scammer.

8. Was Ed's scam that he set impossibly high standards for himself?

Ed always thought he could do better, and that delivering less than his best was deceptive, that was his personal scam. Consider this example: after he had hung up the phone after an amiable discussion with Dr. Weinard, he admonished himself and said that he should have done better. He had the same reaction after he had "inserted" himself in political conversations with his trustee bosses.

	But
	Is it possible to scam oneself? Maybe, for a slacker, but for a hard-working, successful professional, it is called setting high standards. It verges on an expectation of personal perfection. Consider high standards first. Setting high standards is one way of pushing yourself to do better. Athletes are a visible example. They achieve a goal, and then having reached their goal, they adjust their next goal to an even higher standard. This is just strategizing. Ed set high standards as a means to force him do his best. High performers also have high personal expectations. This tendency can be overdone—in part because people do not understand themselves. Ed both knows himself and fails to know himself. Ed knows a great deal about others, and he knows many things about himself. But there are parts hidden from him. He is like other people in this regard. Grant (2018: 3) studied and wrote about how well people know themselves and concluded, "Any time a trait is easy to observe or hard to admit, you need other people to hold up a mirror for you" (Grant, 2018: 6). I held up a mirror for Ed, but he did not see what I saw.
	Ed may not have met his own standard, but that was no scam.

I found no scam after examining eight "scam" scenarios. None fit. Ed's request was simple, and I pursued it diligently. He had me looking deeper, forcing me to question what I saw. In the end, it was Ed's classical teaching process. He had forced me to look hard, to be skeptical. Ed's statements about a scam were oblique reminders do my best, and to report what I saw and understood, even if it was uncomfortable.

An editor of this material provided a new insight. She noted that Ed's response could be a classic case of "imposter syndrome." According to Wikipedia, "Impostor syndrome is a psychological pattern in which one doubts one's accomplishments and has a persistent internalized fear of being exposed as a 'fraud' despite external evidence of their competence…." The article continued, "Studies suggest that more than 70% of people experience the impostor syndrome at some point in their career." It is associated with stressful situations, and perfectionism could be a cause. That all fits. Ed knew that he was not perfect, but knowing it and accepting it are different.

Is Qualitative Research a Scam?

If I could not find Ed's scam, perhaps the fault was with the researcher or the methodology. I was the qualitative researcher, and if there was a scam, perhaps the scam was mine. As a neophyte researcher, I thought I could watch a strong leader, think hard on it, understand it, encapsulate it, and practise it. Maybe I was too naïve. Two central problems created doubt about the process.

First, my application of the process was imperfect. To pick two examples, I never understood what was going on with Jake Harris or with Ann Spencer, Ed's secretary. Instead, I focused on observing and understanding Ed. I did learn about others, but it was peripheral.

The point is, by focusing on one person, a bigger, wider world of people and events—all in play with my subject— were left unattended. Further, a skilled researcher might have asked better questions. There were spots where I failed to ask about something I questioned. Not asking Ed to detail his scam might have been one. But if asked, would he have answered it or redirected it as he had done previously, for other unproductive queries? I also engaged in the opposite of ignoring inquiry opportunities. I had my own questions and asked them. In interviews, I probed—some might have called it "leading" the interviewee. I thought that it was the right strategy then and still do now; I trusted myself.

Second, being a part-time observer introduced the potential for missing critical details. I did not observe everything in an ongoing series of events. Catch-up was therefore necessary, and some context may have been lost. For example, I could not track the source of ideas. Ed liked that, as no one could be identified as having the good ideas or the bad ones. Missing context could be important because one small thing has the potential to redirect subsequent action. Consider how lucky I was to have Ed tell me that he had helped staff coordinate their presentations at the September 28 board meeting. Their actions contrasted sharply with the lack of coordination between Dr. Weinard and his team the night before. Consequently, the board saw teachers as caring professionals. I assume that timing had me miss other equally important events.

Do such shortcomings invalidate qualitative research, my research? While I brought personal shortcomings, I had good prior experiences in qualitative research, including classes, projects, and teacher evaluations. And methodological shortcomings exist no matter what. Science can be a minefield for methodology errors.

The two illustrations above go to the heart of qualitative research; they consider validity. Doing valid research is not just about asking the right questions or being there at the right time. No one asks just the right question, and no one can be there for everything. The grizzled contrarian, Harry Wolcott, a well-regarded qualitative scientist, knew something about validity. He knew that understanding did not require knowing everything. He thought that researchers needed to "recognize the difference between what we have actually observed and what we think it means, what we hope it means, or what we insist that it ought to mean" (Wolcott 1981: 261). Demonstrating the utmost in validity requires more:

"What I seek is something else, a quality that points more to identifying critical elements and wringing plausible interpretations from them, something one can pursue without becoming obsessed with finding the right or ultimate answer, the correct version, the Truth." (Wolcott 1990: 146)

Methodological limitations are discussed in more detail in Appendix D: Participants, Places, and Sites, with District Schools Listed Alphabetically.

I tried to find Ed's scam and failed. I tried to understand the Truth of Ed's leadership and settled for what seemed plausible.

Part VI: Concluding Remarks in Two Parts

CHAPTER 15

Concluding Remarks

This investigation formally began with Ed Noyce's arrival at a school to discuss his new staffing predicament with principal Paul Brigg. It continued to the bleak anticlimactic moment when Ed realized that while the Paragon Alternative School proposal was dead, Dr. Weinard's issues would need more attention.

I started with two goals: learning that would assist me in my job, and to share my findings and graduate with a well-earned PhD. Neither goal was met perfectly, but both were met imperfectly.

While I was no longer working in the field of education, this study has helped me, and it may help someone else. My personal gain came from watching a skilled professional act professionally. I also had sufficient time to produce a working model of Ed's leadership.

Critical aspects of Ed's leadership path are summarized in the challenging Table 10. This table must be read across, in rows, as columns are not aligned—despite appearances. The purpose of this table is to show the progress of my thinking from the first meeting with Mr. Joe Pivott to a final contribution by Ed Noyce. Explanatory notes follow after the table.

Table 10: Critical Aspects on Ed's Paths to Leadership

Sections		Chapters		
Part 1:	Introduction	Chapter 1	Intelligence	Affability
Part II	Ed's Key Traits	Chapters 2-3	Thinking and understanding, Searching for Data, "Big Picture" reality, Weighing choices: • Trust and respect • Balance	Self-discipline, Honesty, Fairness, Pleasant, Honouring commitments, Integrity
	Composite Ed	Chapter 4	Satisfactions Dissatisfactions Disturbing	
Part III	Leadership Processes	Chapter 5, Chapter 7, Chapter 13	Trust and respect, Focus on students, Scanning the environment, Consensus	Co-operative teaching, Time, Respect role differentiation, Balance • Work/Life
Part IV	Normal Leadership: Student Accommodation committee	Chapter 6, Chapter 7	Trust: • The role • The people Focus on the people Respect Balance: • Work solutions	Time Intensive processes: • Scanning • Thinking • Co-operative teaching • Consensus Implementation (if adopted by the Board)
Part V	Leadership in a Crisis	Chapters 8-13	Trust: • The role • The people Focus on the people Respect Balance: • Work solutions • Work/Life	• Time Intensive processes: • Scanning • Thinking • Co-operative teaching • Consensus Implementation (no implementation if no consensus)
Part VI	Concluding Remarks	Chapter 16, Chapter 17	Conclusion: • Ed's leadership process followed a pattern Two Beliefs: • leaders all need to spend time, have feelings for their enterprise, and focus on their business. Vaill (1986) • leaders find unique paths to professional success. Ed Noyce's reaction	

Leadership is complex. Ed is complex. Table 10 describes a journey of understanding that began simply enough, with intelligence and affability. From there, the features and values inherent in Ed's particular brand of "intelligent" and "affable" were examined. Ed's nature led him to work that he liked and was good at. Work was satisfying, but it came with inherent dissatisfactions, and unfortunately, to aspects that made him wonder if it was all worthwhile. Thus, we understood the man, but leadership required more.

To lead his district, Ed needed to understand events and to plan, and this meant that he had to have more data, and had to put together a wider, bigger district picture of reality. To implement whatever decisions were reached, he had to get everyone on board with the plan. He did this with his colleagues and superordinates by cooperative teaching, weighing all their choices, and building a consensus. With consensus, decisions were ready to implement.

Detailed observations revealed a pattern, summarized as eight leadership processes. Six came from the initial observations, one more was added when "normal" leadership was examined relative to the work of a board committee, and a final, eighth process was discovered in the emotional context of a crisis.

The final events in this journey started out as normal leadership, but gradually changed. In the end, the district was in crisis; some staff were in crisis, and Ed faced a personal crisis. The crisis was created by his board, and was occasioned when the board's political solution created an administrative, pedological problem. It was a political solution because it involved a choice of values. The board would have to approve or reject a new school whose structure and mission were unlike that of their existing schools. Its values were different. It was an administrative problem because the proposal was flawed, and the professionals recognized the challenges inherent to its implementation—should that school come to pass. This amalgam of politics and administration tested Ed and his leadership model. Ed managed, and his leadership may even have been enhanced, but it drained his energy. (The chronological comparison of normal leadership and normal-morphing-into-crisis is highlighted in Appendix L: "Two Case Studies—Summary Timelines.")

In the end, through normal times and in crisis, Ed's leadership sustained itself; it was a cycle of a problem emergence, exploration, and solution. Within the eight leadership processes, three stand out. First, Ed focused on trusting people. Second, Ed was a teacher and led by teaching. His distinctive teaching style required time-intensive processes of data gathering, cooperatively reviewing, thinking about, and evaluating the data, until eventually reaching a consensus on what needed doing. Third, implementation followed. But wrinkles sometimes occurred; not all issues could be addressed consensually. Implementation of the two cases which were followed closely were not seen in my limited time in the field, but I looked around and saw that decisions were implemented: Middle Schools were created. An International Baccalaureate came into being: Schools were closed and opened. Staff were hired and promoted. Sometimes Ed had to make the decision, and he did. It could be stressful. Such stress was managed by the critical last process, the external process invisible when restricted strictly to observations of work, namely work/life balance.

Two Beliefs on Organizationally Effective School Leadership

I needed a dissertation to graduate and failed, but I did meet the next best standard—the completion of this project. Here, I finally inventoried Ed's leadership processes, just not in time for formal recognition. While this is now finished, I can make no claim about leadership beyond Ed's. He was a sample of one, and what I learned was not generalizable to the many. Still, my experiences support limited and generalized theorizing, namely, by citing two basic beliefs.

The first is that leaders all need to spend time, have feelings for their enterprise, and focus on their business. My observations started from this, Vaill's theory (1986). I utilized his theory and fine-tuned it to provide the detail and specificity observed with Ed.

The second belief is that leaders find unique paths to professional success. I believe that no one led the way Ed did. But there are many successful school leaders, and I knew some and informally watched them. All of their paths were different. Their leadership styles reflected their unique skills and experiences. I offer a suggestion in this vein—namely, that to understand someone's leadership, look first to the choices they make early in their career. Early on, Ed learned that utilizing the ideas and approaches of others improved results. Second, on seeing that he did not like some approaches to leadership, he left one district and moved to Wapiti Falls. Ed's list of strategies grew as Ed learned more, but they all started with his early choices. Ed's early choices reflected the principles or values that led to continued growth. All else followed.

The data in this study is old, and while still valuable in my eyes, its messages may be dated. But the methodology is not. I looked for more current examples of qualitative leadership studies. This methodology can still be found, but the approaches are different. Researchers have generally avoided the open-ended approach I took. Their approach is more focused, and their scope is narrower. (See Appendix M: "Selected Qualitative Studies of Educational Leadership: 1997–2017" for examples.) I discovered the hard way that my study did not easily lend itself to a dissertation. Over a period longer than a single generation, this paper is the third of a trilogy: Feilders (1982) wrote about a superintendent of a large American district; Wolcott critiqued an elementary school principal (1984); I followed with this study of an effective Alberta superintendent. Despite limited appeal, this approach may still have something to offer.

A generation ago, I watched an effective school superintendent. Does it have any value now? I think it does. It was important to me, and it can be of value to others. "Effective" is effective, irrespective of the time. Ideas are adaptable. The paths are innumerable. Consistency matters. Understanding creates opportunity.

Ed Nears Retirement

Well past my formal observation period, I continued to follow Ed Noyce's career. Nearly a year after my last observation, the local newspaper awarded Ed Noyce with a rhetorical dart, no rose, a piercing projectile instead. Ed had "blasted" the minister of education, Edmund McSeain, for releasing superintendent salaries. Ed had said that it was "to some extent" an invasion of privacy. The newspaper declared, "Noyce is wrong; McSeain's right." The paper's beef was not because Noyce was paid too much. His salary, relative to neighbouring superintendents, was in the middle range, nowhere near the top, and they were not saying that any of the salaries were too high or too low. "Too low" would never be said in Wapiti Falls. And the paper had had lots of time to attack his salary, as his board had released his exact salary a year earlier. The beef was that Noyce had the temerity to say that Alberta Education had broken their own rules and was therefore acting unethically. Ed thought Alberta Education, having established the rules, that they should follow them or change them. It was just that; Ed thought they should lead by example. This particular dart was exclusively aimed at creating a little controversy. The paper hoped it would sell newspapers. Perhaps Ed said it knowing that such truths would bother some. Speaking plainly sometimes becomes easier as retirement nears.

For Ed, normal leadership continued for another year. Then he retired. His career accomplishments were recognized in a gala celebration. Two articles in both Wapiti Falls newspapers shared the news. The *Wapiti Falls Cascade* on Sunday, February 11, 1996, started with "Superintendent Noyce retires: [...] Citing burn-out and a desire to pursue other interests, Ed Noyce will retire as a public-school Superintendent in August." Ed had been in Wapiti Falls since 1981 and superintendent since 1990. The article gave his recent accomplishments, "a key role in developing learning disabilities and gifted programs, the Family School Wellness Program, the strategic planning process, reorganizing middle schools, and a 'hack' computer model." Ed was quoted, "We've got an excellent board with two more years until the next election. So, the transition is guaranteed to be smooth." His parting comments were instructive, "More than anything else, Noyce said, he'll miss interacting with staff, parents and students. It's so much fun to watch kids working, learning, and growing."

The *Sunday Rapids* reported, "He says this is a terrific district here, and the schools get support from the parents and the community, adding 'there's a lot of neat things happening between our schools.'" Ed was pleased with what had been done and expressed confidence in the future. He also tweaked an alarm, disarmingly soft, about money, "There are going to be budget decisions until we start getting a more reasoned approach to funding schools." And he still enjoyed the whimsical, "Maybe at some point in time there'll be an opportunity for some part-time work, maybe 40 to 50 hours a week."

Curiously, in the list of key accomplishments during his tenure as superintendent, there was no mention that he had brought in a second large high school, introduced the International Baccalaureate program, or faced down education crusader Dr. Phil Weinard. That particular crisis had passed and was all but forgotten.

When asked, did he miss his former higher profile? "Not at all," Ed said, several times, and his practice of staying away from crowds, avoiding any limelight—away from any chance of being dragged into discussions and evaluations of schools and its personnel—confirmed it for me. I recently saw new schools named after his former principals and asked, "Had he been asked about having a school named a school after him?" "No," there had no such approach, and "if he had been, he would decline." He explained, there are too many good people to remember them all, and in short order, who would know who they were? Sour grapes? Not likely.

Overwhelming Admiration

I have finally come to my end of this tome. In this account, I have detailed Ed's work and found that the original adjudicators had correctly judged him as "organizationally effective." He did his job very well, but I could have found other candidates who also did their jobs extremely well. Ed was smart and smooth, but his package of skills and attributes would have likely been similar to other "organizationally effective" superintendents. But I did not observe them or think about their work. I did observe and think about Ed's work, and it was very good. No doubt he was not the only superintendent doing high-quality work. People are different, and leaders lead differently. Ed taught me a great deal, but I would not have and could not have led as Ed led. In fact, before leaving the field, I was busy seeking out my own style of leading.

Nevertheless, this project of detailed observation left me very impressed with Ed's work. Someone described it as "overwhelming admiration." Their judgment is accurate.

I was not surprised that Ed asked me to critique his work. It might have been a compliment. Had he thought I could point out things that could make him better? But he didn't ask me that, he asked me to find his scam and report on it. I looked but could not find it. Why would I think I could? Why did he think I could?

Ed was an excellent superintendent, but we have seen that Ed was not perfect. The three letter campaign—two letters from Dr. Weinard and Ed's own letter to an Alberta Education department head—were not the actions that he championed. He had valid excuses for being out of character then—the letters from Dr. Weinard were disingenuous, and the letter to Dr. Toth was payback. So what if that particular day, October 5, was long and arduous—that day had me learning about and discussing the three letters, and observing a very full day with a senior admin meeting, preparation for and being attentive in the black hole of Student Accommodation Committee meeting, a meeting with a downtown lawyer, a call to buck up a fellow Student Accommodation Committee member, the crucial evening meeting with Dr. Weinard and parents, and sundry other interactions. He even shared an unsigned letter he had received with its litany of complaints about what was happening in their district—under Ed's watch. In total, this day turned out not to be Ed's best day. And yet it was. His objective for that day was met; parents made their decision regarding the Paragon Alternative School, and that debacle would soon be over.

Ed was an extremely able leader, but I could quibble with some aspects of his total approach. First, Ed relied on a system of centralized delivery of special education services. The province was doing the opposite. They incessantly promoted a local school delivery model. Both approaches were defensible, but only one was the current fashion. And one was less costly than the other. Ed's choice was the less costly. Better funding—equitable funding—would have helped the district, and allowed Ed's to follow the province's leadership. Indeed, it would have made everything easier. Over and over, the lack of funding—funding such as my district had—forced Ed's district to be more frugal than their neighbours, more frugal than my district.

Second, at the time, the public—outsiders all—complained that schools accepted lame excuses for the unacceptable behaviour of students. Bad behaviour was tolerated. In response, many schools adopted a policy known as "zero tolerance." Ed's district subscribed to it, and Ed said that he agreed with it. If he did, I never saw it carried out as "zero tolerance." Think about what was learned when one student was expelled from the district. She had her faults, and her behaviour, as Ed well understood, was unacceptable. But he questioned it and asked, was she treated fairly? As a student with native heritage, was her treatment equitable—not better, but equitable? Ed was not sure that it was, and he promised to, and did, give it further attention. Perhaps a "zero tolerance" policy served a purpose, but I never understood how "zero tolerance"—intolerance in other words—was defensible. Maybe we have learned something since my days with Ed. But I would be wrong on this count. As a pandemic and police brutality merged in 2020, I read and heard "zero tolerance" in use once more.

Third, Ed kept thinking that the province would address their and his equity problem. They had not done so, but Ed kept hoping they would. His entire district did the same. Ed oversold the idea that the province would help. Others knew that the politics were against that. But did Ed have any choice but to hope?

And finally, my last criticism, Ed liked "tuneful" music, while I like rock 'n' roll.

Why had Ed asked for what I could not do—to find his scam? Would it be to avoid any extra attention? Ed certainly did not want a research report that made him stand out. Disguised or not, someone—in addition to myself—would know him and might applaud his work and him. But a critical evaluation, or capturing a cryptic, cynical view of his leadership would have been less auspicious and quieter. Aggressive criticism, that would have better served Ed's preference for anonymity.

Ed was very good, but I found him to be "overwhelmingly admirable" for what I believe to be an excellent reason. He faced down a district and personal crisis. He could have avoided the Paragon Alternative School fiasco by simply shutting Dr. Weinard out. Many of his colleagues in the district would have done so; others outside his district had done so. But Ed did not take that approach. He devised a plan to rationally determine if Dr. Weinard's proposal suited his board and their bosses, the parents and electors of Wapiti Falls. It was Ed's leadership that brought his board together, and that encouraged teachers and administrators to evaluate their practices. What could be more admirable than holding on to one's principles in service to others?

CHAPTER 16

Concluding Remarks: Ed

Following the restart of this writing project, I kept Ed Noyce informed. He agreed to the disguises of people, places, and buildings. That left dates and events intact. He agreed to be "Ed Noyce," and was agreeable with all the other replacements used. The photos I submitted were interesting, but he couldn't locate either the site or people. That made sense because some photos were disguises, and non-identifying features had been selected. Ed thought the story was acceptable, the accuracy reasonable. He sometimes wondered who was being described and, if it was him, why were his "warts" absent? I admitted that I had been unable to solve his alarming request, to root out the details of his "scam." But Ed wasn't sure what he had said. Had he forgotten or was it a non-denial denial? His involvement with me in that final task looked suspiciously like his normal leadership process; leave people alone to work things out, and redirect them if the direction is wrong. He didn't redirect me. Forgotten or tolerant, either way worked.

We talked about his work during that half-year of observation and he noted that he had been fortunate during my time with him. Over his career not everything had gone as he wanted, as he had foreseen, or as I had seen them. He had had his disasters. Finally, he asked what I thought might happen through all of my effort. I thought, maybe my home institution would be interested, or maybe another university. Maybe I would have to self-publish. I just knew that I needed to finish it. And deep down, I thought, what a guy, interested in what I wanted. Ed was still mentoring me. I asked for a written comment. He agreed and provided it:

> "It is rare for one to have the opportunity to review, several years later, a segment of one's working life in considerable detail, complete with annotations and commentary. Having agreed to participate in this study, that is precisely the unexpected experience presented by this close examination of daily activities over the period of time recorded. I am grateful to the researcher for his attention to detail and his kind, and frequently very generous, interpretations of these events from the past.

> "I must confess that many of these discussions, meetings, and decisions had been erased from memory to the point of having to struggle to place people, places, and happenings in context with the reality that brought them all

together. Later in retirement, those events still quite vivid are the ones that did not evolve quite so well. There are no 'do-overs' in day-to-day life. But when actions and decisions have the potential to significantly affect the lives of others, it is inevitable that some of those actions and decisions will be regretted. Those particular moments have remained crystal clear in memory, while so many others have faded into obscurity.

"It would be appropriate to expand just a little. In my teenage and early adult life, many opportunities to assume leadership roles were presented. The usual small-group experiences in school and university, of course, but also more significant leadership roles in larger groups led me to believe that I might have a potential career in educational administration. But they also led me to understand that when I relied heavily on my own judgment, the results were not always stellar. Hence, the evolution of the administrative style referred to in several places in this document. For myself, involving others in decisions that affect them, and in decisions that have the potential to change dramatically the course of an organization was a survival mechanism, pure and simple. I appreciate that this approach would not fit with all leadership styles. But it seemed to work for me.

"I would like to express my appreciation to the researcher for his efforts in ferreting out the details presented in this study. It was a monumental task in the observation and data collection phase, and a similarly monumental task in the interpretation and analysis phase. It would have been easy to cut a few corners and simplify the task. But that could have resulted in very different conclusions.

"I am also grateful to those staff members, school board members, and others who agreed to participate. It can be quite threatening to have an unknown observer attending meetings at which private feelings and opinions are being shared. Yet, to the best of my recollection, no one showed even the slightest hesitation having an unknown observer recording their every move. The researcher deserves much credit for the way he managed to put others at ease."

Tables

Table	Appears in	Title	Page
Table 1	Chapter 6	September 12 – Issues Discussed in Student Accommodation Committee Meeting 4	82
Table 2	Chapter 6	Committee Member "Finds" in the Field Notes of Meeting 6	88
Table 3	Chapter 6	Ed's Leadership Processes as Observed in Student Accommodation Committee Meetings	89
Table 4	Chapter 8	May 26 to June 10: Paragon Alternative School Events Summary	101
Table 5	Chapter 8	June 23 to September 8: Summary of Paragon Alternative School	104
Table 6	Chapter 8	September 12 to 27: Paragon Alternative School Summary Notes	108
Table 7	Chapter 10	September 28 to October 2: Paragon Alternative School Discussion Notes	136
Table 8	Chapter 13	A Count of Key Leadership Processes Related to the Paragon Alternative School	162
Table 9	Chapter 14	Were There Hidden Scams?	170
Table 10	Chapter 15	Critical Aspects on Ed's Path to Leadership	178
Table 11	Appendix E	Observational Tallies and Ed's Workday	207
Table 12	Appendix F	June 7 – Items Raised During Student Accommodation Committee Meeting 2	213
Table 13	Appendix G	Seating Plan in Student Accommodation Committee Meeting 4, September 12	219
Table 14	Appendix K	Grade 9 Mathematics Achievement Test Results – 1992	242
Table 15	Appendix L	Two Timelines: Student Accommodation Committee Highlights and Alternative School Highlights	245

Appendices

Appendices provide the reader with details that the body of the text does not include. Some appendices help the reader understand the educational system better, provide a compilation of terms and people for reference, and add details left out of the main account.

Appendix	Title	Page
Appendix A	Ethics, Validity, and Reliability in Qualitative Studies	189
Appendix B	A Primer on Educational Structures in Canada, in Alberta, in Wapiti Falls	193
Appendix C	A District Lexicon	197
Appendix D	Participants, Places, and Sites, with District Schools Listed Alphabetically	201
Appendix E	Observation Dates with Time Observed	207
Appendix F	June 7 – Tabular Account of Student Accommodation Committee Meeting 2	213

Appendix G	September 12 – Notes on Seating Plans Relative to Accommodation Committee Meeting 4	219
Appendix H	October 5 – Sample Discussion from Student Accommodation Committee Meeting 6	221
Appendix I	September 28 – Narrative Discussion on the Paragon Alternative School	225
Appendix J	September 29 – Narrative Discussion on the Paragon Alternative School	233
Appendix K	September 30 and October 2 – Narrative Discussion on the Paragon Alternative School	241
Appendix L	Two Case Studies—Summary Timelines	245
Appendix M	Selected Qualitative Studies of Educational Leadership: 1997–2017	249

APPENDIX A:

Ethics, Validity, and Reliability in Qualitative Studies

Of the two basic research designs, this account describes a qualitative study. The other design is quantitative, which often consists of studies featuring statistical interpretations of experimental tests. Qualitative studies are different. They are naturalistic, observational studies. The roots of the two words reveal the differences: Quantitative is the quantity of something—numbers. Qualitative refers to the qualities of a phenomena. Both types of studies are scientific, but quantitative is deemed a "hard" science, and qualitative is referenced as "soft." The reference to "soft" may be why qualitative science seems preoccupied with validity and reliability, as they are seen as suspect by hard scientists. A short word on qualitative research is useful background to this preoccupation.

Delamont is an interesting practitioner and a creative wordsmith. She calls qualitative research a "voyage of discovery" (Delamont 1992: vii) undertaken to make the "familiar strange." She was talking about studies where details ruled, details usually left unnoticed, and therefore strange. She recommends ample preparation (reading), early analysis, self-awareness, and respect for the "the views, perspectives, opinions, prejudices and beliefs of the informants, actors or respondents" (Delamont 1992: 7).

Bogdan and Biklen's 1982 text introduced me to qualitative research in educational settings. Their key points: data are analyzed inductively; that is, rather than proving a hypothesis, hypotheses are formed from, or grounded in, observation. "'Meaning' is the essential concern" (Bogdan 1982: 29); the natural setting is the "source of data, and finally, the researcher is the key data collection instrument" (Bogdan 1982: 28). That last part is important, and worthy of repetition; the observer is the "instrument." Shouldn't there be scientific alarm bells ringing now? Probably, but there is a solution.

As the researcher is the instrument of data collection, strategies are required to corroborate evidence. Triangulation is part of that strategy. It is the use of multiple data sources—observations, documents, multiple informants—that helps establish the credibility of qualitative findings. Another major contributor to credibility comes about because qualitative researchers spend sufficient time in the field to amass copious data, and hence repetitive observations. Consequently, researchers know the setting, and they know what is routine; they are thus prepared to recognize what is forced or fabricated. Informants wanting to put on their best show would find it harder to mislead an observer who is there day in and day out. Notice the skepticism. It is typical of qualitative science, in fact, of science in general.

This particular study falls under the rubric of "ethnology," and that makes the researcher an ethnographer. Creswell describes the ethnographer as listening to and recording "the voices of informants with the intent of generating a cultural portrait" (Creswell 2013: 292). This study also relies on three ethnographic constructs: naturalistic observations, deconstruction of observations, and reconstruction of these same observations. Naturalistic observation was the practice of collecting data by watching the subject in his normal work environment. My field notes, collection of document and photographs, and interviews were the products of the naturalistic observations. Deconstruction consisted of cutting the observations into component parts, followed by identifying and naming these parts. This is the process through which Ed's leadership processes were found and listed. Reconstruction was the analysis of the events relative to the parts identified earlier. Here, events were reconstructed to create Ed's cultural portrait, his story.

Ethnography has further distinctions. The ethnographic process followed here is called "participant observation" or hyphenated as "participant-observation." This term seems self-explanatory, but it may not be quite that simple, as there is a continuum between total participation and total observation. There are other discombobulating facts relating to ethnography and participant-observations. Consider the thoughts of these two qualitative scientists.

Goffman (1989), a researcher with Alberta roots, used humour, and was loose and uncomfortably revealing. "I only want to talk about…participant-observation—observation that's done by two kinds of 'finks:' the police on the one hand, and us on the other" (Goffman 1989: 125). His point: participant-observers look to reveal others, and therefore, because real people are involved, caution and care are required. His solution was to be sure of what is seen and understood, and that requires sufficient observation. His expectation was to spend much more time in the field than I had, and to compensate, I provide an abundance of detail.

Contrarian Wolcott (2005) provided further insights. At seventy-five years of age, nearing the end of a forty-three-year career, Wolcott had become an elder statesman for participant-observers. He delighted in fieldwork. One reason was that it allowed him to watch people without fear of censure—that is, fieldwork encouraged him to stick his nose into other people's business. He was fun, clear, generally diplomatic, and consistently common sensical. "I cannot imagine initiating a study in which I had no personal feelings, felt no interest or concern for the humans whose lives touched mine, or failed to find in those concerns a vital source of inspiration and energy" (Wolcott, 2005: 158). That is definitely not a description of the cold, hard facts of quantitative science. For him, qualitative research was an art, and the researcher was an artist. When asked, what's next for the researcher, Wolcott's typical answer is "it depends," and with this hedge, he eloquently shared why this is so.

Beyond the "it depends" defence of qualitative science, Wolcott had concrete guidelines for researchers. He recognized that data collection and analysis would always challenge researchers and, therefore, had to be addressed. Consider his thoughts on data collection: Is it right, ethical, Wolcott asks, for an observer to watch, record, and analyze events that would normally be private? What should be included? What should not be included? To illustrate, consider the extreme. Do researchers talk about murder, violence and abuse, fear and insecurity, and love/hate relationships? Wolcott thought that determining "how much to tell and how best to tell it" (Wolcott 2005: 259) was critical. Decisions had to be weighed artistically and personally. Ethnographers must not abandon their human qualities because of work.

Beyond ethical considerations, observing it correctly with valid, truthful data and plausible meanings, when everything was personal, extra care was required. Two parameters, validity and reliability, help addresses these issues. Validity refers to the accuracy of data. Reliability refers to how well the data matches the events observed.

The first parameter, validity, is nuanced, but it starts simply with this observation. How much more accurate can data be than what is observed firsthand? But there is more, because validity relates back to the data collection instrument; again, validity depends on the researcher! Unable to observe and record everything, researchers must select what they record. And having selected what to record, how can the researcher set aside their preconceived ideas? Wolcott is referring to bias and recognizes that biases cannot be avoided. Everyone has views and opinions that matter to them—perhaps more so if they deny their existence or fail to understand own their limitations. Good technique, however, mitigates biases. Good technique consists of thorough planning, careful and explicit description and analysis, openness, full descriptions of what is seen, and explicit explanation of where the data leads. Above all, it is telling the researcher's own story. That is not a misstatement, for Wolcott believes the product is the researcher's story; he appreciates that there are other stories. He tells us to own it, to make it our best. That brings us to reliability.

The second scientific parameter required is traditionally regarded as reliability, which means replicable. Experiments are replicable. Observations are not. Observations are always one-off events and are therefore incapable of being repeated exactly as witnessed. In qualitative science, consistency is the substitute for reliability. While consistency is not replicable in the quantitative world, it is as persuasive. Being persuasive is not easy or obvious. Analysis is persuasive when purported patterns are supported with concrete descriptions, and when the perspectives of participants are preserved. In short, the cultural portrait or story has to fit; it has to make sense; it has to be believable.

Valid and reliable data creates credibility and that hinges on good technique. How does the researcher demonstrate good technique? Wolcott tells how in "Confessions of Trained Observer" (1981). He lists them, using his own views and those of others: Record everything. "Look for nothing in particular" (Wolcott 1981: 255) but notice what "stands out in a flat setting…'bumps'…interruptions" (Wolcott 1981: 255). "Look for contradictions or paradoxes" and "for the key problem" (Wolcott 1981: 256). Researchers should talk little and listen a lot. Share feelings, not judgments. For clarification, ask a participant and add it to your field notes. Get feedback at all stages. Check findings against the raw data. Write accurately and well. Trust the reader with data; more is better than too little. Look for meaning, but recognize that meanings can never be precise, and hard as we try, our story is not quite their story. Therefore, recognize, appreciate, that you are "not quite getting it right" (Wolcott 1981: 259).

Wolcott's final advice is twofold. First, good technique ensures validity, reliability, and credibility. Second, do what can be done.

Wolcott did not stress skepticism, but others have. It is relevant here because it became relevant to me. Every document is intended for an audience, and this audience can be played. And for the spoken word, every word was intended to serve a purpose for the speaker. Given the contradictions of purpose and accuracy, what can be believed? Remember, deception is subtle.

Return once more to the instrument of data collection—the participant-observer. Then look to my data collection. The longer I stayed, the more opportunities I had to become less part of the landscape and more of a player or participant. The advantage of being one of the players in their drama, as every observer turned participant no doubt thinks, is that secrets kept from an outsider will be shared within the group. Thus, the insider is granted access to more authentic observations. The danger is that in "going native"; observations get complicated. The "native" observer has less objectivity, and counterintuitively, data reliability and validity are reduced—not improved. Could this be happening to me? During data collection, I wondered if I was supplanting an incumbent's role as my subject's main confidant. When the "natives" invited me to participate, were they being polite, or had I crossed a thin line, becoming a volunteer member of the team, of their team? In the write-up phase, was I showing "overwhelming admiration" or the admiration due? Finally, was this concern legitimate, or was I overthinking it? I took these concerns as a reminder to pay attention, to be cautious, to be careful. Did I succeed?

APPENDIX B:

A Primer on Educational Structures in Canada, in Alberta, in Wapiti Falls

This short introduction, a primer really, is the offering of a lay person. It is here because some readers may not be familiar with Canadian educational structures and specifically with those of Alberta. From Federal and provincial structures, I describe power as I have known it. Power had an important role in Ed's history (and my own). Power became a personal research interest. My bias was that power was always present, always important, and seldom discussed. Finally, I place the community of Wapiti Falls in context as if it were something close to an actual community. The reader who wants and needs to know more, should consult actual authorities rather than rely on my personal experiences, on my memory of the educational foundation courses that I and many of my student colleagues uniformly maligned, and on my recollection of legislative highlights which were gleaned from every reading of a new School Act or other substantive legislative change. I begin with Canadian education.

Education became a responsibility delegated through the BNA Act, the British North America Act, which created Canada and its provinces and territories in 1867.

In turn, each Canadian province or territory delegated partial authorities to local education agencies. Note that each province, and I assume, each of the territories, also held on to substantial authority. In Alberta, local educational authorities had delegated responsibility for operating schools and collecting school taxes in their local political jurisdiction, while the province maintained responsibility for curriculum, staff qualifications, and additional taxes. In return, the province made substantial financial contributions in the form of capital and student operational grants. At one time, local taxpayers were expected to provide fifty percent or more of the school district's operational costs. At the commencement of this study, the portion of local contributions was under careful scrutiny. Changes appeared imminent.

The BNA Act was primarily legislative. Like the 1774 Quebec Act, the British made no effort to affect the dominant religion of their dominions. This minimized friction. Canada was Christian and the state-sponsored educational system supported the Christian faith of the majority, be it Protestant or Catholic. In the vast expanse of what would shortly become the North West Territories—NWT—the majority religion was mixed, and the public system could be either Protestant or Catholic or both. This dual religious convention was brought forward in 1905 when Alberta and Saskatchewan were carved out of the NWT. Consequently,

Alberta could have two publicly funded schools, a public (usually Protestant) system, and if minority faith voters so choose, a separate (usually Catholic) system.

As in all of Canada, elected citizens run their jurisdictions—nationally, provincially, and locally. The party that won the majority of electoral representatives formed the government of their respective jurisdiction—province, territory, or nation. The federal leader whose party won the federal election became the Canadian prime minister. The provincial leader whose party won the provincial election became that province's premier. Prime ministers and premiers, in their turn, appointed their fellow elected representatives to head each government department. These representatives are called ministers (of the crown).

As previously stated, every provincial department of education has delegated some of its authority to locally elected bodies called boards of education. These boards serve a legislative or policy setting function within their defined, non-overlapping jurisdiction, and they hire and pay staff to educate the jurisdiction's students. Now look to Alberta.

In each local Alberta jurisdiction or district, the senior staff member responsible for implementing local policy is the superintendent of schools. The superintendent also manages the staff of the district. He or she is assisted centrally by professional and support staff, and in the schools by teachers and other non-professionals. Schools are smaller units within a jurisdiction and are managed by principals who report to the superintendent or their appointees.

Professional staff—primarily certified teachers—are members of the Alberta Teachers' Association, a union that is also known as the ATA. All certified teachers are union members except for the superintendent and the deputy superintendent.

Most Alberta jurisdictions have two public boards, a public system, either Catholic or Protestant, and a separate system of the minority faith. Many localities also have one or more non-public, private schools that are often staffed by trained teachers. Federal schools for Indigenous students are also found on or near some First Nations jurisdictions. They operate under federal rules.

As previously stated, each province or territory is responsible for education through the boards of education, which they created. They do this by maintaining substantial authority over boards of education, and by providing and controlling large cash infusions. Alberta took their responsibilities seriously, and exercised power as they saw fit. Accordingly, the minister of education exercised legislative and monetary power over boards and board chairs. To make it work, each political appointee—minister or chair— was represented in their work with educators, respectively, a deputy minister or a school superintendent. At one time superintendents reported to the Deputy Minister. This was changed in the 1970s, making superintendents solely responsible to their local board. In this study, the deputy minister thought he should have both titular and legitimate power over superintendents. Some superintendents challenged this. Some ignored it. Ed was confused by it. Control or power has relevance in this study because it was part of the operational milieu.

So why draw attention to the differences in power? This was because power was there to be exercised. Superintendents were, at one time, appointed provincially and placed in a school jurisdiction, leaving the province with essentially all the educational power. When the province transitioned to locally hired superintendents who required only nominal provincial approval, locally elected boards suddenly had power, which in turn led to some superintendents experiencing employment difficulties. A number were fired. Time smoothed over the rash of firings but did not totally solve the problem.

Additionally, elected school boards could be dissolved by the province and replaced for a time with a provincial authority, specifically by an official trustee. Overall, board–superintendent conflict, while uncommon, did exist, and board dissolution was rare, but not unheard of. Still, the province was viewed as supportive of both superintendents and local boards. These understandings made for workable, but challenging environments until money became tighter—1995 and for a time thereafter? Money changed the dynamics of power.

To illustrate the importance of power, note that during Ed's and my educational careers, twenty years after the changes of the 1970s, the effects were still working their way through the system. I served my career in four jurisdictions. One of my boards was divided into two jurisdictions. This smaller unit was subsequently dissolved by the minister of education (1984), and in my next and last jurisdiction, my board was dissolved through a forced amalgamation (1995). Power was significant enough that, for this study, I anticipated watching how Ed would apply power. Then, during observations, I discovered that Ed had "inherited" his position in Wapiti Falls when his board and their superintendent came into conflict. At his acceptance, Ed vowed that his leadership practices would not be modelled after his predecessor, a once-powerful superintendent.

This study took place in the Wapiti Falls Consolidated School District #1, a system located in Wapiti Falls, a city of about 50,000 residents at the time. Its enrollment of over 8000 students in June 1994 made it the larger of the city's two public systems. Both were public, but one was known as the public system and the other as the catholic (separate) system. That fall, the Wapiti Falls public district was planning to employ upwards of four hundred fifty certified teachers and perhaps two hundred fifty noncertified staff. The catholic districts had their own staff, superintendents, and ratepayers. Overall, a healthy competition, existed between the two systems.

APPENDIX C:

A District Lexicon

Term	Used by	Meaning
according to script	Ed	Following the path predicted by Ed—if not the exact path, close enough for Ed to announce that it had.
ballistic	Ed	Extreme. (I found only one recorded usage but somehow remember hearing it more often.)
big picture	Ed	Including all the known data into a descriptive mental picture of the district.
bizarre	Ed	Eccentric and irrational, with a tinge of annoyance.
"Brother 'arris" "Brother Nolan"	Ed	Reference to a staff member, and only heard used within the senior administrative family: "Brother 'arris" was Jake Harris. "'arris" was a corruption of the family patronymic. Brother Nolan was the trustee, Paddy Nolan.
coming down the tube	Everyone	Information expected, but not yet received. Some Alberta Education announcements were slow to arrive, while others that were said to be "held up" were never received.
crossovers	Ed and Student Accommodation Committee members	Students whose attendance crossed over district boundaries, as opposed to students who moved out of school attendance boundaries but stayed within a district. Crossovers were an issue for both city districts—public and Catholic—but were tolerated. With crossovers, the district received per capita provincial grants, but not the taxes assessed in their home district. Rural students who left their rich districts and went to either of the relatively poor Wapiti Falls districts did not take their "big money" taxes to the city district. This was part of the "equity" problem. The other part was that tax inequity served political rather than educational interests. See equity.

crunch time	Bill Bersche	Last opportunity to finish financial calculations.
equity	Educators	Equitable funding was a funding principle that would ensure that every Alberta student had equal programming opportunity. Improved equity would let all districts offer comparable programming irrespective of their local tax capacity—wealth. Overall, rural districts received more tax revenue from oil infrastructure than urban districts received from houses and businesses. Rural districts were generally wealthy. Politically, rural districts also had more legislators while urban district had fewer legislators but more residents.
fat boy	others	A member of the local IT team—information technologists or computer programmers. I was told that on one memorable occasion the IT staff dressed up in hockey referee jerseys to emphasize their slim physique. The "fat boys" were parodying themselves.
gassed that move	Trustee Paddy Nolan Ed	Dropped that idea as non-viable. Gassed: spent or exhausted, drained it of its energy (Merriam-Webster, online, May 2020).
glued together	Ed and others	A puzzle solved or finalized. The antonym, "unglued," indicated arrangements that were no longer working, arrangements that might fall apart.
good boy	Ed	A person effective in their job, someone doing the right thing. Offputtingly "sexist" now, it did not seem so at the time. I do not recall hearing "good girl," which would have been even worse.
hot spots hot topics	Ed, Paddy Nolan	Areas of concern in Student Accommodation Committee discussions. They included French programming, schools and busing, and boundary principles. The committee chair added school closures to a growing list of hot spots.
just like (fill in the name)	Everyone	Referent power. District staff and others identified with Ed, and Ed identified with numerous others. The speaker signalled their empathy. Ed also used the term to refocus or change directions in discussions.

interesting	Ed and others	A neutral filler meaning nothing, indeterminate interest, qualified interest, no interest, negative interest, or ambiguous interest. "Interesting" was given when a reply was expected or needed. Its role is to fill empty verbal space.
leakage	Student Accommodation Committee	Students leaking out of their own attendance area by attending an out-of-area, but within district, school. It is synonymous with slippage. Leakage, slippage, and crossovers all came with student grants, but cross-overs left big "tax" money behind.
magnet school		A school with a specialized program that attracted students to it. Note: magnet school is a common educational term; it is widely accepted jargon.
makes all kinds of sense	Ed and others	The facts were coming together to provide clear direction. It culminated the discovery process initiated by Ed. The phrase implied success and efficacy. It also signified that it was time to move on to another item of interest.
oh man	Ed	Everything happening at once. Recognition of and resignation to overwhelming events ahead.
once in-always in	Ed and committee members	Wapiti Falls students living outside of a school's official attendance area were permitted to attend any school if the principal of the receiving school made the determination that the school had and would have space for the student throughout that student's years in the school. Accordingly, schools were "open enrollment" wherever there was space. In district policy, this was known as "Principle C."
Papa Phil	Ed	While never said in his presence, this term referenced Dr. Phil Weinard. Dr. Weinard took exception to any appellation that did not reference his medical title. In the Wapiti Falls School District, even slightly derogatory terms for Dr. Weinard were strictly used in private. Using such a term was as mean as it got.
powerful stuff	Ed	A good idea. An idea with the potential to contribute positively to work or attitudes. Student celebrations were powerful stuff.
process, not an event	Ed and James Thorborn	Decisions were still in flux, as more data was constantly coming in. The effect was to continue to gather more details until decisions were appropriate or required.

puzzle	Ed	Bits and pieces of data that were likely part of an unsolved problem, but which had not yet been assembled into a "big picture."
ripples	Ed and others	Changes or comments having a cascading impact throughout the system. Slight waves that might grow significant.
seeking to understand and be understood	Principal Paul Briggs	Listen and learn before trying to get your way.
slippage	Ed and members of Student Accommodation Committee	Occurs when a student "slips off" to another attendance area but within the district. It is synonymous with leakage. See "leakage" for equity implications.
speechie	Ed	A speech therapist.
take care	Ed	It signalled the imminent end of a telephone call. Other closing statements were also used.
Thursday, anything happens	Ann Spencer	Thursday's were often hectic and predictably unpredictable An over-generalization used for emphasis. It also worked for any day ending in a "y," leaving "anything happens" as the only constant.
worth the wear and tear on the chicken	Ed	A process, while challenging, would yield positive results.
wing nut	Ed	Someone counted on to repeatedly change position. He or she was unstable or unsure of their direction. Unpredictable.

APPENDIX D:

Participants, Places, and Sites, with District Schools Listed Alphabetically

Participants	Location/Details	Notes
	A-8 Air Force Camp	WW II military buildings and grounds in Wapiti Falls.
ATA		Alberta Teachers' Association. Membership in this union is mandatory for all public school teachers, as well as all central office certified staff, except for two—the superintendent and the deputy superintendent.
Babiuk, Ron	Alberta Education	Alberta Education consultant, Alberta Education coordinator of charter schools My personal friend Deceased
Bakker, Susan	Central Office	Department secretary for the student services coordinator
Bakker, Zach		Son of Susan Bakker
Belterlaben, Sam	Kananaskis Middle School	Principal
	Beaver Landing	Small Alberta town in Shortgrass Region. Home of researcher and his school district's central office
Bersche, Bill	Central Office	Assistant superintendent of business services
Big Rock		A rural community transitioning to an urban centre in greater Calgary
Bowdage		Family complainant, possibly pursuing sexual harassment charges involving their daughter in Grade 5
Bondar, Herb	Central Office	Student services coordinator

Boyce, Jerry	Snipe Lake Middle High	Former principal of Snipe Lake School who was referenced in June 1994 retirement ceremony. Later in a private conversation, Ed filled in details concerning a problematic school evaluation and his subsequent resignation.
Byron	Wapiti Falls Education Foundation	Foundation president, a city lawyer, and community volunteer
Briggs, Paul	Pawoki School and Etzikom School	Principal at Pawoki School (spring 1994) Principal at Etzikom Community School (fall 1994)
	Calgary Mercury	Major provincial newspaper
Cameron, Agnes		Community representative on the Student Accommodation Committee, and a former trustee and board chair
Cashel, John		Parent member, Student Accommodation Committee, and a local realtor
	Celebration Hall	City facility, formerly part of the A-8 Air Force Camp in Wapiti Falls
Cobb, Mark		Teacher and union representative (ATA)
Digby, Ab	Central Office	Curriculum coordinator (spring 1994) Assistant superintendent, human resources (fall 1994)
Dymtriw, Mike	Maintenance staff	Maintenance worker, president of CUPE local (Canadian Union of Public Employees)
	Edmonton Diary	Major provincial newspaper
Emerson, Gavin	J. M. Pivott Community School	Principal
Funder, Albert	Board	Trustee
Gatenby, Eileen	Waputiuk Elementary School	Principal
Guard, Barry		Leader of The Tailgate Jazz band during Ed's youthful career as a professional musician
Harris, Jake ("Brother 'arris")	Central Office J. M. Kovach School	Assistant superintendent (spring 1994) Principal at J. M. Kovach School (fall 1994)

Hendriks, Marvin	Alberta Education, Regional Office (Calgary)	Education consultant, Alberta Education
Hepworth, Barney	Central Office	District computer specialist, probably a "fat boy." See Appendix C: A District Lexicon.
Hislop, Willis	Calgary	Guest presenter, and a junior high school principal in Calgary
Hoffman, Esther	Calgary Board of Education	Board chair
Howard, Don	Central Office	Deputy superintendent
Jacques, Lydia	Board	Vice-chair (spring 1994) Chair (fall 1994)
Jenkins, Sandra	J. M. Kovach Elementary School	Vice-principal
Kanouse, Charles	Viewfield School	Principal
Kroome, G.		Local writer of a letter to the editor, *Wapiti Falls Cascade*
Lawrence, Harry	Coalspur Middle School	Principal
Lindsay. Loren	Orchestra Leader	Renowned orchestra leader during Ed's youthful career as a professional musician
Llewellyn, Dennis	Snipe Lake Middle School	Retiring teacher who spoke glowingly of Ed at Dennis' school luncheon retirement ceremony
Lynch, Rex		Parent member, Student Accommodation Committee
Mackellar Jeff,	Nakiska (Elementary) School	Principal
Mallet, Dr. Patrick	Urban British Columbia school district	Guest presenter, and deputy superintendent
	The National Press	One of Canada's premier news agencies
Natalia		Retiring teacher
Neally, Kimberly	J. M. Pivott Community School	Teacher, worked in a portable classroom
Nilsson, Beata	Principal of an Ontario School	Guest presenter, and principal
Nolan, Paddy (P.J.) ("Brother Nolan")	Board of Trustees	Trustee, local lawyer, chair of Student Accommodation Committee.
Noyce, Ed	Central Office	Superintendent, informant, subject, and friend
Noyce, Marie		Spouse of superintendent, and friend

O'Connell, Margaret	Board of Trustees	Chair (until August 1994) Trustee (starting September 1994)
Oliver, Karen		Parent member, Student Accommodation Committee
	Our Alberta	Weekly news magazine
Palmer, Milt		Former superintendent, Ed's predecessor
Petersen, Magnus	J. M. Kovach Elementary School	Principal (Retired June 1994)
Pivott, Joe (J. M.)	Central Office	Long-retired superintendent (emeritus) of Wapiti Falls
	Post Office (Old)	Refurbished heritage building in Wapiti Falls
Ramots, Gwen	Board of Trustees	Trustee, member of Student Accommodation Committee.
The Rileys		Family in Wapiti Falls. Ed said they had "history," which I assumed meant past encounters of interest.
	Roseray County	An Alberta rural municipality near Wapiti Falls Consolidated School District #1.
Sharon	Calgary Regional Office	Alberta Education consultant
Sherry, Wayne	Central Office	Central Office staff member, previously acting secretary-treasurer in Beaver Landing, researcher's hometown and home school district.
Spencer, Ann	Central Office	Secretary to the superintendent
Stanley, Howell	Calgary Public	Superintendent
Stickle, Lisa		Local teacher and board presenter
Stimson, Rita	Goodwater School	Principal
	Sunday Rapids	Free-circulation weekly paper in Wapiti Falls
Svarich, Peter	Board of Trustees	Trustee, local lawyer
	Tallgrass Human Resources	Association of human resource department heads serving a large geographic region that included Wapiti Falls

	Tallgrass Region	Informal group of prairie school districts serving the huge geographic region including Wapiti Falls and Beaver Landing—Saskatchewan to British Columbia. Prairie ecosystems include the vague terms shortgrass, tallgrass, and parkland. Here, the low population "shortgrass" region where I lived was informally subsumed by the higher population "tallgrass" region where Ed lived.
Thompson, Ruth	Central Office	Assistant secretary-treasurer
Thorborn, James	Central Office, Ormand Mitchell High School	Principal designate/executive assistant (to July 1994) Principal (from August 1994)
Toth, (Dr.) Arnold	Alberta Education	Director of testing (and, in Ed's view, a de facto supporter of Dr. Weinard's school proposal.)
Virtanen, Katja	Goodwater Elementary, Central Office	Principal (to July 1994) District coordinator of elementary education (from August 1994)
	Union Gas and Electric	An international utility company located in Roseray County
Wapiti Falls	Wapiti Falls	Smallish Alberta city
Wapiti Falls Cascade	Wapiti Falls	Local newspaper
	Wapiti Falls Consolidated School District #1	An Alberta public school district
	Alexo Elementary School	
	Coalspur Middle School	
	Christian School	A private (Fellowship) Christian School and lessee of the former Pawoki Elementary School (fall)
	Etzikom Community School	
	Goodwater Elementary School	
	Kananaskis Middle School	
	Kananaskis Elementary School	
	Walter MacEwan High School	
	Nakiska (Elementary) School	
	Ormand Mitchell High School	

	Pawoki Elementary School	Closed (June 30, 1994); Pawoki principal Paul Briggs moved elsewhere that fall. The building became Christian School (from September 1994)
	J. M. Pivott Community School	
	Snipe Lake Middle School	
	Waputiuk Elementary School	
	Windfall School	Mentioned in school closure discussions.
	Wapiti Falls Education Foundation	Byron, president, local lawyer James Thorborn, executive director
	Wapiti River	Area river
Weinard, Dr. Phil		Educational crusader/reformer, medical doctor
Wilder, Harold		Professor at local college (future trustee and board chair)
Wong, Janice		Teacher with a full-time, two-school assignment

APPENDIX E:

Observation Dates with Time Observed

This table was originally constructed to tally my observational times. It was adapted to count the hours Ed worked and to identify key activities.

Table 11: Observational Tallies and Ed's Workday

Week	Date Observed	Times	Total Hours	Notes
	Tuesday, May 17			Ed Noyce identified as subject. Interview appointment made.
	Thursday, May 19	16:00 – 17:00	Time not counted	Entry interview with Ed Noyce. Agrees to participation. Leads building tour.
	Friday, May 20			Attend Joint Meeting: CASS 09:00 – 12:00 and 13:00 – 14:30 (CASS = Conference of Alberta School Superintendents)
Week I	Thursday, May 26	07:50 – 12:00 12:00 – 16:30 19:00 – 20:30	10:10	First full day of observation Lunch meeting: board committee examines new teacher contract proposal Student art show: 19:00 – 20:30
	Friday, May 27	08:10 – 12:00 12:00 – 17:35	9:25	Dale's late arrival. 08:05 hours District retirement luncheon (Ed admitted that he normally worked 5–6 hours on the weekend.)

Week II	Tuesday, June 7	08:05 – 12:00 12:00 – 16:36	8:31	Central Office admin retreat at Ormand Mitchell High School Student Accommodation Committee, Luncheon (Next Accommodation meeting held on June 21.) (Ed confirmed that he caught up on mail at home.)
	Wednesday, June 8	07:47 – 12:00 12:00 – 16:55 18:46 – 21:30	10:10 (Ed's private meeting. Adjust 1 hr 42 mins)	Senior admin meeting Ed's meeting with County of Roseray—1:42 hrs.—while Dale had lunch with the Wayne Sherry family. Dale and Wayne talked about the district Regular board meeting
	Thursday, June 9	07:45 – 12:00 12:00 – 17:55	10:10	Lunch at Noyce home. 16:00: Central Office retirements 17:55: Ed and Marie depart for Walter MacEwan High School year-end function (Note: Hours not counted when Dale absent.)
	Friday, June 10	07:58 – 12:00 12:00 – 16:40	8:42	Wapiti Falls retirement luncheon. Ed attends evening function (another retirement?) (Time left out of Ed's work hour count) Ed's weekend work: enrollment data for Accommodations Committee
Week III	Wednesday, June 22	07:45 – 12:00 12:00 – 16:30 18:45 – 23:05	10:15 (Ed's private lunch: adjust 50 mins)	Senior admin meeting Ed and son have private meeting (son's vehicle accident): 12:10 – 13:00 Regular board meeting features update from Dr. Weinard
	Thursday, June 23	07:43 – 12:00 13:00 – 16:30	7:47 (Ed's private lunch adjust 1 hr)	Ed & son had private meeting (vehicle accident): 12:00 – 13:00. Dale used the time to read Dr. Weinard's compilation of selected research.
	August 17 to August 19			Attend Joint Meeting: CASS Summer Conference. Arranged further observations and interviews with Ed.

Week IV	Thursday, September 8	08:00 – 12:00 13:20 – 16:52	7:32 (lunch: of 1 hr, 20 mins omitted)	Dale had lunch at Wayne Sherry's home and returned late to the office, while Ed attended an unrecorded luncheon event.
	Friday, September 9	07:50 – 12:00 12:00 – 16:30	8:40	Lunch at Noyce home. Ed takes computer home for weekend work. Interview schedule completed.
Week V	Monday, September 12	07:50 – 12:00 12:00 – 18:07	7:57 (interview: adjust 3 hrs, 10 mins)	Ed Noyce interview: 9:30 – 12:20 Ed at private meeting: 12:20 – 13:10 Howard interview: 13:30 – 15:00 Bersche interview: 15:00 – 15:50 Accommodations Committee meeting
Week VI	Thursday, September 22	07:45 – 12:00 12:00 – 17:30 19:00 – 21:00	4:51 (interview & lunch: adjust of 5 hr 24 mins)	Thorborn interview: 9:00 – 10:30 Cameron interview: 10:45 – 12:20 Lunch on my own: 12:31 – 13:15 O'Connell interview: 13:15 – 14:05 Jacques interview: 15:15 – 16:05 Attend Joint Meeting: CASS. Evening 18:00 – 21:00 (not included)
	Friday, September 23			Central Office: 8:00 – 8:30 CASS Meeting with Ed: 9:00 – 12:00 Lunch: Ed and Dale at separate events CASS Meeting with Ed: 13:00 – 14:00 Update with Ed: 14:00 – 15:00
Week VII	Tuesday, September 27	07:48 – 12:00 12:00 – 16:40 18:50 – 22:15	10:48 (interview: adjust 2 hrs, 29 mins)	Private, student expulsion hearings: 7:48 – 8:25, and 8:30 – 8:34 Lunch at Noyce home, test, 12:00 – 13:20 Bondar interview: 13:30 – 15:14 Pivott interview: 15:25 – 16:10 Paragon Alternative School meeting with school staff and board Obtain three of Dr. Weinard's documents

	Wednesday, September 28	07:45 – 12:00 12:00 – 16:45 18:50 – 22:00	10:08 (interviews: adjust 1 hour, 59 minutes)	Senior admin meeting Marie Noyce interview: 10:15 – 11:40 Lunch at Noyce home: 11:40 – 13:00 Spencer interview: 13:00 – 13:34 Regular board meeting w/ committee (in camera) regarding alternative school
	Thursday, September 29	08:00 – 12:00 12:00 – 17:00	6:15 (interviews & lunch: adjust 2 hours, 45 minutes)	Lunch on my own: 12:05 – 12:30 (Ed attends to personnel matter over lunch: 12:05 – 13:28) Dymtriw interview: 12:30 – 13:20 Ab Digby interview: 14:30 – 16:00
	Friday, September 30			Telephone/fax update Received Ed's letter by fax: Re: Dr. Weinard achievement test claims
Week VIII	Wednesday, October 5	07:45 – 12:00 12:00 – 16:30 18:40 – 23:45	13:50	Senior admin meeting Accommodations Committee meeting: 11:50 – 13:30 Regular board meeting with Weinard and school council representatives Committee portion (in camera)
	Friday, November 25			Attend Joint Meeting: CASS
	Thursday evening – Friday, December 8 & 9			Attend Joint Meeting: CASS Issues @ Wapiti Falls Ed leads Dale on tour of district office renovations Final acknowledgement to Ed
Observer Total Hours	16 days		145 hours, 21 minutes	
Ed's Total Hours			155 hours, 36 minutes	Totals, plus interviews, plus excluded time, minus lunches at Noyce home, minus Ed and son's personnel meetings. No record is recorded as zero time.

| Ed's Average workday | | | 9 hours, 52 minutes | Ed also had work beyond the observation period—private meetings, and celebrations such as graduations, retirements and other events. Therefore, my observational totals understate his average workday. |

As stated, this table was not designed to compile Ed's time at work. Its intention was to count my time. Still, it provided a long and detailed account of both of our times.

There are challenges and limitations to the table. After careful compilation, I still found issues on my final reading.

This table records times as precise, while it actually contains many approximations. To explain, Ed might start for home, but was sidetracked and stayed longer than the record showed. Notes give only some such details. Sometimes, I forgot to record times.

Careful attention was paid in converting observational times to work hours, but as every scientist knows, with every conversion, error is introduced. It might have been better to include a qualifier, such as "more or less" or to have used the scientific notation of +/- (plus-minus) for all records of time. I had this internal debate and decided that it was too late to improve the record and asked myself, to what end would better precision achieve. For example, Ed worked a good long day, whether it was recorded as nine hours, fifty-two minutes or between nine and ten hours.

For accuracy, a spreadsheet was used to calculate the totals and averages. Adding hours and minutes together gets confusing, but when time is recorded entirely as minutes, and then converted by the spreadsheet, the tally is easy.

APPENDIX F:

June 7 – Tabular Account of Student Accommodation Committee Meeting 2

Student Accommodation Committee Meeting 2 was held in a small meeting room in the district office's resource centre. The call to order came at 12:08 hours, followed by introductions of the seven committee members and the observer. A table summarizes this meeting. Its purpose is to highlight the breadth of topics raised, to note the general involvement of committee members, and to consider Ed's involvement.

Table 12: June 7 – Items Raised During Student Accommodation Committee Meeting 2

Raised by (if known):	Issue/Comment/Other	Ed's Response (if any):
Paddy Nolan, Committee Chair	Asked Ed to review progress to date. Members all had a package developed and circulated by Ed and his secretary.	Reviewed attendance areas, their establishment criteria, and answered related questions.
Unattributed	Strong feelings expressed over crossovers, specifically Catholics attending public schools. Committee learned that crossovers also happened in the opposite direction. (Nothing was said about rural students crossing over into the public district.) Time: 12:24 hours.	Crossovers were problematic for both public districts.
Gwen Ramots, Trustee	Note: Gwen's comments were not recorded here, as the observer's focus was on Ed's involvement, and being new to the committee, I struggled to keep up.	
Agnes Cameron, former Board Chair	Thanked Ed for providing excellent information.	

Unattributed parent member	How many non-resident (rural) students were enrolled in district schools?	The answer could be easily obtained by an examination of their handout. Members looked at the materials, seemed satisfied, and the question was not pursued further.
Gwen Ramots	(Again, Gwen's question was not recorded.)	Ed struggled to answer while eating a luncheon sandwich. (Ed finished chewing and swallowed. Thereafter, he avoided eating during committee meetings.)
Agnes Cameron	Interrupted Ed's struggled response to Gwen by asking, was the committee looking for drastic changes in attendance areas? The question hung out—left unanswered. Agnes continued, and drew chuckles over an incident from her past: back when she was board chair, a policy change drew student protest, picketers, and media coverage. (To me, her unspoken message was that board work was serious, with serious ramifications.)	
Paddy Nolan	Asked Ed to read the board policy and answer questions.	Ed did so.
Unattributed parent member	Since parents shopped for schools, how did this affect Windfall School students? After a generous discussion, this parent's question was left unresolved.	Ed referenced a list in the committee's package.
Agnes Cameron	Requested clarification, explanation on a policy matter.	Made notes (presumably for minutes, his investigation and a subsequent revisions).
Unattributed	Would a new school be built in the growing subdivisions to the east of their new high school?	Advised that the district held nine future school sites. This knowledge generated related questions and comments. Ed disputed one developer's promise of the imminent construction of a new school. Time: 12:41 hours
Unattributed	Discussion on wide range of topics: principles, program specialization, educational fads, equity of opportunity, and on the province's political leadership—supporting it, fighting it, or giving up on changing it.	

Paddy Nolan	Summarized and invited further discussion of board principles and parent choices. As to busing students, the board would bus an entire community to a school rather than splitting the community among various schools.	
Gwen Ramots	Commented about the district's open boundaries. She then asked if her understanding was correct..	Confirmed Gwen's claim.
Agnes Cameron	Requested clarification and history from Ed.	Indicated that district always tried to leave a student in a school to finish the program where possible. When asked again, he provided further details. (In future discussions, this became known as the "once in-always in" rule. It illustrated how "Principle C" was applied.)
Paddy Nolan	The committee should think about guiding principles for school boundaries, attracting/recruiting students, and specialized programs.	Nods in agreement.
Various committee members	Terms and questions thrown about. (Again, it was a struggle to keep up with field notes.) Further wide-ranging discussion took place on various topics including on the coherence of attendance areas, making sense of the system, common sense, grandfather clauses, and continuity within the system.	Responds, often with examples.
Unattributed	Disruptive student movements—uprooting students from their existing schools—drew substantial discussion and disagreement.	
Unattributed but general	Board efforts were recognized and appreciated.	
Unattributed but general	General discussion on the committee's role and mandate. Questioned if they were to focus on principles, propose major changes, or just clarify practice? Should they propose simple or extensive revision of existing attendance areas? Overall, what did the board want?	
Paddy Nolan	The board wanted an independent view. He added, "Don't worry about the board."	

Agnes Cameron	Countered Paddy's "don't worry" claim by saying it would soon be "an election year." (The implication that I understood was that whatever they decide would have political implications.)	
		Suggests that the committee look for "hot spots" and named some.
Agnes Cameron	The issues were complicated. Then admitted, "I don't know" if we can find solutions.	
Unattributed	Further wide-ranging discussion.	Answers specific questions posed. Others begin to use Ed's terminology such as "slippage," "crossovers," etc.
Agnes Cameron	Compliments Ed: his knowledge, his sense of timing, etc.	
Unattributed	Wide-ranging discussion. (Note: the pace was fast and hard to follow.)	
Agnes Cameron	Asserts that there is a problem of excess student space because elementary schools have lost one grade. [Grade 6s were removed from elementary schools and Grade 9s were assigned to a high school These moves created Grade 6 to 8 middle schools. Further, with Grade 9s in high school,. the district could fill both the old and new high schools.]	Notably offered no comment—neither further explanation nor mitigation. (She may have been wrong on space available in elementary schools. Moving grades was undertaken to fit of existing student populations into existing schools. Further, I wondered if the change to a middle school philosophy was actually secondary to the real need of fitting in all the students.)
Agnes Cameron	French immersion enrollment has dropped from initial enrollments. Was this expected?	Yes. Gives reasons and adds that this was normal.
Paddy Nolan	Think about their next meeting: the date and time; the decisions needed, and the suggested discussion topics including French immersion and school amalgamation—school closure.	

Unattributed	What practices helps attract students, to fill schools?	Suggested that a local college professor be invited to a meeting. (Ed may have thought this educator was particularly knowledgeable, but we soon hear a hint of other perspectives.)
Unattributed	Windfall School's recruitment ad was raised as a future discussion item.	Asked about his response to the ad, Ed said only that he was aware of it. (He did not seem unduly upset, said simply that he did not support it, but someone still ran it.)
Unattributed	Someone disparaged the college professor's motives. (Note: the observer may have the order wrong. There was tension over small school enrollments, and the possibility of imminent additional school closures. Someone seemed to distrust this professor or perhaps a general distrust for "learned folks," attitudes that were not uncommon in Alberta.)	Ed did not respond. (My assumption was that this professor had made his views on small schools known.)
		Asks for and gets permission to offer direction for future discussion. Once more Ed names hot spots—French immersion and its delivery, low and high enrollment schools and related busing, and boundary principles. Members nod in agreement. He made no mention of school closure(s).
Unattributed	Next meeting dates and times discussed. They settle on June 22.	
Paddy Nolan	Proposed that the committee discuss boundaries, and noted that one school, J. M. Pivott, had a geographical area too small for a K to 9 school.	

Paddy Nolan	Suggested that the Pivott School would better suit a K-5 student configuration. (It was currently K-9 and come next fall it would be K-8. Also note that K is kindergarten. The number—5 or 8—is the senior grade enrolled. As previously outlined, Ed followed up on this suggestion with the school's principal)	Ed explains the history of enrollment at Pivott School. The board wanted to reduce grades, but the community liked it as is. He mentioned portables but did not elaborate on issues with them.
Agnes	The Pivott School grade configuration was strange.	
Unattributed	Someone wanted to know more about portables, their number and location.	
Paddy Nolan	Moving programs would help.	Moving programs by a division—elementary, middle school, etc.—would be considered a school closure and therefore subject to lock-step provincial rules.
Paddy Nolan	Directed Ed and staff to investigate ideas for school boundaries over the summer.	
Gwen Ramots	Asked about specific aspects of Valleyview School.	Promised to check it out.
	Meeting ended at 13:33 hours.	

As parenthetical notes explain, this table above contains some holes. The comments of some people were missed. Topics were missed. Streets and locals were totally foreign, and consequently not recorded. It was my first meeting with this group, and it showed. My solution, as always, was to focus on Ed, which meant that less attention was paid to others. It worked initially, and as familiarity improved, so did the notes and insights.

APPENDIX G:

September 12 – Notes on Seating Plans Relative to Accommodation Committee Meeting 4

It may be unusual to depict where committee members sat for meetings but think back to growing up. In our family, each individual had a regular chair. There were reasons for the order; some of it involved discipline. In school, students always had their assigned seats. The same held true when men lived away from home, in construction camps. There, some individuals always sat at the same table, the same bench, in the same spot on the bench. Those who needed this familiarity, sitting next to friends, meant that discussions could be continued, and non-verbal exchanges understood. Some seats or areas seemed to have their own status. Having worked in four such camps, I learned that it was best not to sit in someone else's spot.

In short, I learned that where you sat affected conversations, specifically in agreement/disagreement, when individuals felt comfortable or alienated, or when sharing little insights and humour. A sitting plan might have been informative on the work of this Student Accommodation Committee, and so, I used some "down" time to create the table below.

Table 13: Seating Plan in Student Accommodation Committee Meeting 4, September 12

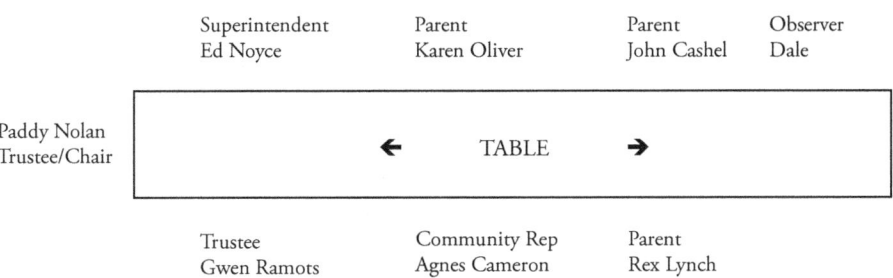

The next meeting of this committee had a different chair placement but maintained the same seating order.

Would this be because we are creatures of habit or of comfort? I also observed musical chairs on one other occasion, in a senior administrator meeting, and made notes on it. Having observed seating order, and finding no obvious connections, I concluded that seating order did not appear as important as it had been in my family, in my teaching experiences, in my board experiences, or in my earlier history in construction camps. Seating plans were interesting, but not enough to create or share more of them.

APPENDIX H:

October 5 – Sample Discussion from Student Accommodation Committee Meeting 6

To review, the Student Accommodation Committee consisted of three parents (Karen Oliver, John Cashel, and Rex Lynch), two trustees (Paddy Nolan and Gwen Ramots), a community representative (and board chair some eighteen years before, Agnes Cameron) and the superintendent of schools (Ed Noyce). This narrative discussion demonstrates how discussion flowed easily and amiably. The participants were now well-informed about the issues, and they skillfully used this knowledge to move the discussion forward, even in disagreement.

This portion of the meeting began at 12:09 hours ,shortly after the meeting began.
- Paddy wondered out loud, were they saving money?
- John talked about closing Windfall School. It would make Flowerdale School more efficient. He then switched topics, asked about French immersion.
- Ed was asked related questions. He answered them.
- Others joined in this discussion.
- Agnes said the changes being proposed will not have lasting impact. In a few years, the board will be back in the same spot.
- Paddy talks about the expenses of buses, and that students will need more transfers. (The district primarily used city buses to transport students to and from their schools. City buses routes end downtown, close to the school presently hosting special needs students. Some special needs students would therefore need a transfer from downtown to J. M. Pivott School. That could be a struggle.)
- John came in again, said that there would be a minimal savings. Further, the committee should not rush to do everything in the name of efficiency. Maybe we should re-look at our decision to recommend closure of Windfall School. Besides, the funding crunch was behind the board. (Equity [special funding] was expected.) Moving would be disruptive. Moving dislocated special education students would be even more so.
- Karen disagreed; it would save money. The money would bring extra teacher time. It would alleviate some of the problems that come from larger classes. They needed to stick to their principles of fiscal efficiency, and as such it was hard to justify small enrollment French programs.

- John would not let her comments go unanswered. He commented that it was inappropriate to tie special education programs and French language learning together. They were too different. French added to the system, and there were extra grants. It did not take money away. And if the costs were higher, the district could charge more. Put in special fees. The committee needed to put forth a better plan.
- Ed said nothing. (Extra fees for special programs might not be permitted by the province.)
- Gwen Ramots spoke of saving one-and-a-half teachers.
- There was further discussion. Rex and John talked about the real savings and the money involved. They worked out some examples.
- Ed suggested that the board should address some of these issues when the dollars were actually on the table. The estimates would be better if they waited.
- Rex talked about French immersion, about cutting through the "principles," the red tape of rules and principles. (Rex thought French was elitist, but supporters thought it principled, even obligatory, in a bilingual nation. He supported keeping schools open which would be less disruptive.)
- John agreed, that is right.
- Paddy asked, would that be the best alternative?
- John restated his issues. He did not want to disrupt special education programs in Kananaskis Elementary. And, if we are serious about having only one school for French immersion, then look elsewhere.
- Paddy asked, what is so different about that population [special education]? Why can't they move?
- John said that they were simply less able; disruptions to their routine would confuse them.
- Agnes agreed, "Yes. I feel my heart to be ruling my head."
- Paddy spoke, but other things were also happening. (Note: the field notes did not capture what this referred to.)
- Rex suggested, maybe we could eliminate the single-track (French only) option. We have no school where it would really work well, and parents were strongly in favour of the dual-track schools. (English and French instruction in the same school.)
- Gwen Ramots thought that most people supported the dual-track.
- Karen countered; single-track schools had worked well for the separate board.
- Ed agreed.
- Paddy talked about fiscal efficiencies. Single-track French immersion schools would be more efficient, but he was open on the decision.
- Agnes asked Ed a question. It concerned the nature of French language instruction.
- Ed informed her, informed all; there was more English instruction as a student advanced through the program. After Grade 3, for example, English language arts was added to the program of studies; time was specifically scheduled for English instruction.

- Paddy liked the concept of French immersion in Kananaskis Middle School. He also liked saving money. He realized that this left Viewfield and Flowerdale at 50 percent of official capacity.
- Rex asked, would they still be viable schools?
- Agnes had further questions about language instruction.
- Ed thought about his reply, and then said, when French language students leave Viewfield and Flowerdale, there would be fewer students left behind. Cuts to staff and ancillary services—technical programs, library, counselling, administration—would follow.
- Agnes understood and thought that forced that the program consolidation measures off the table. It would not suit parents or students.
- Paddy Nolan asked, if the committee was comfortable going forward on the relevant alternative.
- The committee paused, were briefly quiet.
- John indicated that he would endorse the dual-track over the single-track; that is, he would maintain the status quo.
- Karen was not sure if we should make that decision.
- Paddy admitted that he could not find more good reasons for the single-track, and then laughed at himself, "And I am the one promoting it."

This portion of the meeting took about half an hour, from about ten minutes in and continued until about halfway through the eighty minutes of meeting time. Again, times were estimates.

APPENDIX I:

September 28 – Narrative Discussion on the Paragon Alternative School

Table 6 in the body of this account covers the exact same timeframe as this appendix and the two appendices which follow. Here additional details might be appreciated by some readers.

On September 28, I was in district offices by 07:45 hours. Ed was occupied, giving me a few minutes to fill out my field records. Yesterday left me with a big unanswered question. Shortly, Ed finished what he was doing, and when I asked for help, he made himself instantly available.

Was an 85 percent level of parent support for an alternative school attainable? Ed doubted it, but Dr. Weinard was fine with it.

This was my big question, and now I had an answer. I thought about what that meant as we traded comments. Ed told me that while principal leadership was prominent on most effective school lists, Dr. Weinard's exemplars did not include principal leadership. My turn: Who were the ladies who offered him support last night, one tapping his shoulder as they left the meeting? He named them, then shared a story: Last night's second speaker had similarities with a principal once employed locally. He did not last. I understood this to mean that he was gone, but I did not ask if he was fired or resigned. It was immaterial. We were done sharing, and Ed's workday began in earnest.

Wednesday's admin meeting started at 08:20 hours. Bill and Ab arrived on time. Don followed. Next came Ruth and then Ed. Bill favoured the same chair location for previous meetings, but this spot was now occupied, so he moved to a new spot. Ed came next, but his usual spot was also taken. No problem as everyone settled in. Chairs and positions were sometimes important, but not so here, at least not so then.

The meeting was soon underway, but before starting, everyone agreed to disperse at 11:20 hours. They had other commitments. Agenda building usually started their meetings, but today Ed started the process. (Was that because last night's meeting of Dr. Weinard and staff was critically important?) Ed was pleased with the meeting and summarized it: "It was all going according to script." His words set the tone. The discussion that followed was wide-ranging: the qualities of the various speakers, the feelings expressed by staff, Weinard's preferred American texts. A strategy slowly emerged. Don Howard, the deputy superintendent, suggested that the board should co-opt Dr. Weinard's agenda.

There was strong interest in this idea, but unfathomably to me, more topics were explored: Dr. Weinard's ego and unpredictability, research on phonic reading programs, press releases, last night's staff survey results (three for the alternative school and ten against), presenting research to the board, getting trustees into schools more, principals for or against the alternative school, and site-based management. Ab Digby, assistant superintendent, human resources, gave some history. Their current centralized text program came about to facilitate student movement between schools. It worked. Principals, Ed noted, would be comfortable picking their staff, but were uncomfortable with the possibility that parent advisory councils might pick principals.

Don Howard, deputy superintendent, had let his suggestion percolate, but now he brought the group back to the possible win/win scenario suggested earlier. It could be the common ground they had been searching for. Since the board is committed "in principle" to a research project, they should adopt the Weinard agenda and do it themselves. They would "have control over it." (As usual with an idea going forward to the board, this suggestion was being vetted in depth.) After extensive discussion, Don summarized, should we present this idea at tonight's regular board meeting? Everyone agreed; they should. Discussion moved on to other topics: a new and eagerly anticipated provincial fiscal framework, recognition programs, and student suspensions and expulsions.

It was 10:00 hours, one hundred minutes in, when I departed for my first interview of the day.

Analysis: September 28 Senior Administrator's Meeting

Would I miss something by leaving then? Undoubtedly, but what I had seen was important and worthy of some analysis before going further.

The administrative team's first topic had come from last night—namely, Dr. Phil Weinard's school proposal. Other topics come up, but they all transitioned back to this theme. Members laughed with each other. With a plan to go forward, they were progressing towards their favoured position, a consensus.

I made a point of watching Ed during the meeting. His ample eye contact, his hand gestures—opening and pulling in contributions—and his body language—leaning into some points and out for others. He was playful, suggested that he would ask Dr. Weinard to elaborate on his approach to teaching the provincially mandated human sexuality program. It was funny, just slightly embarrassing! My notes recorded this comment with a question, was that sarcasm? There were mild signs of Ed's nerves—perhaps—stifling a burp, tapping, and pointing a pencil. None were totally unusual, but they seemed more pronounced, more animated than on other occasions, on boring occasions. And while on this track of questioning what was going on, I noticed that deputy superintendent Don sometimes held back information and sometimes volunteered it. Ed did the same thing. Was there a right time to be open, and even when that right movement arrived, it did not necessarily mean being open about everything?

Of course! Later, I asked Ed about being sarcastic. He agreed; he could be. So what? That would be normal. A few more examples of sarcasm popped up; each surprised me. Did staying longer mean seeing deeper?

Back to thinking about the meeting taking place in front of me. While I was the observer tending toward participation, Ed was a participant tending towards observation—watching, listening, thinking, waiting, inviting, and always preserving his non-threatening manner. Observing was his preference. He participated when he had to intercede or prod, but mostly he waited. He helped everyone discover the best path forward, and to do this he turned away personal feelings. This was, after all, cooperative inquiry.

The first eighty minutes of this morning's observations, the district's senior administrators had been enormously productive, all of it relative to the coming crisis. The next twenty minutes focused on other matters—the cost savings of faxing over using the mail, a provincial fiscal framework paper expected Friday, student recognition, and student expulsions. I left to attend to my scheduled interviews and reflected on the positive attitude seen minutes earlier. I felt their optimism when I departed. What insights, I wondered, would the rest of the day bring?

Continued Observations: September 28, early afternoon

Done with the day's interviews, I returned to Ed's office and found him on the phone with his board chair, Lydia Jacques. She was asking about the media. His advice: say as little as possible. Their talk turned to the meeting with Dr. Weinard. Ed summarized: "It followed the script as I had it." Dr. Weinard's guests were not helpful, but he thought they were. Unfortunately, Ed said, there was still no more clarity about the alternative school proposal. The board would need to talk about their response. Snippets of conversation showed the rapport between Ed and his board chair: mocking the self-described "jock" principal, pretending that Dr. Weinard's supporters would be taking the proposal "back to Calgary." When Ed offered to share his notes, I was suddenly alert. Whereas I took notes constantly, Ed took notes infrequently. I looked and saw a mass of tiny script on a tiny sheet. The conversation continued until Ed alerted Lydia that he had a media interview in a half-hour. He returned to his telephone conversation, saying,, Phil was not available. Today, he was working at his medical practice. He acknowledged principal Charles Kanouse; he did a great job last night. And he let Lydia know that Phil Weinard had retreated from his promised tour of a Wapiti Falls School. It was now set for mid-October. Nearly done with agenda building, he shared the new direction that came out earlier, at the senior administrators' meeting, framing it as a way for both parties to succeed. Perhaps they could have a win/win. Details were promised that evening, at the board meeting.

Finished, Ed started a call to principal Gavin Emerson when Bill Bersche, assistant superintendent of business services, stepped into his office. Bill asked about French immersion, but he and Ed were soon talking about the meeting last night and wondering what educational topic would be on television that night.

Ed had previously said that he liked the local TV station; the district and the station were mutually supportive. They helped each other.

Bill left, and Ed returned to his interrupted task, his call to principal Emerson. He reached him and began the conversation by referencing the media's request to tape next week's meeting. Dr. Weinard, however, had requested no video cameras. Ed had agreed to this request, and in its place, he thought he would suggest that the media do their interviews before and after the meeting. Next, the talk turned to anticipating the discussion and encouraging attendees. This done, Ed returned to the topic of Dr. Weinard's request for no video cameras. No video meant that they would avoid a spectacle, akin to the "O. J. Simpson trial." (Cameras had helped turn that murder trial into a media event and popular showstopper.) With the call over, Ed filled me in. If Phil says anything, it would be a put-down of the superintendent and board.

Ed had more to say on the topic, telling me that he planned on challenging Dr. Weinard's claim that public schools cannot do well. He thought his showdown would occur after the meeting with parents.

That would definitely be done off camera. Ed had spoken of challenging Dr. Weinard many times, and he said that he had already had one showdown. I had missed it. Whatever, I knew that any face-off with Ed would be low-key—said, done, and gone.

Was Ed's deft touch, or even his reticence to make a scene, a strength of his leadership? Nothing showed otherwise. When I heard this promise repeated once more, the detail of his assertion seemed to be more than previous talk of challenges. I regarded it as further evidence that Ed was ever closer to the zenith of his tolerance.

While on another call, Ed was advised that the media team had arrived. He finished his call, went outside, faced the camera, and began. He enjoyed it. He was easygoing and able to throw in some chuckles. I left briefly and called back to my district. On my return, Ed surprised me. After numerous interviews, he had finally noticed how attractive this young woman, his interviewer, was. I teased, and he laughed with me.

Was Ed opening up to me, or was he stressed, his formidable discipline diminished?

At coffee, Ed chatted with Ab Digby, digging into Ab's knowledge as a former curriculum consultant. Ed was learning about the contrasts between the reading series Phil Weinard had named and that used by the district. Their conversation extended beyond textbooks, to personalities and strategies. Don Howard, deputy superintendent, listened in, then added his view: if the district did not take on his suggested research proposal, someone would do it in a private school. (I saw that as classic "them or us" mentality.) Ed did not react and instead turned his attention to learning from the district elementary specialist, Katja Virtanen. His specific probes focused on the merits of different reading series.

Back in his office, Ed took a call from principal Jake Harris, the Jake Harris of previous dust-ups. Days earlier, September 8, we saw that Jake was worked up. He had sought Ed's support then and received it, but somehow some need was left unsatisfied. Jake was worried again; now he was sure that the alternative program would be coming to his school, and this would mean that he would be out of a job.

Jake was providing the piece missing from an earlier puzzle, namely that he was afraid of being let go, released, fired. A string of problems seemed to be settling on him, tangling him up with every turn.

Ed asked, where did you hear that? He listened and responded, Phil did us some good last night. They shared other details, including a discussion of a media person known for promoting Dr. Weinard; these two were seen as a tandem team. And while this nationally syndicated columnist was at the meeting, he was not seen chatting with Dr. Weinard. Was something amiss in their relationship?

Ed and Jake's back and forth continued. Ed said, we went overboard on promoting "whole language." Some of the current criticism would have been legitimate five years ago.

Would Ed's relaxed manner, his calming tone, placate Jake? It may have worked because Ed switched tactics, began asking questions, asking for advice.

Who did Jake predict might be interested, possibly interested, in working at the proposed school? What did Sandra, his vice-principal, think, feel?

Ed already knew something here; Sandra had tapped Ed's shoulder while leaving the meeting. It might have meant many things, but I saw it as support or agreement. Perhaps by focussing on her, Ed was seeking more knowledge or wondering about confidences shared within the school. Or maybe he wanted Jake to think harder, to dig a bit deeper.

Then the conversation turned from Jake's crisis to real school issues—current matters—the language arts curriculum. I knew this signalled that the conversation would soon end. It did, but there was no work stoppage.

Ed began returning calls. When one particular principal on his priority call list was unavailable, he left for a school on a topic unrelated to Dr. Weinard.

It was now 15:45 hours, ever closer to quitting time, and Ed was back in his office and on the phone with principal Charles Kanouse. He told principal Kanouse that thirteen surveys were completed last night.

These were the results I learned earlier. No one mentioned the number of teachers at the meeting. Some of the attendees were trustees, and others were from the central office and elsewhere. Most attendees, however, were teachers, and most of them did not respond to the survey.

With their chit-chat done, Ed said, "Thanks, Charles. I appreciated your comments last night." Ed listened, learned that Dr. Weinard had not been able to set a meeting date at his school. Ed acted surprised, but he had already heard about the delay, from several sources. No matter, he enjoyed the dialogue: "Yes, put the onus on him." "Yes, and when he comes, he will have his mind made up… "Oh man!" […] "That's right!" He crossed his legs, uncrossed them, leaned to one side, tapped his pencil, dropped it, picked it up.

Then the conversation turned, with Ed leading: The district could access funds to do research in a small way. If Phil found one positive experience, he would want to apply it in every school. In medicine, one improvement affected every practitioner, but social research was different. We could give Phil a methods course as a Christmas present.

Charles followed along, played along. Then, Ed turned serious; he dropped his beef—his current frustration. Phil dropped names from the research but had not read the whole article. By 15:55 hours, Ed was summarizing, thanking Charles for his comments from last night, "much appreciated." And he invited him to the meeting next week. "Take care." (The seeds were planted; Ed wanted someone with Charles Kanouse's knowledge at the meeting next week.)

Done with calls for the afternoon, Ed told me that a presentation scheduled for tonight's board meeting had been re-worked to reflect what they learned last night. He had worked with the presenting team. (Staff were eager to help their district respond to what was increasingly seen as a threat to their system.)

Normal work continued: a memo to the teachers' union, French immersion enrollment, the district's wellness program. Ed left work at 16:45 hours with a promise to be back by 18:50 hours. That would be just before the regular board meeting. This stretch of normal amounted to forty minutes.

That evening Ed was already in the office when I arrived. He was with the sound technician, offering suggestions for improving the mike pick-ups. Ed's knowledge as a musician was being put to good use. The technician was attentive and receptive to the help offered. Don, the deputy superintendent, arrived next. He visited with the presenters. Others were also present, chatting before the meeting began.

This was the regular board meeting, and proceedings began on time, 19:00 hours. Business proceeded normally—the adoption of minutes, and then the presentation of administrative and trustee reports. Their first item under new business was "Auditory Discrimination In-Depth Program." Deputy superintendent Don Howard introduced their new district coordinator of elementary education, Katja Virtanen. She spoke about the program and introduced her team. Two of them, teachers from two different schools, would start the presentation. This part of the program was called Reading Recovery, and it originated in New Zealand. Ed listened. Twenty minutes in, another teacher was up, leading the presentation. She had been on a sabbatical leave to the University of Alberta, and suddenly embarrassed, she just found several spelling errors. She acknowledged her mistakes and then continued with new details, further information, and she recommended that a support group be formed. Another staff member, Lisa Stickle, stood, ready. She had test results displayed in a convenient chart. Trustees, and others in attendance, followed along.

This team had it together, a presenter in front, while two others, out of the direct line of sight, worked the overhead projector. Then they switched roles. Lisa began a mini-lesson on vowel sounds. Don commented, four months for students to complete it. He was immediately corrected by a presenter. No, it was forty-five minutes a day, and completed over six weeks. The presenters continued. Results have been positive. Trustee Paddy Nolan asked for clarification. Was this suitable for all students?

A team member answered, this program was like phonics, so not every student needed it. Most kids moved from phonics to whole language. There was a waiting list for this program, eighty to one hundred students.

(Apparently, these teachers thought that Dr. Weinard was partially right; phonics was important for some kids, just not all kids, and not all the time.)

Ed apologized on behalf of students; English was a hard language to learn. Teacher training was especially important. Tonight, I learned about the "athletic 'e' jumping over a consonant."

Mark Cobb, teacher union representative and regular attendee, addressed the board. A boy from his class had been in this program. Lisa had worked with him and did a great job.

Trustee Paddy Nolan, obviously interested, had another question, can we do more, add more? Ed indicated they were going as fast as they could. He could see that trustee Nolan wanted more, and he added more forcefully, this is a high priority but there are other kids and other program needs.

Don Howard, deputy superintendent, talked about doing a research paper on it.

Trustee Albert Funder was eager; he too wanted more teaching along these lines. Trustee Paddy Nolan restated his earlier support.

Again, Ed answered, but with still greater emphasis, if you give us "more money," we will do more, but until then we will strive for balance. We "need to keep things alive" for other students, too.

The district had the power of taxation. They could raise taxes but that would have a political price and would fly in the face of the province's incessant mandate, "no tax increases." Ed had pushed out with his comment on "more money." He knew that it would not happen; higher local taxes, for schools, was effectively off the table. Trustees understood.

Clearly, this presentation had interested trustees. And as Ed had suggested earlier, their reworking of the materials would reflect well on teachers and the district.

The message delivered was that staff cared about students, that they did their best for students, and that they utilized more than one approach to get it done for students. They utilized their teaching skills, together. Conversations were easy. Teachers admitted their vulnerabilities; they admitted their mistakes and corrected each other. They were approachable, handling questions easily, respectfully. While the Weinard crisis had refocused the presentation, neither Dr. Weinard nor his alternative school were actually named. It was clear, however, that in the face of an imminent threat, teachers and the entire district were pulling together. Their presentation was really an attack ad absent the name calling. It looked political because it was political, just not political in the sense of challenging the board.

From this point on, the meeting continued with oblique references to last night's meeting with Dr. Weinard. Don introduced a discussion on French instruction and the team talked about coordination now that they had only one consultant for French and English language arts. (To save money, two consultants had been replaced by one.) The topic changed to a recent school evaluation. After Ed introduced the evaluation report, the school's principal, Gavin Emerson, gave further explanation of the process and results. There were no easy solutions; teaching was about more than using certain readers or teaching harder. This was an indirect reference to the Weinard presentation, but everyone recognized the tone and got the message.

By 21:18 hours, trustees were up. Their regular meeting had ended at just over two hours. Some participants were invited to media interviews. Ed, for one, was captured with a reporter leading him out of the board room. Surprisingly, no reporters pursued the "Auditory Discrimination" presenters.

The remaining trustees moved to a committee room. This room was their preferred location for discussions of personnel or strategizing. There, they waited for their missing colleagues to return.

The board's previous chair—that fall, she declined to continue in that role—Margaret O'Connell, chatted with me about the meeting last night. She had not liked it and was not impressed with the alternative school program. Trustee Peter Svarich listened in. Ed entered the room, and chairperson Lydia Jacques left, presumably for another interview. My chat with Margaret continued, but my notes did not. I was busy and paying attention to her. Trustee Paddy Nolan joined in. He agreed; Dr. Weinard's presentation was not impressive. In fact, Paddy had left before it finished. Questions about the numbers in attendance were discussed, and guesses made—about one hundred attendees. Bill Bersche, assistant superintendent of business services, had the exact count; it was eighty-one.

By now, everyone involved in media interviews had returned, and the in camera meeting was convened. Trustee Nolan had questions, detailed questions, about Dr. Weinard's presentation and about his concept. Several other trustees discussed getting more help to Dr. Weinard. They wanted to help him clarify his proposal and suggested that they adjust meeting dates previously agreed to. Trustee Nolan disagreed, if you try to help him and if he then failed, he would blame the "helpers." Trustee Loren Svarich stated that Dr. Weinard just does not know how to talk to teachers. (Was this legal pandering, an example of how Svarich, as a lawyer, would excuse a wayward client?) This view did not wash with his fellow trustees. Ed talked about Dr. Weinard's ego, about helping him save face. He asked, what would happen if there was not parental support? He then requested that trustees hear out a proposal from their deputy superintendent.

Don elaborated on the morning's discussion. The district should do action research. He spoke at some length, and as he elaborated, there were nods around the table. Trustee Albert Fundy agreed, but thought it was an offer that Phil would not accept. Everyone loosened up, felt their stress dissipating. The board had an olive branch. They were coming together. This executive portion of their meeting ended at 21:55 hours.

Ed and I lagged behind for another five minutes to review events. Ed indicated that it had been a good day. I inquired about Paddy Nolan, thought that he was going somewhere with his comments. He had impressed me. Ed agreed, but said that he was inconsistent, and that Ed could not predict what Paddy would think or say. Ed then turned the tables, why did I think it was important? I offered no real answer, but my hesitation gave Ed opportunity to volunteer his thoughts. He had been "sharp" with Paddy, "give us more money" sharp. Ed was not pleased with himself, but he was pleased with Don and his presentation. Don had scored "some brownie points" with trustees. Previously off-putting to some trustees, Don had grown into his role. Tonight, he had given his board a way out of their dilemma.

For Ed, Don's success was important while his own reaction to Paddy was viewed as unacceptable.

APPENDIX J:

September 29 – Narrative Discussion on the Paragon Alternative School

As indicated in the previous appendix, this is another, more detailed, account than provided in Chapter 8, Table 6.

Thursday, September 29, began in confusion (for me). I arrived at district offices early, only to realize that I had forgotten my laptop computer and briefcase. I needed them and left. When I returned, at 07:58 hours, Ed was behind a closed door. I used the free time to add notes about the previous night.

The night before, former board chair Margaret O'Connell, who I previously saw as distant, had invited me to sit next to her during the executive discussions. We chatted, leaving me unable to simultaneously participate and maintain field notes. Part of our conversation seemed significant—Margaret O'Connell hoped that Dr. Phil Weinard would reject any school in Wapiti Falls. Failing that, she hoped that parents would just say that Dr. Weinard's ideas would not work in their schools. And then her final, fallback plan was to have me tell Dr. Weinard that he should just move elsewhere with his plans—anywhere but here! Some of her fellow trustees were listening, and they reacted by laughing. I laughed too, but added, that would be a "No."

Left unsaid was my commitment to avoid anything that had me talking to Dr. Weinard. Still, I thought it was interesting. I was becoming more than a mere observer, and I could become a potential messenger. While not quite an insider, perhaps, if I would just pony up—a small break from the acceptable protocol, from watching to influencing—I might be invited into their circle. Would "almost membership" bring better information, or would such information be corrupted by a newfound identification with the group, being part of their "in" group? This was the classic dilemma of "going native." (Appendix A: "Ethics, Validity, and Reliability in Qualitative Studies" provides further explanation of "going native," and other qualitative research considerations.)

Secondly, I had time to reflect once more on Don's presentation of a win/win idea—namely, taking on in-house research. I knew I had heard it before, but where? I decided to check details later, and when I did, I found several references. Ed had talked about action research in our interview on September 12 but said nothing when Don introduced it on September 28 to the senior admin team. And in an interview the next day, September 29, Ab talked about it being an idea he had previously suggested. And hadn't James Thorborn talked about it in his interview September 22? Don had also confused me by a referring to this very idea in his interview September 12 and then agreeing to sit on it until he thought the time was right to bring it back again. And what had been said when I wasn't in the district or at the table with them? In the end, I realized that they could not source the idea, nor could I.

Ed was out of his meeting now. I found out that he had been with the nearly infamous "Brother 'arris"—Jake Harris. Jake again. Jake was clearly a good administrator—he had been given his choice of assignments when positions were tight. And he had good support among the staff. They recognized and appreciated his work and his personality—Herb attended the staff meeting with Dr. Weinard for the stated purpose of hearing and supporting Jake—and no one ever said a bad word about him. Still, during my observations, he required more of Ed's time than others. Not that Ed ever held back any help he could offer or complained about his time with Jake or about Jake, period. While this account is a compilation of noteworthy events, Jake's name comes up more than others. In a word, Jake was interesting. Using a computer word count of this document, the most common person identified—outside of Ed—was Dr. Weinard. Dr. Weinard's mentions are fitting, as he was the educational crusader bringing a crisis to the district. The second most referenced name, with a quarter of Dr. Weinard's mentions, was Jake. Jake had about twice the counts of Ed's deputy and his assistant, and at least three times the next most commonly mentioned others—senior administrators, principals, public, and trustees. Jake's name comes up because he was a complex person feeling events that tested Ed. As a researcher, I appreciated Jake because he kept creating issues of cognitive dissonance that might have confounded Ed, that might reveal something of Ed's performance under stress.

Ed brought me up to date on Jake's newest issue: Jake was still concerned with the Weinard proposal, still afraid that he would be out of a job. Ed had previously addressed this issue, several times, but Jake could not shake his fears. And so, as Ed explained, this morning he had stuck to his message, refined it, and offered an emerging theory—namely, that Dr. Weinard had too much negative baggage to make an alternative school work here. But Ed added a caution, Dr. Weinard's failure here would not end the debacle, as he would continue to bad-mouth Wapiti Falls and Ed.

I began to think about what I saw as a significant problem materializing. Even on extraction from this crisis—no alternative school—the damage would be ongoing; Dr. Weinard just would not stop. Did Ed's own thoughts take this theme further? Did he think that this damage was self-inflicted—the administrative approach to his board's "approval in principle" was Ed's plan, after all. Had Ed brought a pox on the district?

Having brought me up to speed, Ed then turned his attention to Arnold Toth, head of Alberta Education's Student Evaluation branch, and then he called him.

Ed and Toth exchanged greetings, and then Ed cautiously and indirectly said that he would appreciate an update on examinations and on the testing consortium. (Bill Bersche was in and out; he needed to talk to Ed about a meeting. At the time, Ed was just listening to Dr.

Toth, and it did not affect the call he was on. Bill soon left.) Ed's lead-in did not produce the information he was looking for, so he became more specific. The reason for his call was that he wanted the "stats" that linked schools to socio-economic data. He listened, heard confusion, but no answer. Finally, Ed spoke directly, telling Dr. Toth exactly what he had heard. One parent—he still did not identify the parent—claimed that relative to communities of comparable socio-economic status, Wapiti Falls' achievement test results were disappointing. Hearing nothing, he finally asked, "Does the name Phil Weinard ring any bells?" Now, he smiled, amused, as he listened, then repeated Dr. Toth's words, the highlights, perhaps for my benefit. Dr. Toth could think of nothing to back up Dr. Weinard's claim. With this denial, Ed let Arnold know that he would call Dr. Weinard and would teasingly ask him to put money on his claim. Shortly, I heard, "No, he has lots of money." (Humour? Maybe.) Ed listened and confirmed his resolve to challenge Dr. Weinard, secure in the knowledge that Weinard had "no legitimate source" for his claims. His claims were false. He listened, agreed, and then ended the call.

Ed, planning his response, and, probably for my benefit, voiced his thoughts out loud, "Do I phone or write?" He decided on writing; he wanted a written copy, "short and sweet." Ed typed. His memo had four lines in paragraph one, two in paragraph two. Paragraph three was just starting. Short. He finished paragraph three, announced that it was done, and added, "one on my to-do list."

I called him out on having a "list." Even after seeing several notes, I was sure he had no to-do lists. And again, he surprised me. He showed it to me—tiny, brief, but real.

Ann Spencer, Ed's secretary, advised him that Dr. Weinard was on the phone. Ed took the call, and they chatted comfortably. Ed seemed to be enjoying it, and then, after a pause in the banter, Ed said that he had not obtained the results from Alberta Education, so "could I get them from you?" Ed listened for an extended period. Dr. Weinard, it seemed, was unable to provide the source data, and the call continued. Eventually, Ed responded, "That is interesting," and said, "Principals Academy in Calgary." And he identified "Wapiti Falls?" The call continued. I heard Ed say, "Your comment is that we should do better?" And then, "That is the same thing," and then indicated that he will "go back to Arnold. If you have it, we should have it."

The call was over, and Ed talked to me, filled me in; Phil heard about this data in a meeting in Calgary. Still, he had not offered to share his crucial and critical evidence, but he had identified it.

I suggested that there might be a mix-up, something linking equity with test results, that rich districts did better, perhaps. Ed listened and reacted with the words, "I have to get back to Arnold Toth's office." He tried and found that Arnold was not available.

Ed continued on to other business—a student moving to Wapiti Falls and arranging a meeting with Byron of the Wapiti Falls Foundation—when he heard a call coming into Ann Spencer's office. Ed waited, poised for that call, and when it arrived, as he had guessed it would, he spoke to a principal. Done there, he was on to another call, to a reporter.

Ed returned to typing. One more task done and suddenly, he left his office at top speed. Arriving at Ann's desk, they talked about the letter; it was his letter to Dr. Weinard. He was back in his office at 09:37 hours where he continued to take more calls. In an interlude, he shared other news with me—immaterial news.

The next significant call was from principal Harry Lawrence at the district's Coalspur Middle School, and it was about the Paragon Alternative School. Ed talked about the data he could not source. He said, Phil has some data, but "it is not what he says it is" because Albert Education has no such data. Having shared this news, it was Ed's turn to listen. Principal Lawrence commented about Dr. Phil Weinard's facial expressions during the meeting with staff, specifically during Jake Harris's speech. A trustee had also watched then and shared her observations. Both noticed Dr. Weinard grimacing all through Jake's talk. It was Ed's turn again, and he shared new information: Dr. Weinard wanted to bring in sponsors to the next meeting, the parent meeting. Ed thought that was acceptable, even desirable; Dr. Weinard's sponsors "should see how Phil talks to teachers." More back and forth: Ed discussed Alberta Education funding changes; he appreciated Harry's attendance at the meeting with teachers; added, "It would be a shame if we gave up the fight. The kids are first." He continued, said, that Jake was down. And then he projected ahead: if we do not get parents out, and if the wrong people show up, we will have only a narrow representation of parents. While Dr. Weinard's external resource people were "not dazzling," we need strong parent representation. If not, trustees will want to swing to what sounds best at the time. He forewarned Harry; they might swing to Dr. Weinard's preferred American language arts textbook, which would be the wrong "territory" for Canadian students. He was nearly done and said, how do we go to parents, offer them some balance? Phil will not get his school in Wapiti Falls, "but Phil will damn us far and wide." Before the call ended, Ed mentioned the action research proposed by deputy Don Howard. Finally, with the real business done, the conversation wandered. I heard "bizarre." These were two signals, wandering among topics and "bizarre," that told me that the call was about to end, which it did.

This barrage of alternative school discussion had arrived quickly, and then suddenly was gone. It started just before 08:45 and finished before 10:00 hours—maybe an hour and a quarter. I thought about what happened. Ed was keeping his principals informed, thanking them, listening to them, and sharing gossip. He expressed confidence that there would be no Paragon Alternative School and then—he was not so sure. He was also saying that upcoming events were important. Trustees could easily change course. Principals need to stay involved, need to help ensure that quality parents came to the meeting. They needed to exercise their influence. It was also clear that Phil would not be forthcoming on whatever data he had or talked about having. He frustrated Ed as I surmised from this micro-minute: Ed, when outside his office, a short distance away in an empty hallway, said something. Was it S.O.B, in full? Had I heard right? No matter, I recognized that tensions were building.

I left, briefly, in response to a call from my home district. On my return, Ed was on another call, and then another. This latter conversation was with a principal, and their conversation concerned Dr. Weinard. This issue would not go away. Ed was repeating previous sentiments; Dr. Weinard's claims about disappointing local results had no factual basis. There were no such statistics. And then, Dr. Weinard would be bringing in sponsors for their October 5 meeting. No problem. The conversation turned briefly to normal business, their strategic planning committee, and then they were back to Dr. Weinard.

It was still early—10:07 hours—and coffee would soon follow, and then a meeting with a staff member from accounting. Bill dropped in again. Ed told him of guests coming to the October 5 meeting. They were probably Phil Weinard's current, or maybe potential, donors. Bill let him know that a cheque for the Paragon Alternative School had arrived, but the donor wanted anonymity. Consequently, the money was sent to the district. Ed jested, maybe it should go into his "Benevolent Fund." Bill left, and Ed returned a call to Rena, a local TV personality. He gave her a contact number for one of the "Auditory Discrimination" presenters from last night's board meeting. He noted, by way of an explanation for me, that the media get a topic, do a live interview, and miss the next topic. The board agenda now tries to anticipate media noteworthy items and alternate them, so that the reporters get all the "hot" topics they want.

By 11:00 hours, Ed was on a call to principal Rita Stimson. It concerned Kumon math, an out-of-scope math instruction program. Principal Stimson wanted to tell parents more about it. Ed offered support and a caution, be careful not to oversell it. Ed told her why; he wanted to avoid the blowback of overpromoting whole language with parents—different programs but the same issue. Again, the conversation wandered. At one point, Ed asked, "How did the media get that? Was it from Phil? Was it from a rookie reporter?" Ed wanted to "put them straight." He called it "weird," but "on script. Papa Phil didn't do himself any good." This conversation, like so many others, had turned into another Phil Weinard critique. Ed lamented: Phil did not have the stats; he simply drew conclusions; he could take lessons from a shoe salesman, and finally, Phil's guests were "gunslingers."

Ed's string of critiques was a bit cutesy, and for Ed, an unusual screed. Understanding the nuances of a conversation when only one party was heard could be challenging, but today's messages were unmistakable. Ed was tense.

Ed called another principal, James Thorborn. He wanted to talk about a student suspension, but James was out, and Ed agreed to call back later.

Eleven minutes later—it was now 11:11 hours—and having talked to his secretary, Ed was returning from the washroom when he saw Katja Virtanen, his elementary specialist. Yesterday, they had chatted about a reading series, but today Ed's focus was narrower. He wanted to learn more about *Open Court*, the reading textbook favoured by Dr. Weinard. She knew the series. Her summation: Lisa Stickle's program was easier and better.

Ed had also promised to get back to principal Harris, so he tried, but Jake was not in his office. He made an appointment to see another principal. He returned calls. One was to someone at the CBC—Canadian Broadcasting Corporation. He explained to me that he had a note, pocketed it, and then forgot it. He would now make good on the request. He tried again but missed this individual. He told a receptionist that he would try after 14:00 hours. He dialed a friend in England; they were coordinating a summer exchange. He reached him and chatted about the dates for a teacher exchange and a band exchange. They chatted about their work, about their respective issues and district debt load.

And all this time, Ed was moving, seemingly uncomfortable no matter the position, restlessly sweeping his hands through his hair, and staying exceptionally busy. He finished his call, hung up, and talked to me about the calls.

By 11:46 hours, he was greeting Bev, a school volunteer. He alerted me, told me that he expected her to become a trustee. He continued filling me in, described events as a media frenzy, and all of it was to do with the Weinard proposal. He concluded; they must be hungry for this to be newsworthy. It was a hope and a dismissal.

Just shy of noon, Ed called Arnold Toth again and reached him, again. This time he made notes, a lot of notes. He shared his fax number, wanted all the details. The call ended, and Ed explained, he would soon have the information he was seeking. Student Evaluation did, after all, release results identified by provincial location and community—all if it non-specific. Dr. Toth was walking back from an earlier dismissal. Fortunately, Ed had learned to check more than once, and to ask rather than pounce.

Ed suggested lunch at his home, and I declined. I had an interview, and I prepared for it in a vacant room. Once there, I could hear Ed and his deputy in discussion, but I could not make out the details. I did not try that hard. (Was this why Don spoke so quietly in our September 12 interview?)

My interview went from 12:30 to 13:20 hours. Finished, I returned to the office, learned that Ed was at a school, in talks with a principal. Curious, I thought he was going home for lunch, but this made more sense. Ed had talked about meeting with a principal to discuss his future in the district. This would likely be that meeting. It was personnel. It was private. Once more, normal leadership emerged briefly.

Ed was back shortly, and we looked at provincial Grade 9 mathematics achievement test averages from Arnold Toth, Student Evaluation's head honcho. It showed results by location, communities identified by cardinal location: East, West, South, and North. Huh? All the descriptors were vague, but all were apparently nearby. One community was described as a "magnet school." A magnet school in Tallgrass? News to me, and like Ed, I was part of this geographically huge educational community, and a resident. Another community was identified as a "university" city, but there was only one city in Tallgrass, and it had no university. College yes; university no! "Farming" communities were everywhere, but "blue collar," that seemed industrial and elsewhere. Further, the scores shared were all over the map; there were no easily recognizable patterns. One could be a school in my district, but there were numerous other Tallgrass communities that would match the stated criteria; likely several would have similar results. Was it even Tallgrass?

I looked at the results and categories and found nothing, so what was the point? I looked for a disclaimer. There was none. Had someone hoped to discover trends or relationships out of some ill-defined definition of a community? It might have been brainstorming, but for what purpose? And if brainstorming, why was it shared with the public? It looked problematic and it was.

It was 13:28 hours, and Ed had met Herb, student services coordinator, to discuss an incoming student, and then it was back to more calls, more in-house sharing, before crisis work would return. Phil Weinard's Paragon school was driving much of the work within the district.

At 13:56 hours, on reaching principal James Thorborn of Ormand Mitchell High School, Ed did a great deal of listening. It was about student suspensions. Thorborn had suspended two students that week, and Ed wanted the letters.

Principals can suspend a student on their own, but only a board has the power to expel a student, and then only on the recommendation of a principal. A suspension can be up to one week. Expulsions are for serious and repeat offences and typically last for the balance of a school year. An earlier expulsion involving Walter MacEwan High School was previously considered here. Since that expulsion, Ed has been learning more about school practices regarding student removals. His follow-up reflected his concerns about a lack of fair and consistent practices. Ed was investigating; were principals being fair?

Ed soon learned more of the details; these two suspensions followed student fights. Knowing more, he indicated his support for principal Thorborn's decision. Still, he wanted the suspension letters.

With their immediate business done, the conversation continued in the typical rambling fashion: "Jake was mouthing off?" He listened and found that Dr. Weinard might be using data that principal Jake Harris had given him, his school's achievement test results. Jake was now afraid that these results would show that his school was not measuring up, and Jake's vice-principal worried about that, too. Next, the conversation turned to the practices of a school counsellor. From what Ed was being told, he felt that the counsellor's comments were not helpful to students. Ed suggested that James talk to the union representative—let them know of concerns early on. Ed went on to mention a fix that was now in place for teacher and intern contracts. (James was previously Ed's administrative assistant, and Ed was evidently comfortable sharing some details on personnel.) Another school counsellor was mentioned. Ed was carefully attentive throughout the call, but he was also restless, fidgety. Finally, I heard, "It's been a slice," and the call ended at 14:19 hours. It had lasted for twenty-three minutes.

No wonder Ed's nervous energy had emerged during this longish call. Why hadn't he just ended it earlier? That was what normally happened; this was unusual. But why would he when he was hearing so much new data? James Thorborn was still part of Ed's network of "ears."

Another interview took me away, from 14:30 hours to 16:00 hours.

I returned to Ed's office and found him hard at it. He told me about his day, and he asked about mine—my experiences, my problems. I had seen this before; Ed was thinking. He was, as Ab had said, being "more pensive." His thoughts were interrupted when he saw colleagues walk by. He waved, pleased to see them, and then he shared the story of the "speechies." It was now shortly after 16:50 hours, and Ed's day was almost done. So was mine, except I had a long drive home.

The long drive gave me time to speculate: Could it be that Ed simply wanted control? Doubtful. One of the problems that day had Ed concerned about people sabotaging their own cause: A counsellor was speaking out of turn. Principals were being arbitrary about student discipline. Such issues could bother Ed, and right now, I saw him dwelling there, in the thick of these matters. I harkened back to a previous concern he had expressed about a trustee and about Don's concern that the student issues "weighed heavily" on Ed. But the big issue—consider all the time spent—was clearly about Dr. Phil Weinard, who was hurting himself and his cause by pursuing questionable interpretations. Confusing—why would Ed be concerned about Dr. Weinard? But then I realized that it was not all altruism. A damaged Dr. Weinard would lead to further repercussions in the district. That would eat up more of Ed's time, and unproductively at that. Ed lived for his district. I decided to phone him next day from home. With lots to think about, my three-hour drive home seemed short.

APPENDIX K:

September 30 and October 2 – Narrative Discussion on the Paragon Alternative School

As indicated in the previous two appendices, an account containing less detail is provided in Chapter 8, Table 6 and in the subsequent analysis. The focus of this Appendix is on just two days, September 30 and briefly on October 2. Of unanticipated significance at the time, Ed' copy of his September 30 letter would play an important role in what became the "Three Letter Campaign of October 5.

From my home district, at about 08:15 hours, I phoned Ed at work, but Ed was already in a meeting. If possible, I asked, would Ann have him call me back before 09:00 hours? He called back shortly.

I had two items to discuss: I wanted to finish my observations on October 5. Was that okay? It was, and then we chatted briefly about my district's and another's amalgamation process. Next I mentioned an upcoming job interview. He suggested that I should get to the kinds of things the new board wanted to achieve and to emphasize their priorities. Get at the human side of things: students, parents, staff, programs. "Glue it together." I was surprised and pleased. Facing his own crisis, he was thinking about my job prospects.

We continued our conversation briefly before I got to my concern. I thought that yesterday's events around Phil Weinard had really thrown him off-kilter. He agreed and elaborated. No matter what the outcome, Dr. Weinard would still bad-mouth the district, and having the ear of the national press, the district would never find peace. He saw no solution, but he thought it was helpful that he had a new and better understanding of the man. We left it at that.

Later that day, I was back in my office after school visits. Ed had forwarded a letter that he had sent to Dr. Weinard. No longer the "short and sweet" letter originally envisioned, he now had a detailed response, a two-pager plus an Alberta Education report.

He started his letter by referencing the September 29 challenge of sourcing the data behind Dr. Weinard's disparaging remarks on local achievement test results. Between Ed and Drs. Weinard and Toth (Alberta Education), the source study had been located. It consisted of test results from six randomly selected schools in Grade 9 mathematics. Each school was described but not named. Ed enclosed the full report—one page. There, results were compiled to show the percentage of students who received "acceptable" and "exceptional" standards. Ed examined this Alberta Education release and found that no results from a district school were included. He unequivocally concluded that claims of inferior district results according to their "socioeconomic status cannot be made from the study data."

Moving on, he shared district results with provincial averages. Local results were better. With these two point made, Ed shared his assessment:

> "If these statistics are the basis for your conclusion that we would be dismayed by the comparison with other districts of similar socioeconomic status, then I offer the following:"

1. There are no comparisons involving socio-economic status and Grade 9 mathematics achievement tests, because the descriptors "white collar or grain farming" were simply types of communities and were not socio-economic indicators.
2. We should celebrate the "District's Achievement Test" results.
3. Having "reviewed the individual school results achieved by the five schools in our district . . . , I find no cause for alarm or even concern."

He wrapped up as follows:

> "If these statistics are not the source of your comments during the meeting with our staff, I would invite you to contact me again. It is important that our Board of Trustees have the full information."

Ed had promised to confront Dr. Weinard's claim, and he did so plainly in this letter. Having read Ed's assessment, examine the data he used. Table 14 superimposes Ed's two line table of district and provincial results, with the six study communities and their test results.

Table 14: Grade 9 Mathematics Achievement Test Results - 1992

	Number of Students	Total Test: Percentages		Problem-Solving: Percentages		Subject Matter: Percentages	
		*ACC	*EX	*ACC	*EX	*ACC	*EX
Wapiti Falls	486	**75.3**	**11.3**	**73.3**	**13.2**	**81.1**	**16.3**
Province	27,888.0	67.4	8.9	64.1	10.7	75.6	12.7
Community descriptors							
Small Rural School in Grain Farming Community	16	100.0	25.0	87.5	25.0	93.8	18.8
Small Rural School in Mixed Farming Community	18	38.9	5.6	27.8	11.1	61.1	0.0
Large Urban School in "White Collar" Community	118	88.0	10.2	88.1	15.3	85.6	11.0
Academic Magnet School in "White Collar" Community	52	100.0	59.6	98.1	59.6	100.0	63.5

Mid-sized Rural School in Grain Farming Community	68	47.1	1.5	48.5	4.4	51.5	1.5
Small Rural School in Grain Farming Community	25	84.0	24.0	84.0	32.0	92.0	32.0

For Wapiti Falls, Bold letters indicate percentage above provincial standards.

* ACC - Percentage of Students Achieving Acceptable Standards.

EX - Percentage of Students Achieving the Standard of Excellence.

Several notes are significant. First, Alberta Education wanted schools to use results for teaching purposes. Since Dr. Weinard was not using results as a teaching tool, Ed had not provided individual school results. He stuck to Alberta Education guidelines. Second, Dr. Weinard may not have wanted to defend "farming" and "white collar" as valid socio-economic statuses. His statement of inferior results would imply that farming was a lower socio-economic status than white collar employment. Disparaging farmers and farm families was just not done in Alberta. Third, while the source of shared district results was never mentioned, some thought that Jake Harris was involved and further that he had said more and provided more than he should have done. If true, had Jake entrapped himself? That went to the heart of his worries; if his new school was not measuring up, he could well be out of a job.

On October 2, the *Wapiti Falls Cascade* published a letter from Dr. Weinard. In it, he replied to a letter to the editor. Previously, a writer had raised issues about Dr. Weinard's proposal, and Dr. Weinard wanted to set that record straight. It was a well-reasoned, respectful letter that addressed multiple concerns. This invitation occurred at the end:

> "I encourage parent council members to attend the 7:00 p.m. Board meeting at the School Board Office on October 5. Come with your interest, an open mind, and tough questions."

Like opinion writers everywhere, Dr. Weinard had responded selectively to the issues raised by the dissenter by sticking to what he regarded as his proposal's strengths.

APPENDIX L:

Two Case Studies—Summary Timelines

Table 15 highlights the temporal order of key features in the two case studies followed here, the activities of the Student Accommodation Committee and the Paragon Alternative School.

Table 15: Two Timelines: Student Accommodation Committee Highlights and Alternative School Highlights

Date	Student Accommodation Committee Highlights	Paragon Alternative School Highlights
Pre-observation	May: Committee formed and had one meeting before study began.	March: Board approved Paragon Alternative School "in principle."
May 26	Full-time observations began. * Observations took place but without mention of Student Accommodation Committee work.	First day of full-day observations. Alberta Education requested a verbal update on the alternative school.
May 27	*	** Observations took place but without mention of Paragon Alternative School business.
June 7	Committee meeting 2: Members still learning. Chair directs Ed to investigate school boundaries over the summer. Ed was already taking work home on the weekend. More extra work.	**
June 8	*	Board discussed alternative school and adopted Ed's recommendations.
June 9	*	**
June 10	*	Ed composed letter inviting Dr. Weinard to board meeting June 22.
June 21	No observations. Committee meeting 3 missed. (Observer did not comment on minutes.)	No observations.

June 22	*	Dr. Weinard attended board meeting as requested. He was critical of the board and the superintendent. Board directed Ed to compose a letter for Dr. Weinard to use with potential donors.
June 23	Ed tours portables. Committee chair had asked about them. Ed was already uncomfortable with portables and this visit did not improve his view—old, smelly, unhealthy.	Ed and the senior administrative team critiqued Dr. Weinard's appearance at board meeting.
August 31	No observations.	Board package contained Ed's proposed alternative school budget, proposed meeting agenda and related news. (Dr. Weinard focused on theoretical concepts while neglecting administrative details. He seemed unaware of this need.)
September 8	*	Ed updates observer: Dr. Weinard has money. He was importing help for meeting presentations. Ed not sure how the alternative school would add to existing school programs.
September 9	Talks to Gavin Emerson, Principal of J. M. Pivott School, about a possible new grade configuration—fewer grades. Gavin and staff were likely reluctant to lose grades but would understand. Ed had planted this idea the previous June without elaboration, then or now.	Ed deals with Ontario educational jurisdiction in order to secure approval for the attendance of Dr. Weinard's guest presenter. The stressed Jake Harris seeks and receives help from current and former colleagues. Ed also does his best to calm Jake.
September 12	Committee Meeting 4: Progress. Recommendations adopted.	Interview with superintendent Ed Noyce. Two other interviews completed. Brief references to alternative school at Student Accommodation Committee meeting.
September 15	No observations.	No observations, but Ed informed me by phone that during a meeting of principals, he received complaints about the possibility of the Paragon School (which principals referred to as a charter school).

September 20	*		No observations, but Ed informed me that plans for upcoming meetings had been firmed up with Dr. Weinard. In the approval process, Ed hears that Dr. Weinard's star presenter had serious issues locally.
September 22	*		Four interviews completed.
September 23	*		**
September 26	No observations. (Committee Meeting 5 missed. Minutes provide a record of progress.)		**
September 27	Ed tours Kananaskis Middle School to visualize changes considered by Committee.		Two interviews completed. Principal from town of Cheyenne sought invitation to Weinard/Teacher meeting. Ed rejected his request but suggested that he attend a subsequent meeting, the parent meeting. Principal Jake Harris read his prepared speech to selected colleagues. Dr. Weinard met with school staff. At this meeting, Jake Harris spoke civilly and persuasively. Overall, staff were not receptive to Dr. Weinard's proposal. Ed did not speak. Nodded a "Yes" to the only question put to him.
September 28	*		Two interviews completed. Deputy superintendent initiated discussion of a possible win/win solution—namely, action research. Ed showed mild signs of stress. Board receptive to idea of action research and were visibly relieved to hear a possible win/win solution.
September 29	*		Two interviews completed. Ed initiated feud with Albert Toth, Alberta Education director of testing. Ed's aggression was unusual.
September 30	*		Ed, in writing, challenged Dr. Weinard's negative interpretation of district students' achievements test results.

October 2	No observations.	No observations, but Dr. Weinard's response to a letter to the editor was printed. In it he invited parents for the meeting of October 5
October 5	Ed updates observer: Chair Nolan had introduced another new direction that required more research for Ed. Committee Meeting 6: Ed and two others lost on a vote. He had supported the process and decisions but thought that the board would not support their recommendations.	"Three Letter Campaign" Parent meeting: The Weinard team spoke a great deal, 56% of the meeting time. Parent questions, the Weinard team's answers, and the chair's procedural guidance took up only thirty-five percent of meeting time. Outside of his brief introductory remarks, Ed responded twice. Parents took no action; they did not want Dr. Weinard's school. Parents had reached a consensus; they quietly took no further action. (Hence, the board would need no further action.) Ed was relieved, and his emotions spilled out.
Post-Observation Notes	Following further meetings, the committee presented their analysis and recommendations to the board. The board did not act on the committee's school closure recommendations.	Normal Leadership returns. While Ed had feared a difficult transition from crisis to normal, from afar, there was no evidence of a difficult adjustment.

*Observations took place but without mention of Student Accommodation Committee work.

**Observations took place but without mention of Paragon Alternative School.

While interviews were referenced in Table 15 further details related to the Paragon Alternative School were not presented. These details make up the entirety of Chapter 9.

APPENDIX M:

Selected Qualitative Studies of Educational Leadership: 1997–2017

Author	Year	Principal Strategy	Description	Comments
Genge	1991	Interview	Interviewed thirteen organizationally effective Alberta school superintendents in an exploratory and descriptive study.	I was selected as a study participant. This gave me a model for a study of an "effective superintendent."
Polite, McClure and Rollie	1997	Observation	Sixteen principals shadowed, each for one fall day, 1996.	These sixteen principals (out of a sample of fifty-eight) participated in extensive, intensive professional development program.
McDonald	2005	Observation	Sixteen principals were shadowed and offered advice/support.	
Garza	2008	Journal entries	Rookie superintendent's diary of his first year.	Autoethnography or diary used.
Miller	2008	Personal interpretation of events	Interviews combined with old survey comments used to examine what the researcher described as the dubious "firing" of a superintendent.	Relied on the detailed personal knowledge of his friend, the fired superintendent, and the comments of various community members.
Herring	2011	Interviews with observation	Study of celebrity superintendent, with interviews of superintendent and various stakeholders. Required six observational days and used instrument developed by dissertation advisor.	Documents also studied.

Forner, Bierlein-Palmer, Reeves,	2012	Interviews	Each of six superintendents were interviewed, plus at least one principal, one teacher and one board trustee from each districts.	Prior personal knowledge of districts and superintendents
Maxwell, Locke, & Scheurich	2013	Interviews	Study of, and rating of, three effective superintendents as equity change agents.	Investigative team had prior, first-hand knowledge of the districts.
Hetherington	2014	Interviews	Several rounds of interviews with eight superintendents on the topic of decision making.	Good study. In my view, the current issues and responses were not dissimilar to what had existed a generation before.
Shields	2017	Interviews	Interviewed six superintendents and assistant superintendents.	Long-time knowledge of purposively selected subjects

REFERENCES

Alberta Teachers' Association. (1994). Member's Handbook. Edmonton, Alberta: Author.

Beck, J. (2019, January 8). "The personality trait that makes people feel comfortable around you." *The Atlantic*. https://www.theatlantic.com/family/archive/2019/01/affective-presence-how-you-make-other-people-feel/579643/

Bennis, W. G., & B. Nanus. (1985). *Leaders: The strategies for taking charge.* New York: Harper and Row.

Bogdan, R. C., & S. K. Biklen. (1982). *Qualitative research for education: An introduction to theory and methods.* Boston: Allyn & Bacon.

Burns, J. M. (1978). *Leadership.* New York: Harper & Row.

Creswell, J. W. (2013). *Qualitative inquiry and research design: Choosing among five approaches* (3rd ed.). Thousand Oaks, CA: SAGE Publications, Inc.

Delamont, S. (1992). *Fieldwork in educational settings: Methods, pitfalls and perspectives.* London, UK: Falmer Press.

Dictionary.com. https://www.dictionary.com/

Downey, L. W. (1976). *The school superintendency in Alberta—1976: A report of an inquiry.* Edmonton, Alberta: Alberta Education.

Feilders, J. F. (1982). *Profile: The role of the chief superintendent of schools.* Belmont, CA: Fearon Education.

Forner, M., L. Bierlein-Palmer, & P. Reeves. (2012). Leadership practices of effective rural superintendents: Connections to Waters and Marzano's leadership correlates. *Journal of Research in Rural Education, 27*(8), 1–14. http://jrre.vmhost.psu.edu/wp-content/uploads/2014/02/27-8.pdf

Gardner, J. (1990). *On Leadership.* New York: Free Press.

Garza, E. Jr. (2008). Autoethnography of a first-time superintendent: Challenges to leadership for social justice. *Journal of Latinos and Education, 7*(2), 163–176. https://www.tandfonline.com/doi/abs/10.1080/15348430701828749

Genge, A. (1991). *Effective school superintendents.* Unpublished doctoral dissertation, University of Alberta, Edmonton.

Goffman, E. (1967). *Interaction ritual: Essays on face to face behavior.* New York: Pantheon.

Grant, A. (2018, March 1). People don't actually know themselves very well. *The Atlantic*. https://www.theatlantic.com/health/archive/2018/03/you-dont-know-yourself-as-well-as-you-think-you-do/554612/

Herring, R. L. (2014). *How does a successful superintendent lead? A case study of Dr. Mark Edwards.* Harvard University. ProQuest Dissertations Publishing (3662091).

Hetherington, R. W. (2014). *Decision-making and the superintendency.* University of Alberta, ProQuest Dissertations Publishing (10100130).

Kuhn, T. S. (1970). *The structure of scientific revolutions* (2nd ed.). Chicago: University of Chicago.

Maxwell, G. M., L. A. Locke, & J. J. Scheurich. (2013). Case study of three rural Texas superintendents as equity oriented change agents. *The Qualitative Report, 18*(11), 1–23. http://nsuworks.nova.edu/tqr/vol18/iss11/2

McCarthy, B. (1980). *4MAT system: Teaching to learning styles with right-left mode techniques.* Oak Brook, IL: Excel.

McDonald, S. (2005). *Studying actions in context: A qualitative shadowing method for organizational research.* SAGE Journals. https://doi.org/10.1177/1468794105056923

McLeod, G. T. (1984). The work of school board chief executive officers. *Canadian Journal of Education, 9*(2), 171–190.

Merriam-Webster Dictionary. https://www.merriam-webster.com

Miller, R. (2006). *A mixed methods study of shared leadership in a K-12 school district enhanced by a case study of the former superintendent's role.* https://eric.ed.gov/contentdelivery/servlet/ERICServlet?accno=ED501191

O'Donnell, B. R. J. (2017, October 9). What studying conflict resolution teaches about personal relationships. *The Atlantic.* https://www.theatlantic.com/business/archive/2017/10/conflict-resolution-donna-hicks-relationships/541857/

Polite, V. C., R. McClure, & D. L. Rollie. (1997). The emerging reflective urban principal; The role of shadowing encounters. *Urban Education, 31*(5), 466–489.

Shields, C. M. (2017). "Is transformative leadership practical or possible? Learning from superintendents about social justice. International studies in education administration. *Commonwealth Council for Educational Administration and Management, 45*(2), 3–20.

Vaill, P. B. (1986). The purposing of high-performing systems. In T. J. Sergiovanni & J. E. Corbally (eds.), *Leadership and organizational culture: New perspectives on administrative theory and practice* (pp. 84–104). Urbana, IL: University of Illinois Press.

Webster's Ninth New Collegiate Dictionary. (1983). Markham, ON: Thomas Allen & Son.

Wikipedia. "Cooperative learning." https://en.wikipedia.org/wiki/Cooperative_learning

Wikipedia. "Imposter syndrome." https://en.wikipedia.org/wiki/Impostor_syndrome

Wolcott, H. F. (1981). Confessions of a "trained" observer. In T. S. Popketwitz & B. R. Tabachnick (eds.), *The study of schooling: Field based methodologies in educational research and evaluation.* New York: Praeger.

Wolcott, H. F. (1984). *The man in the principal's office: An ethnography.* Prospect Heights, IL: Waveland Press.

Wolcott, H. F. (1990). On seeking—and rejecting—validity in qualitative research. In E. W. Eisner & A. Peshkin (eds.), *Qualitative inquiry in education: The continuing debate* (pp. 121–152). New York: Teachers College Press.

Wolcott, H. F. (2005). *The art of fieldwork* (2nd ed.). Altamira Press.

Zeigler, H., E. Kehoe, & J. Reisman. (1985.) *City managers and school superintendents: response to community conflict.* New York: Praeger.

CPSIA information can be obtained
at www.ICGtesting.com
Printed in the USA
LVHW060909240621
690963LV00003B/128